Praise for *N*

"Lauren McKeon looks be̲y̲ of male power to see what we truly need to achieve a more equitable world—not simply more women at the top of government and business, but more freedom to define and create a world that doesn't abide by the dated rules of the patriarchy. Drawing on a variety of women's stories and lived experiences, McKeon shows us that there are plenty of ways to live outside the lines and create change rather than wait for it." — Gemma Hartley, author of *Fed Up: Emotional Labor, Women, and the Way Forward*

"Lauren McKeon is one of the most important journalists writing about feminist issues in this country today. This impeccably researched and reported book is a revelation, an inspiration, a punch in the gut, and a fierce rallying cry. It's a definite must read for anyone who cares about women's current reality, and women's future in this country and beyond." — Stacey May Fowles, author of *Baseball Life Advice: Loving the Game that Saved Me* and co-editor of *Whatever Gets You Through: Twelve Survivors on Life after Sexual Assault*

"Lauren McKeon has written a bold, searching, and ultimately hopeful book about what it would mean for women to be truly powerful in the world. Not the kind of power that requires a token change at the top, but a radical overhauling of social structures to create a more progressive and inclusive society. There is much power to be found in her wise, eye-opening book." — Elizabeth Renzetti, author of *Shrewed: A Wry and Closely Observed Look at the Lives of Women and Girls*

"Lauren McKeon has long cemented herself as a writer whose insights are biting, effective, and necessary. And unsurprisingly, *No More Nice Girls* is no different. In this book, her work is meticulously researched and brilliantly argued, and she's not afraid to confront us with information and perspectives that are as uncomfortable as they are true (see: *very*). That said, Lauren's ability to engage with instead of dictating to is powerful and unifying, specifically as she provides the type of ammunition needed for readers to abandon existing comfort zones or truths fabricated for self-preservation. She urges us to learn and listen (but *actually* listen). She's patient, but forceful in offering her many (many) facts. I've never liked the word *nice*, and liked the idea of aspiring to be nice even less. Thankfully, Lauren makes *nice* a non-word—a notion or descriptor that means nothing and does nothing. She sets us free of the rhetoric associated with niceness, and exchanges the burden of playing by the rules for the data, statistics, and emphasis on intersectionality that will help us, collectively, to obliterate them." — Anne T. Donahue, author of *Nobody Cares*

The Walrus Books

The Walrus sparks essential Canadian conversation by publishing high-quality, fact-based journalism and producing ideas-focused events across the country. The Walrus Books, a partnership between The Walrus, House of Anansi Press, and the Chawkers Foundation Writers Project, supports the creation of Canadian nonfiction books of national interest.

thewalrus.ca/books

Also by Lauren McKeon

F-Bomb: Dispatches from the War on Feminism

NO MORE NICE GIRLS

GENDER, POWER, AND WHY IT'S TIME
TO STOP PLAYING BY THE RULES

LAUREN McKEON

ANANSI

Published in Canada in 2020 and the USA in 2020
by House of Anansi Press Inc.

www.houseofanansi.com

House of Anansi Press is committed to protecting our natural
environment. As part of our efforts, this book is made of material from
well-managed FSC®-certified forests, recycled materials, and other
controlled sources.

24 23 22 21 20   1 2 3 4 5

Library and Archives Canada Cataloguing in Publication

Title: No more nice girls : gender, power, and why it's time to stop
playing by the rules / Lauren McKeon. Names: McKeon, Lauren, author.
Identifiers: Canadiana (print) 20190172657 | Canadiana (ebook)
20190172681 | ISBN 9781487006440 (softcover) | ISBN 9781487006457
(EPUB) | ISBN 9781487006464 (Kindle)
Subjects: LCSH: Women—Social conditions—21st century. |
LCSH: Women's rights. | LCSH: Equality. | LCSH: Feminism. |
LCSH: Sex discrimination against women. | LCSH: Power
(Social sciences) | LCSH: Social control.
Classification: LCC HQ1155 .M35 2020 | DDC 305.42—dc23

Book design: Alysia Shewchuk

*We acknowledge for their financial support of our publishing program
the Canada Council for the Arts, the Ontario Arts Council, and the
Government of Canada.*

Printed and bound in Canada

CONTENTS

Introduction

ON NOVEMBER 8, 2016, I tried to pretend the TVs at my gym did not exist. I'd shown up that night to my weekly class expecting to walk out sweaty and exalted. If America elected a woman as its leader (as all the pundits and polls suggested the country would), then, surely, Canada would follow. Anything felt possible. I imagined a cascade of broken status quos — belligerent white men in crisp suits falling like dominos. But over the next hour, disbelief replaced excitement. At one point, our class melted away from our workout stations to pool, lost, around the TV. Women muttered *shit*, *what*, *no*, over and over again. That night, I couldn't sleep. I stayed seated on my bed, cross-legged, stunned. It didn't matter that I wasn't American, or that one of the wokest men on Earth supposedly ran my own country. Electing a blatant misogynist to one of the world's most powerful positions symbolized something: we were fucked.

Since then, the question of women and power has undergone something of a renaissance — largely because we've been forced to confront, once again, how much of it women still don't have. Quite literally overnight, many of us went from believing, with good reason, that we'd never been closer to equality—and power—to reckoning with just how far away from both women truly were. In response, women woke up, gathered, and demanded change. All around the world, they protested. The momentum from the Women's March on Washington built into #MeToo and a very public reckoning with the everyday ways in which women's power and autonomy are constantly undermined.

Watching it all, I was galvanized. But I also felt as though I was stuck in a not-so-fun house of magic mirrors. *Come one, come all! Watch as the road to equality shrinks, stretches, distorts!* Sometimes it seemed as if our fury, powerful in its own right, could propel us anywhere we wanted to go: into public office, into the C-suite, into a world in which we had bodily autonomy. Other times, as the anti-feminist backlash grew louder, bolder, and more expansive, it seemed as though women were in our most precarious spot yet. I began to think of feminist power as a paradox: from some vantages, we seemed closer than ever to achieving it; from others, we'd never been further away.

I have spent the bulk of my journalism career investigating the ways in which women navigate, and in many cases push back against, the expectations of the world around them. In doing this, I now realize, what I've really been asking, consciously or not, is how women disrupt and reimagine power structures, how they gain power both in and over their lives. Many of the women I've interviewed are pioneers in their fields, often ones dominated by men, and you could say they are subverting from within. Others are pushing at established power structures from the outside, rallying from the grassroots. They are all inspiring and amazing. But is what they're doing *working*? These past few years have illuminated some stark, and seemingly contradictory, truths. Despite immense progress, no amount of success can immunize women against the toxic, sexist environments around them, and it is not uncommon for women to be utterly alone: one of few in their field, the only woman in management at their company, or the only one breaking a certain convention.

The more I heard their stories, the more I wondered: Even if a woman won the next American or Canadian federal election, what would that victory gain us? Or, put another way: Do we have the very concept of women and power all wrong? I'm not saying I want all the feminists to give up the fight, retreat to their kitchens, and let one pucker-mouthed man and his acolytes burn the planet. I want women to attain the same powerful positions afforded to men, in equal numbers. But it's also dangerous to see that status, in and of itself, as a panacea to centuries of Western civilization, all built on foundational histories of sexism, misogyny, and violence against women. A woman prime minister certainly wouldn't "cancel out" this seemingly new brand of misogyny, dredged up for all the world to see. In fact, the past few years have revealed that any woman, or member of another equity-seeking group, who stands where white, straight, cisgender men usually do is certain to face violent backlash. Or, as University of Cambridge classics professor Mary Beard argues in her short manifesto *Women & Power*, throughout time women have been placed in, or near to, positions of power simply to fail. To illustrate her point, Beard borrows from Greek mythology, referring to Clytemnestra, who rules over her city while her husband fights in the Trojan War, only to be murdered by her own children after she refuses to cede her new leadership upon his return (well, okay, she also killed her husband rather than go back down the patriarchal chain). Or more recently, Beard suggests, consider Theresa May or Hillary Clinton.[1] For women, power is messy from every angle.

Perhaps, then, it's finally time to start rethinking feminism's one-time end goals, to ditch our old checklists for equality. Yes, let's not abandon our strategizing toward getting more women to the top, but let's also examine a deeper, less considered problem: that is, what the view from "the top" looks like for women once they're there. What if we could redefine not just women's path to power but the very concept of power itself? Or, more radical yet: What if we stopped focusing on playing the game better, ditched the rule book, and refused to play their game at all? What would power even *look* like to us if we weren't always visualizing it within the context of men?

I've often heard the path to power described as a ladder. Through hard work and talent, a person can pull themselves up, rung by rung, right to the very top. Or at least that's the myth. In reality, if somebody is born with privilege, money, a lighter skin colour, or sometimes a certain appendage between their legs, they're likely to start higher up on the ladder. Their climb to prime minister or president, billionaire or boss, is easier, softer, less sweaty. I imagine it's as if their metaphoric ladder is lined with velvet, their climbing shoes plush Gucci loafers. And when they get to the top, a dozen flying cherubs shower them with Dom Pérignon, possibly while playing tiny golden trumpets. They are accepted and celebrated—or else so feared that they are unquestioned. People want a piece of their power; they want a hand up to the next rung.

But for those who haven't historically dominated positions of power, the ladder metaphor rarely works. It isn't that a few rungs are broken, although they probably are; it's that the path hardly ever looks like a ladder at all. Think of it as a maze instead — one with a lot of traps and dead ends.[2] Forget the luxe shoes and Champagne. Women and others who've been historically excluded from power are more likely to battle gargoyles, to traverse rickety bridges (if there is a bridge at all), to leap over rusty spikes in the road. And god help them if they don't do it all while smiling. If a woman does manage to make it mostly through, she should be prepared to smash, crash, or otherwise break through a glass ceiling at the end. (Sounds violent; bring Band-Aids.) Once at the top, she'd better brace herself for constant doubt (her own and others'), harassment, suggestions that she doesn't belong there, and no job security whatsoever. If people are happy that she's there, they might be even happier when she topples.

How bleak. How bleakly *familiar*.

We have long positioned power as something that doesn't come easily, or even naturally, to women. It is seen as something women must fight for, a club they must break into, a first they must become. Laced into all of this language is the message that power, by definition, is masculine — is for men. How often do we read articles about male CEOs or politicians that ask, "But how did you manage to overcome your challenges as a *man*?" The answer is: we do not.

Perhaps worse, the traditional solutions to righting this imbalance have too often been as troubling, depressing, and even belittling as the problem itself. Not long after we got "glass ceiling" as the problem, we got "girl power" as a solution. What started as a riot grrrl concept quickly became co-opted by commercial interests. The Spice Girls, in particular, tapped into the idea of power for women as something rooted in prettiness and confidence—something that could be achieved simply by believing in yourself. Girl power told us that we could be badass warriors with good lipstick; it did not necessarily encourage more difficult conversations about pay gaps, workplace inequity, systemic sexism and racism, and so on. At its best, girl power preached—and still preaches—the supposedly revolutionary idea that woman and girls can do...*things*. Anything! At its worst, though, it's infantilizing drivel, grounded in advertising and not much else.

Options beyond girl power aren't much better, either. In particular, there's the hard-to-kill suggestion that a successful, powerful woman must be more like a man. That mindset gave us boxy pantsuits and impossible standards, and it also gave us career self-help books such as *Nice Girls Don't Get the Corner Office* (first printed in 2004; reissued in 2010) and *Play Like a Man, Win Like a Woman* (2001). More recently, women have been asked to #GirlBoss their lives—an effort that combines the pink philosophies of girl power with the adult desires of popular feminism, and sometimes, strangely, the be-like-a-man appeals to women to toughen up. To be a #GirlBoss, women must walk a tightrope: they must be a boss, but not bossy; authentic, but Insta-trendy; real, but not harsh; beautiful, but effortless; killin' it, but not thirsty; busy, but glowing with Goop-ified self-care; vulnerable, but just the right amount; tough, but just the right amount; confident, but not extra; warm, but not weak; decisive, but not rude; your bitch, but not *bitchy*. And on and on.

No wonder we're still on the losing end of power. As of 2019, women accounted for only 4 percent of Canadian CEOs, and 10 percent of top executives.[3] Of the top 100 best-performing companies in Canada, only one is run by a woman.[4] If that weren't depressing enough, consider the pay gap for those few women who do make it to the top. Nationally, among all workers, women earn eighty-three cents for every dollar a man makes (a chasm that widens further for women of colour, Indigenous women, and women with disabilities). As one might expect, the gap shrinks, slightly, for women in senior management, who make eighty-six cents for every dollar a man makes. But then climb on up to the C-suite, where women make a shocking *sixty-eight* cents for every dollar their male colleagues make. This accounts for about $950,000 less income each year, making the pay gap most striking for women who are, arguably, the most successful. Researchers at the Canadian Centre for Policy Alternatives who conducted the study call this the "double-pane glass ceiling." Better grab more Band-Aids.

The wonky pay gap is only one example of gender inequality (and one we'll return to later), but it reveals how complex the knotty intersections of power, leadership, agency, and achievement can be for women and other excluded communities. We're told things will be better once we've mirrored the same power and positions men have traditionally attained; it's the marker of our merit, our success, our *equality*. To overcome hurdles on our paths to power, we're told to play within the system, but better, smarter. To use it to our advantage. To get to the top of a company, to win public office, to report our assaults, to put ourselves out there. And, if we somehow manage to do all these things, and balance all the impossible, contradictory expectations of the perfect boss/survivor/public figure, and find the semblance of success, then the bullshit will stop, or so the promise goes. In truth, by nearly every measure of equality, things are likely to be just as bad or *worse* for the rare woman who manages to achieve traditional power. This all sounds completely hopeless — except it isn't.

Back in September 2018, during the height of the new North American trade talks, I attended the second Women in the World Summit Canada. This one-day little-sister event to the star-powered flagship held every year in New York City is the brainchild of famed magazine editor Tina Brown. The conference opened with an address by Brown herself, followed by a panel on economic bias with jaunty-sock-wearing Justin Trudeau, International Monetary Fund managing director Christine Legarde, and another famous journalist, Katie Couric. But it was Canada's foreign affairs minister Chrystia Freeland, the star of a panel called "Taking on the Tyrant," who walked onstage to a standing ovation. The event program further described her panel as "Two remarkable women who speak truth to power tell us what's at stake in the global rise of authoritarian Strong Men."

As the crowd cheered, and Freeland beamed and waved, panel host Heather Reisman, chair and CEO of Indigo, leaned over to the second panellist, *New Yorker* staff writer Masha Gessen, and explained, perhaps redundantly, "She's loved." Freeland does not have a stereotypically powerful presence. That is, she adopts none of the old "be a man" (bad) advice. Arguably, this is a huge part of her popularity. Freeland's allure can be credited to who she is, sure, but it's also what she represents: a new kind of power that's completely, deliberately at odds with a very old, very masculine one. You could, as Women in the World did, call that masculine model "tyrannical power": a re-emerging, populist- and authoritarian-based leadership, heavily reliant on sowing chaos, division, and fear. We see it in Donald Trump, but also in Brazil's president Jair Bolsonaro, Italy's Matteo Salvini, leader of the country's right-wing League party, and even Ontario's premier Doug Ford. We see it in a lot of men (and, surely, some women).

While speaking out against such leadership has made Freeland beloved among many women, elsewhere it has earned predictable backlash. After he learned about her participation in the panel, Trump himself responded with an assertion that "We don't like their representative very much."[5] Meanwhile, some Canadian media characterized her participation as "antics," "grossly irresponsible," and a "plot" to anger Trump. *Maclean's* asked: "What if Donald Trump has a point with Chrystia Freeland?"[6] (Never mind that Trudeau, you know, basically opened the conference, or that it was he, not Freeland, who actually mentioned the trade talks. *That nasty, naughty, bitchy woman did it!*) Such backlash exposes the depth of our aversion to women in power, but it exposes something else, too: how scared someone like Freeland makes those who occupy, and benefit from, the current models of power.

Freeland is only one, small iteration of this new, oppositional power. Others are #MeToo, Black Lives Matter, March for Our Lives — grassroots movements that have grown big enough to shake the world. We can see this new vision for power at the individual level and also at the collective level, distinctly different from the institutional and structural power that so often governs our societies, governments, and lives. In addition to being in opposition to the status quo, it asks us to contemplate how change might occur outside current systems, how power might grow from collaboration and community, and, yes, how it might also destroy those systems and social structures that were never built with our success in mind—ones that were often designed to keep us out.

This book is not about self-empowerment; there are plenty of other, better books for that (if anything, dear reader, you can expect a thoroughly feminist killjoy critique of the pitfalls of empowerment; #sorrynotsorry). But this *is* a book that offers, and argues for, solutions: ones that invite us to reinvent our ideas of success, leadership, and, ultimately, power. Broadly, it's about how we've been hoodwinked. This is about looking at the devastating imbalance of power that exists across all industries and aspects of public life, and it's about the many roadblocks women face on the way to power. But more than that, it's about pulling back the curtain and looking at how much things truly suck for women when (*if!*) they finally reach the top. Throughout much of the modern feminist movement, women have spent substantial time, resources, and energy putting everything we have into replicating men's visions of success and power, only to discover that things look more unequal than ever once we do. Too often, shattering that ceiling means we're left walking, day in and day out, on a bunch of broken glass. That's not to say this is a book that focuses on asking us to mourn the privileged; this is not about feeling sorry for those who've amassed wealth and influence. Rather, it posits that traditional views of power are limited and will not, in the end, give us what we want. Progress. Equality.

I would never dissuade women from striving to break into male-dominated industries, or other spheres of life, both public and private. But if we ever want to win, some things must happen in tandem: we must also disrupt our entrenched systems *as* we change the face of power. So, this book is also about why women, for example, remain vastly under-represented in the science, technology, engineering, and math (STEM) fields, *and* it's about why, even among those who do hold STEM degrees, men are more than twice as likely to actually work in science and tech as women are.[7] It's about how women have advanced exponentially at work and at home, and yet in 2018 more than 80 percent of them had also experienced sexual harassment and/or assault.[8] It's about how one post-doctoral researcher gathered 3,000 names of Indigenous women who have been murdered or gone missing in Canada and the United States in the past century — and estimates the total sits closer to 25,000.[9] It's about the nature of power, what kinds of power have and have not been historically afforded to women, and how those boundaries have harmed us.

Which means this is also a story about who has had power within the feminist movement, and how, far too often, the movement has sought to remedy power imbalances through policies and initiatives that help elevate white women and no one else. This is a discussion of what we mean when we talk about representation, diversity, and inclusion. It's about how, for example, the organization Women and Hollywood reports that women represented only 15 percent of directors on the top 500 films of 2018, but adds that it only considers gender in its statistics, not race, sexual identity or orientation, or even age.[10] And also how, in 2017, a little over 30 percent of American newsroom leaders were white women, but just 2 percent were Black women, less than 2 percent were Hispanic and Asian women, and only 0.28 percent were Indigenous women.[11] If we're going to change the status quo of power and leadership, then it's essential that we also ask *whom* we're changing it for.

As a white woman, I understand that society grants me power that it does not grant other women. I walk through this world with extraordinary privilege, and this, in effect, means that while there are some things I can instinctually understand about the power deficit by virtue of my own experience, there are many more things that I cannot. Which means that a lot of the research and reporting I completed for this book centred on exploring that privilege and listening to others whose experience with power is more layered than mine. As part of this intersectional approach, I also thought deeply and often about how I, too, have contributed to power imbalances and inequity, how I *benefited* from them. Middle- to upper-class white women — white feminists — seem to have a truly hard time doing this, instead tricking ourselves into thinking that because we've experienced one form of oppression we understand what it means to experience all forms. I've met too many women who vehemently champion #BelieveHer, but simultaneously refuse to believe Indigenous women and women of colour who say the world needs to do better. This book asks such women to consider that if all women are set up to fail, it stands to reason that Indigenous women, women of colour, women with disabilities, homeless and precariously housed women, and those who are LGBTQ+ are only set up to fail more and to fall harder. If that makes you uncomfortable, good, then this book is for you, too.

This book is also careful not to describe women, trans or cis, as well as those outside of the gender binary, unless it is relevant to the discussion of power, unless a person references it themself, or unless a man would be physically described in that same situation. Too much of media coverage focuses on women's appearance. Too much of it focuses a gendered lens on her personality. And this also is an expression of power. If you find yourself missing those superfluous descriptions of her hair, face, body, clothing, or the way she moves, then I invite you to think about why that matters so much to you.

Finally, while I've used the word "woman," it is, undoubtedly, not only women who find themselves on the losing end. While we cannot talk about power imbalances without also talking about things like race, ability, poverty, and sexual orientation, we also cannot ignore the very concept of the gender binary itself. Breaking the power imbalance is also about supporting transgender women and those who are non-binary and gender nonconforming, and acknowledging how society's ingrained ideas of men and women, masculine and feminine, are at the root of what limits us. Stepping outside the system in new, creative ways also means stepping outside gender constructs, what we expect men and women to be and do, and whether we even need ideas like "man" and "woman" at all. Because, fundamentally, having a seat at the table might not do a damn thing for us. Being there doesn't mean anybody will listen to us; our presence does not mean default change. This is not about demanding a seat at the table at all. It's about building our own fucking table, and making it look completely different.

One year before I was born, Audre Lorde wrote her famous essay "The Master's Tools Will Never Dismantle the Master's House." In it, she explains, "They may allow us temporarily to beat him at his own game, but they will never enable us to bring about genuine change. And this fact is only threatening to those women who still define the master's house as their only source of support." Lorde was, prominently, also talking about the divisions between white and Black feminists, and white feminism's refusal to acknowledge and centre those differences. Just as the patriarchy had a vested interest in keeping feminists occupied with the "master's concerns"—forcing a vast amount of energy to be expended merely to educate men on women's existence and needs—so, too, did racism have a vested interest in keeping Black feminists occupied with teaching white women. I mention Lorde now because she was right, of course, but also to stress that while we're currently examining power imbalances against a new backdrop, the problems, and even some of the solutions, have a long history.

In researching and writing this book, I'd often think back to how I learned—or rather relearned—how to punch. I'd joined the Toronto Newsgirls Boxing Club, one of the first woman-owned, explicitly trans-positive clubs in North America, after years of participating in clubs that were technically open to everyone but in reality dominated by men. Or, at the very least, by masculinity. One of the first things the coach told me was that I was punching all wrong. Taught by men, in a very traditional style, I angled my fist to hit with my first two knuckles—as people have, essentially, been taught to punch since the beginning of time. My new coach told me that she'd studied it, along with biomechanics researchers, and discovered that for women the most powerful punch looked different. Shift to your last two knuckles, she implored me, just try it. I remember being so skeptical. It ran contradictory to everything I knew about this sport I loved. I remember rolling my eyes. I remember thinking, *I already know how to do this.* Then I tried it. I've never looked back.

My hope is that we can all learn how to do that—how to shift, how to discard the master's tools—and in doing so find a different sort of power. We'll curl our hands into new fists, adjust our angle, and just smash. And when somebody asks us what we're aiming at, we'll answer simply and powerfully. We'll say: *Everything.*

CHAPTER 1

Power Hungry

Our problem with women and power

O N HIS FIRST DAY of leadership, Prime Minister
Justin Trudeau performed a perfect feminist victory.
Standing outside of Rideau Hall in Ottawa, a Remembrance
Day poppy adorning his lapel, Trudeau announced his
newly formed gender-balanced cabinet. The move vaulted
Canada to fourth in the world in terms of the percentage of
women in ministerial positions, up from twentieth. But it
was Trudeau's famously curt answer to a reporter who asked
him why gender parity was so important to him — "Because
it's 2015" — that earned him international attention, not to
mention a fair amount of gushing. Jezebel said it was "the
sexiest" thing about him.[1] *Newsweek*, *The New York Times*,
Slate, and others all published positive coverage of Trudeau's
cabinet, focusing on the pithy comment. "Coolest thing
I've seen in a while," tweeted the actor and UN Women
Goodwill Ambassador Emma Watson. "Love U Canada."[2]

Of the fifteen women Trudeau named to cabinet that day,

one, in particular, stood out. The new justice minister and attorney general of Canada, Jody Wilson-Raybould, a lawyer and former regional chief of the B.C. Assembly of First Nations, was also the first Indigenous person to hold the high-profile post. It's unlikely that either Wilson-Raybould or Trudeau himself would ever have guessed that several years later he'd push her out of her position, or that she'd resign from cabinet altogether. Certainly, it seems difficult to fathom that, in the fallout, Trudeau's flawless feminist image would, rightly, come under fire. Much of the ensuing controversy surrounding Trudeau, Wilson-Raybould, and, eventually, several other female Liberal Party members would be mired in conversations about corporate influence and government interference. But simmering underneath the dominant media narrative, the conflict between Trudeau and Canada's own Squad indicated something else, too: that gender parity on its own is not enough to fix a system rooted in power imbalances. Trudeau did not get to wave his 2015 wand and then walk away like, *Ta-da! The patriarchy is cancelled.* No matter the good intentions, by early 2019 it was clear that the patriarchy was still thriving—even in Canada's imagined feminist paradise.

The first public sign that something was wrong came when Trudeau shuffled his cabinet in mid-January 2019. Suddenly, Wilson-Raybould was the new minister of veteran affairs, a move that was widely seen as a demotion. Onlookers could be forgiven for being puzzled, which many were. The former attorney general had accomplished a lot in her three years in the position, much of it groundbreaking. To a letter responding to the crush of media and constituent curiosity,[3] Wilson-Raybould attached an appendix that reminded everybody she'd introduced thirteen pieces of legislation, including the legalization of (and corresponding legal framework for) medically assisted death and, also, cannabis. She'd changed the Canadian Human Rights Act to add gender identity and expression to its list of prohibited grounds for discrimination, and legislated the first major change to the country's sexual assault laws in a quarter-century. Overtly, the letter was all gratitude and grace, but it also seemed to have an underlying message: *This did not happen because I was bad at my job.*

Within weeks, media did, in fact, break a story that offered up another reason for the shuffle. Wilson-Raybould, reported *The Globe and Mail*, was booted from her post because she wouldn't bow to Team Trudeau's pressure to interfere in the prosecution of corporate giant SNC-Lavalin. As some Liberals attempted to control the damage and combat accusations of corruption and corporate favouritism, however, another narrative emerged — a deeply sexist one. Two days after the SNC-Lavalin story broke, The Canadian Press ran a story that deployed several anonymous Liberal sources.[4] The story attempted to paint Wilson-Raybould as nothing short of a "nasty woman." The reporter, a woman, wrote that Wilson-Raybould was neither "universally loved" nor "doing a bang-up job." The story continued, explaining that she was known to be "a thorn in the side of the cabinet" whom some insiders called "difficult to get along with," a person who was "known to berate fellow cabinet ministers openly," and also a minister who "others felt they had trouble trusting." Another anonymous source was quoted as saying, "Everything is very Jody-centric." Whether the characterization is true or not, it's worth noting that such traits are largely considered unremarkable in male politicians. Surely, it seems unlikely that not being "universally loved" or having an alleged big ego would be reasonable justification to turf a

male politician who was simply, ethically, doing his job—
even if it defied the prime minister's wishes.

Fellow politicians, from all parties, were outraged over
the article's publication and called on Trudeau to denounce
the Canadian Press story and the insiders who were interviewed for it. "When women speak up and out, they are
always going to be labelled," tweeted fellow Liberal MP
Celina R. Caesar-Chavannes. "Go ahead. Label away."
Conservative MP Michelle Rempel, a person who agrees
with the Liberals on very little, tweeted a furious multi-
part thread, writing that "If 'she's in it for herself' . . . equates
to 'she stood up and did the right thing' then way to go."
Rempel, who also called the accusations against Wilson-
Raybould "gendered af," ended her thread with a meme
that showed Trudeau and Wilson-Raybould standing side
by side. She'd written "dinosaur" across Trudeau's chest and
"meteor" across Wilson-Raybould's, captioning the image:
"Angry women are free women."[5] Sure, it could have been
mere politicking, but she also wasn't wrong. Meanwhile
Liberal lobbyist Lisa Kirbie (a woman who has been called
difficult herself) had pinned her criticism to the top of her
Twitter page: "The blatant sexism in the anonymous
attacks against this powerful woman is shameful."

But it was the Union of B.C. Indian Chiefs that, at last,
addressed the intersections of power, colonialism, racism,
and gender. The Canadian Press story, and those sources
who spoke for it, they stressed, invoked stereotypes that
were particularly damning of Indigenous women. In an
open letter, the union demanded Trudeau "immediately
and categorically" condemn the characterization of Wilson-
Raybould. Those who signed the letter called the portrayal
"disingenuous," adding that such statements "perpetuate
colonial-era, sexist stereotypes that Indigenous women

cannot be powerful, forthright, and steadfast in positions of power, but rather confrontational, meddling and egotistic."[6] They had a point. For a man who campaigned heavily on values of both reconciliation and feminism, Trudeau's silence seemed incongruous at best.

In the end, Trudeau did denounce his fellow Liberals — albeit in a roundabout way, through his press secretary, who commented in an email to the Aboriginal Peoples Television Network.[7] That email, though, came five pointed days after the initial story. It was surely long enough for the sexist, negative portrayal of Wilson-Raybould to linger, and certainly ample time to set the stage (at least for some) for how she'd be viewed as the controversy unspooled: that is, basically, as an uncooperative, unreliable *bitch*. In fact, shortly after her eventual testimony on the whole SNC-Lavalin affair, one B.C.-based Liberal MP dismissed her comments as "sour grapes," said she "lacked experience," "couldn't handle the stress," and suggested her father, a prominent hereditary chief, was "pulling the strings." (The MP later apologized.)[8] There are many lessons to be gleaned from this mess, to be sure, but I found myself constantly returning to one of them, perhaps the most troubling of all: disrupting power, it would seem, is far trickier than making a token gesture, however grand or well-meaning, and calling it a day. In the end, what good is gender parity if women have no power to do their jobs?

Power: Working for Men since the Dawn of Time

The treatment of Wilson-Raybould was perhaps shocking, but was it surprising? If the Trump era is marked by a certain type of male leadership, it's also marked by a very specific backlash against women and those who stand up to that leadership. Trump, after all, cannot seem to mention Hillary Clinton without calling her "crooked," a sustained and successful effort to throw shade. Whatever he may be, Trudeau is clearly not Trump, and yet he benefits from the same systems and social climate that helped Trump rise. Those systems favour (and have perhaps always favoured) a hyper-masculine view of leadership and power: authoritative, unbending, tough. A good leader does what needs to be done, won't be pushed around, and speaks *his* mind. Trump has brought these qualities into almost-cartoonish relief as he Makes America Macho Again, with many world leaders following suit, an arsenal of misogynist stereotypes at their disposal.

What's more, whether it's from experience or instinct, many women understand that these cherished "strongmen" qualities would not translate especially well were they to exhibit them. It seems naive to think this disparity did not factor into the belief that Trudeau could get away with pressuring Wilson-Raybould in the first place. As has been much discussed, she later testified that Trudeau and others within the party had pressured her repeatedly.[9] Such experience with power also likely played a part in his apparent belief that he could quietly shuffle *her* out of power, an acquiescing smile on her face. This imbalance — not friendship — was further on display every time Trudeau subsequently, consistently, referred to Wilson-Raybould as Jody, not Minister, not even Ms., as she did not go silently, to his "disappointment."[10] (The Union of B.C. Indian Chiefs had previously called Trudeau out for doing the same with another female Indigenous leader. Can you imagine either woman publicly referring to him as *Justin*?)

In so many ways, Wilson-Raybould's push out of power

was Canada's own Clinton moment, our own attack on a Squad of powerful female politicians—one that few of us even noticed. We may be nicer about it, many people around the country realized, and we may have (some) leaders who claim feminism, but our systems work just as hard against women who try to seize more power than we think they ought to have. Here, our leaders don't call women "nasty" and they don't talk about grabbing her "pussy" on camera, but they still don't want her to challenge their authority with her own thoughts, ethics, or decisions. Trudeau reportedly grew angry with Celina Caesar-Chavannes when she told him she wouldn't be seeking re-election (she later left the Liberal caucus to sit as an Independent). "He was yelling. He was yelling that I didn't appreciate him, that he'd given me so much," she told *The Globe and Mail*, adding Trudeau was also worried about "the optics of two women of colour leaving."[11]

Then, in early April 2019, after Wilson-Raybould revealed she'd secretly recorded a conversation about SNC-Lavalin with the clerk of the Privy Council, Trudeau ousted both her and Jane Philpott, who had been critical of the Liberals' handling of the situation, from the caucus. He told media that it was the "will of the caucus" and that "the trust that previously existed between these two individuals and our team has been broken." Condemning Wilson-Raybould's actions, he added that he had tried to address the women's concerns and did not want a "civil war" within his party. "If they can't honestly say that they have confidence in this team," Trudeau admonished, "then they cannot be part of this team."[12] He received a standing ovation.[13]

There's an underlying message in all this: women are meant to be liked, supported, and celebrated only so long as they behave. Women like Wilson-Raybould, Philpott, and Caesar-Chavannes can achieve power, sure, but rise too high, get too assertive, speak your mind too often, and it will be snatched away. Fingers crossed the landing is soft when you're pushed off the highest rung you've climbed to; it probably won't be. So, ladies, play nice!

The former attorney general of Canada is far from the first example of what I like to call "be sure to play nice" syndrome — and, unless things change, far from the last. We might also turn again to Clinton, who is perhaps the most famous of the contemporary cautionary tales for women. Her stunning loss has garnered the same type of "where were you when" lore as the moon landing. We all remember that she was expected to win in a landslide. Renowned statistician Nate Silver was the most conservative of the analysts, putting her chances of winning at 71.4 percent[14]; the Princeton Election Consortium put it at a whopping 99 percent.[15] That, we know, did not happen. Only one model, Moody's, which had correctly predicted every president since 1980, noted a caveat in its declaration of Clinton as the eventual victor. "Given the unusual nature of the 2016 election cycle to date," wrote Moody's analytics economist in his report, "it is very possible that voters will react to changing economic and political conditions differently than they have in past election cycles."[16] Meaning, the model could account only for trends and numbers, not how voters felt about Clinton herself. The analyst might as well have said, "Look, we've never tried this thing with a lady before."

Many women felt Clinton's loss as their own — a stark reminder that we really hadn't come so far at all. Like me, Amanda Kingsley Malo cried when she found out Clinton's predicted landslide was stuck in fantasyland. The Sudbury, Ontario, kindergarten teacher told me that she didn't even like Clinton all that much to start with, but when Clinton lost she felt broken. It was a weird feeling; it wasn't even her country. But as she reflected on those moments, she realized her feelings of devastation ran deep. Kingsley Malo was twenty-nine years old, and Clinton was the first woman she'd seen run for the top spot in government as a candidate representing a major party. She started to think more keenly about the ways in which being a woman had affected her life, and the job and political opportunities she'd missed out on. A past Liberal Party community team organizer, Kingsley Malo decided to create Politics Now, an organization dedicated to training and supporting women candidates in Northern Ontario's municipal elections.

Politics Now launched in March 2017, to coincide with International Women's Day. To prepare for the launch, Kingsley Malo gathered some statistics. The nine cities in Northern Ontario had eighty-five available council positions. Women held only eighteen of those seats, and at the time none of the cities had a woman mayor. North Bay, Ontario, had never elected a woman mayor, and the town was founded in 1891. Of the few female mayors who had ever held office, many (though certainly not all) served only one term. The numbers didn't surprise Kingsley Malo at all. She thought back to being a student in the 1990s, when her teacher would tell everybody, "The sky is the limit," but she only had to look at the row of photos depicting every prime minister of Canada to know that wasn't true. When she later learned that Kim Campbell, Canada's only woman prime minister (June 25, 1993 to November 4, 1993), had lost in the general election, that wall looked even more depressing.

"I had to learn there were more men named John than there were women who had ever been prime minister of our country," she said. "Men have heard the same messaging as us and they tell us we're equal now. Yeah, we *say* that. But when I was a kid growing up and people said, 'Amanda, you can be anything, even prime minister,' it felt very much like there was an asterisk next to it." The message girls and women hear, she added, is more like, *You can be prime minister, but look what happened to Kim Campbell.* Or, *You can run for office, but look at Elizabeth May.* An asterisk will reveal that in August 1993, before she went on to lose, Campbell was the most popular Canadian prime minister in thirty years,[17] and she was still leading the polls in mid-October.[18] It will reveal that Campbell went on to lead the Conservative Party's worst defeat in Canadian political history, in which she also lost her seat.[19] And it will also show that Green Party of Canada leader Elizabeth May was blocked from three federal campaigns' worth of national leader debates before the rules were changed for 2019's election.[20]

It can be tough to watch the slow progress. Kingsley Malo helped ten women get elected in Northern Ontario's 2018 municipal elections. She spent a lot more time, though, thinking about the sixteen women she worked with who did not get elected. Did she really make a difference? A lot of people, she told me, assume her end goal is gender-equal councils or cabinets. But that's only the beginning. Truly inclusive politics, she stressed, strikes down barriers for everyone: people of colour, those with disabilities, those with low income, Indigenous people, and so on. The problem, she added, is that everybody is still treating politics like a man's game. They're playing by the rules—often changing themselves, but rarely changing the game. Candidates are expected to fit into a diversity model that's not really built for them, to adapt to the Old Boys' Club and somehow succeed that way, triumphing over the very people the game was *built* to favour. Kingsley Malo is prone to punctuating her sentences with incredulous laughter, and she did so as she said this, thinking about the absurdity of it all.

Our Own Best Chance

The new-old brand of testosterone-fuelled leadership is not, needless to say, universally beloved. There are many Canadians, a lot of them young ones, who believe in a feminist government. In September 2018, the MATCH International Women's Fund released the findings of a cross-country survey of Canadians aged eighteen to thirty-seven, focusing on what role people believed the government should play in achieving gender equality. Nearly three-quarters of respondents expressed the belief that it was the government's responsibility to invest in gender equality worldwide, and roughly half of them wanted Canada to play a big or a leading role—including through funding.[21] I asked Jess Tomlin, the organization's president and CEO, about the motivation for commissioning the study. "Transparently," she said "[we wanted to know] can we make this an election issue? Can we not make this an issue at the margins? Can we actually use this momentum—use this fever pitch moment—to accelerate an agenda in this country for gender equality?"

When I asked Tomlin if anything surprised her about the survey's findings, which also delved into whether people believed gender equality was achievable within their lifetime, she paused and then answered in the opposite direction. "I'll tell you what didn't surprise me," she said, speaking of the survey's female respondents. "What didn't surprise me was that the older she gets, the less optimistic she is that she'll see gender equality in her lifetime." The survey found that 84 percent of men and women between eighteen and twenty-three said they were optimistic the Western world would reach gender equality within their lifetimes. With age, that optimism waned, dropping to 70 percent among those between twenty-nine and thirty-three years old. That wasn't surprising, Tomlin said, because the older we get, the more we have to live in the world. "We teach our girls that they can be anything and they can do anything and there's nothing standing in their way, but that's bullshit. *Right?*" she emphasized. "She can believe that up until she has her first experience where she's sexually assaulted." She can believe it until "somebody decides to follow her home from work, or she realizes there's a boys' club, or she's passed up for a promotion, or she suddenly gets a glimpse of what he's making versus what she's making."

This reality made her wonder about what she could confidently teach her nine-year-old daughter, what dreams of the future she could instill in her. "I am feeding her the lines," she said. "If you want to be a taxi driver, if you want to be a CEO, if you want to be the prime minister of Canada, there's nothing that's going to stand in your way." Tomlin was, in fact, unknowingly echoing the same messaging Kingsley Malo heard as a child—messaging that she grew up to believe was, indeed, bunk. Tomlin knew it too, just as I know it, just as those older women who answered the MATCH survey knew it. The "you can be anything" lie is something we have long wished we could whisper into truth. "But it's like death by a thousand cuts," said Tomlin. "The older you get and the more experiences that you have, the more you are worn down. And that breaks my heart. I do not want [my daughter] growing up without hope and resetting her expectations of what she can achieve because she happens to be on the wrong side of the gender equation."

Still, she found the results of the MATCH survey encouraging — a sign that her daughter's generation would encounter a less restrictive world. Laughing with the admission that the research firm itself would possibly not agree, Tomlin told me that she chose to interpret the optimism of the younger generation as action. Every day, ordinary people, she said, were becoming activists in a way she'd seen spark global transformation. Fundamentally, she added, that's how change happens: when people hold their local government systems, policies, customs, norms, attitudes, and beliefs to account. When they demand a new way. That is different, she said, from methods by which mainstream populations in countries like Canada traditionally approach social advancement. "[It] has been, 'You elect a great person, you trust these establishments to do right by you,' and now people are saying, 'Hell no.'" They may believe the government needs to help push for change, but they also don't want to wait for it. "People are saying, 'We're going to completely disrupt the system, we're going to completely disrupt the status quo, and we're going to rebuild it for ourselves.'"

Or, *some* of us are. A day after Trudeau booted Wilson-Raybould and Philpott from caucus, roughly fifty delegates from the political leadership program, Daughters of the Vote, participated in an event in which they were to sit in their own MPs' seats in the House of Commons to be addressed by the national leaders. When the prime minister arrived to speak to them, some of the delegates, all between the ages of eighteen and twenty-three, turned their backs on him.[22] On the whole, though, it took longer than I expected for the SNC-Lavalin fallout to develop into skepticism about Trudeau's feminism. Expectedly, when it did happen, Conservative Party opportunism drove much of it, leading the charge to call Trudeau a "fake feminist."[23] The conversation quickly devolved into who was a better option for young women: Trudeau or then Conservative Party leader Andrew Scheer. "If the leader of the Opposition wants to be a better feminist than me, I wish him good luck," Trudeau quipped. "That would be a great thing." On Twitter, former deputy prime minister Sheila Copps toed a similar line: "Trudeau has not said bitch to anyone. Even though it may apply. The Feminist rumblings from the media are certainly questionable. Who is more feminist than Trudeau? Andrew Scheer?"[24] Soon, people were ridiculing both Trudeau's avowed feminism *and* the women who questioned Trudeau's avowed feminism. If feminists now took down Trudeau, the logic went, they had better be prepared for what they would get: a supposedly far-worse option.

That many people still seemed to believe the future of equality hinged on the choice between two privileged white men says a lot about our perceptions of women and power. It tells us exactly what we think about the *possibility* of a woman in power. Until we can interrupt that bland, hegemonic narrative—until we can finally see a diverse collection of women as our own best hope for equity—we'll keep replicating those same iterations of power endlessly. It's as though we're making a paper-doll chain of paper white men, one that might as well be titanium for how unbreakable it sometimes feels. It's time we grabbed some scissors.

Why We Don't See Women as Leaders

I'm worried Alice Eagly is telling me to be patient. I'd contacted the social psychologist after seeing her open the Behavioural Approaches to Diversity conference at the Rotman School of Management in Toronto. The blatantly feminist event was held in a very masculine space, and invited participants to ponder whether everything they knew about promoting diversity in organizations was, in fact, wrong. (The spirit of rebellion carried on to organizers who seemed delighted that the acronym spelled out BAD, branding it on everything from notebooks to portable chargers.) I'd called Eagly because I wanted to know why we still had such difficulty seeing women as leaders, and what, if anything, it had to do with our perceptions of power. As a much-lauded professor at Northwestern University, the author of several books and more than two hundred articles (her work has been cited 90,000 times!), Eagly is one of North America's leading researchers on women and leadership — and the stereotypes that help and harm us on our way there.

She began studying leadership, she told me, because she believes that, out of all the factors that might shift gender equality, leadership is the most important one. Yes, it would be "nice," she added, if 50 percent of physicists were women, but she doubted that parity would immediately change the fundamental nature of science. There would be no guarantee that parity in science would, as a matter of fact, lead to new frontiers. (I'm less sure of that, but we'll look more closely at how women are upending the bro-filled tech world in chapter 8.) Leadership, on the other hand, would affect everything. "Because leaders," as Eagly put it, "control resources."

Things were already changing, she added, and had been changing for a while. *Slowly*. Eagly had spent a lot of time looking at the past half-century's worth of U.S. public opinion polls. Those polls assessed the ways in which people viewed men and women — or, essentially, the public's changing gender stereotypes. And gender stereotypes had changed, just not in the ways one might have expected, considering the country's enduring inequality. Perhaps surprisingly, as of 2018, men and women were generally viewed to be equally competent, she said. In cases where people did not view them as equal, women were seen as being *more* competent. Women were also seen as being more communal. All of which explained why women were seeing improvements in the workplace, generally, and also in education.

However, women were also still in an "agency deficit," with men consistently surpassing them. Unfortunately, agency—that is, the ability to be assertive, competitive, and confident in your competence—is also seen as synonymous with leadership. Women, added Eagly, are in a double bind, of the same sort we've seen with Clinton, Wilson-Raybould, and countless others. They are often punished for acting agentic—that is, not playing nice. At the same time, the belief persists that women should be selfless, modest, and communal, but that those same women lack agency. In other words: women are seen either as pushovers or as monsters, neither of which are fit for leadership. So while women are rising, they are *not* consistently rising to leadership. We are advancing, but not necessarily to positions where we can make the most change in organizations. Our competence can open only so many doors.

As someone who's often been called "too nice for leadership," I feel this deeply. Navigating workplaces with kindness and a willingness to hear others' opinions has, repeatedly, been misconstrued as a sign of my weakness and an inability to take charge of a team. I've been chastised for refusing to yell at colleagues, and I've been coached not to ask for feedback. Bosses have told me not to offer mentorship, even as they've acknowledged that advancing in the workplace is still easier for men in my industry. They've told me I cannot "make friends" with everybody, even though it's painfully clear I'm very far from being the office social butterfly. At the same time, it seems unlikely that screaming at my co-workers, refusing to listen to them, and using silly admonishments like "that's my final word" would get me anywhere, either. So people are surprised when they can't steamroll over me, but they keep trying and trying.

The really sticky part, explained Eagly, is that stereotypes are not arbitrary, as much as we'd like to believe they have no grounding. To believe women can be agentic, we need to see more women being agentic, and doing so successfully. Or, put another way: many people don't believe women can be agentic—that they can be leaders—because they don't see enough women in those positions. "It's very much a step-by-step process," said Eagly. "How did women get to be considered so competent? Well, we started all going to college. *Right?* And sticking in there and getting those degrees." This, she stressed to me, happened over a period of decades. It was a gradual escalation of the widespread public perception of women's competence. The same slow process needs to take place for women to achieve equal representation in positions of power, whether it be in government, business, or elsewhere. Her voice rose to a mock pout as she insisted, "We can't just say, 'Stop thinking women aren't agentic, that's not fair!'" She continued, "You have to see it. To get there, women have to work against the grain. Social change is not easy."

There's another way of approaching the power gap, though. Rather than accepting the solution of a slow, long haul to equality, we can work to divorce agency—and its corresponding qualities of aggression and competitiveness—from our definition of good leadership. During her Rotman keynote, Eagly floated this idea, noting that one way to shift the perception of female leadership is for groups and organizations to *decrease* the value of agency. In doing so, they become less hierarchical and foster co-operative relations, elevating democratic and collaborative leadership styles. Such a structure would no longer default to an aggressive, alpha, Type-A personality at the top, but instead would allow for many expressions of leadership—or even no leader at all. She was less enthusiastic about that option when I spoke with her, clarifying that leadership (and, by extension, power) will always require that someone have a dash of agentic qualities. A woman cannot just walk into a room, she explained, and let those in the room decide for her. She cannot run a company or a country by consensus alone.

So while Eagly seemed to agree that feminists can work toward bending leadership models, she also stressed that alternate modes won't fully close the power gap. To her mind, there will always need to be agentic leaders in power, and the toughest, most urgent goal will be getting people to see women as naturally agentic—fully capable of, and suited for, making decisions and leading others. The good news is that women don't necessarily have to win elections for perceptions to change. Speaking of the then-approaching 2020 U.S. presidential election, Eagly, who joked that she's "old," was hopeful. Many women had tossed their hats into the ring for presidential nomination after seeing so many women run for the 116th U.S. Congress and a record number of them win. It was the biggest jump in women Congress members since the 1990s, and it happened after women saw Clinton run for president and lose.[25]

By this logic, the way we talk about women and leadership also has to change, argued Eagly. Both feminists and the media in general often focus on the worst statistics, the ones that seem the grimmest. But why don't we ever talk about the areas in which women have made gains? She cited one statistic that she was particularly sick of hearing: that women make up only 5 percent of the CEOs of companies on the S&P 500. If you look instead at CEOs across all organizations, 28 percent are women.[26] That isn't wonderful either, but it's a whole lot better than 5 percent. Ignoring these women only perpetuates the myth that women can't lead. It ignores all the women who have climbed to power in universities, in non-profits. It makes people say — Eagly's mockingly plaintive voice returned here — "Oh, there are so few women leaders. Come on now!" she shouted. "Don't you live in the world?" She had a point: the very way we talk about leadership, and power, often excludes women, and the areas in which they've already made so much progress in flipping power dynamics.

It's for these reasons that Eagly also believes it's time to retire the "glass ceiling" metaphor. Like me, she sees women's route to leadership as a labyrinth — although hers isn't quite so dire as the one I envisioned. The glass ceiling has a hopelessness to it, she said, because it is by definition a solid barrier. The labyrinth metaphor does not deny that women have challenges men don't. "It presents a challenge with the spirit of go! GO! Figure it out," she told me. "Get through your labyrinth."

I understand what she's saying, and it's something I've heard others say for what feels like my whole life. It boils down to this: just keep going. Still, I cannot help but wonder if there are better ways to achieve access to institutional power, ones that don't culminate in offering up potential leaders like sacrificial feminist lambs. And I cannot help but wonder if Eagly and others have too quickly dismissed alternative power models. Why do we have to keep playing (and losing) the same game to get ahead? Solutions that shuttle women through old systems—albeit hoping that women will change the system themselves once they, fingers crossed, get to the top—don't only seem to reward the most privileged, the most able to lean in, or the luckiest, they also seem to be taking forever. It's possible to view these results as encouraging, as Eagly does, and for good reason, but the process itself is exhausting—and even more so for women of colour, Indigenous women, and those who are LGBTQ+.

Finally, I couldn't take it anymore. We were looking at centuries of ongoing struggle for political and economic equality ahead! Hope was just *fine*, I said, but wasn't this gradual change making a lot of us justifiably impatient?

Eagly blinked at me. "Right," she said. "Social movements are supposed to make people angry."

A Million Reasons to Be Mad

Ontario MPP Jill Andrew was running late. It was mid-October 2018, and the politician, body positive activist, and community co-owner of Glad Day Bookshop, the world's oldest LGBTQ+ bookstore, was set to open Toronto's annual G Day. The one-day event, which started in Vancouver, is meant to help girls aged ten to twelve prepare for the next phase of their lives: adolescence. In many ways, it's also meant to reclaim the term "rite of passage" and mitigate the onslaught of BS that is, already, bearing down on them as they go from "girl" to "woman." There were about a hundred girls gathered that day in the Toronto Public Reference Library, and the delayed opening gave them a chance to chat excitedly as they waited. How often did these girls get to attend something that was all about them? They were practically fizzing. A teenage volunteer buzzed past me. "I'm sorry. I'm very hyped," she said, smiling broadly. "I've been talking to girls all morning!"

Eventually, Andrew rushed in. The organizers encouraged everybody to take three deep breaths for "Jill and ourselves."

Andrew turned to the group. "The first lesson," she joked, referring to the city's transit system, which had unexpectedly closed for maintenance that morning, "is always be prepared." Andrew went on to explain what a member of provincial parliament does, exactly, and mentioned her newly earned doctoral degree. The encouraging and also uncomfortable truth is that Andrew, as a Black, queer woman in power, brings a presence that often upends the status quo — a vital "see me, be me" moment for the girls, who hung on to her every word. Andrew's prepared speech was both engaging and inspiring. She talked about being different as a source of power; she told the girls they were good enough just the way they were. But it was her unprepared commentary, offered in between the other speakers' talks, that struck me most deeply.

"We're allowed to cry," she told the group. "We're allowed to be happy." She took a breath, and when her voice came out it was booming. "But can I also say we're allowed to be angry." The girls started cheering. Their parents and guardians began cheering too, voices roaring. Andrew repeated herself: "We're allowed to be angry!" We don't have to smile, she added. Dozens of little heads nodded. "Every day we're told to smile. Smile. *Smile*. We don't have to!" Cries of "Yeah!" echoed around the room. I wanted to shout with them. I cannot imagine anyone ever having told me that when I was a little girl; I cannot imagine being brave enough to believe it.

Much has been made of women's renewed fury in recent

years, a lot of it called forth in the wake of Trump's win. Several books came out on the subject in 2018 alone, and I heard from many women I interviewed that year that they'd never been angrier. As Jess Tomlin put it: "I'm hearing and feeling a lot of rage. It's this idea that you can't unsee things." She went on: "And because there is this global sort of mass awakening right now, we're seeing establishments crumble, we're seeing celebrities crumble, we're seeing traditional power structures be questioned. It's all so much." You can't ignore it anymore. Certainly, many people don't want to.

Tomlin's right. We have a lot to be angry about. The wrath of the #MeToo movement alone has made it strikingly clear that many claims about equality come littered with the same asterisks Amanda Kingsley Malo saw when she looked at her classroom wall. Clinton's loss—or Trump's win—has often been marked as the spark that ignited the calls to burn it all down. It's worth remembering, though, that our current rage is happening against a backdrop of inequity that has lasted my lifetime and more. Too often the semblance of success and power for *some* has obscured a deeper truth: these systems were never built for us to succeed. I mean, it took until 2018 for us to stop singing "sons" in our national anthem, a change that prompted much backlash and a vow from some politicians, including former Conservative Party leader Andrew Scheer, to never use the new gender-neutral language.[27]

Of course, it's more than these fairly superficial things. Unless there is monumental change (or one of *Twilight*'s vampires takes me as their lover), I will not be around to see the global gender gap close. As of 2018, that was expected to happen in 108 years across the 106 countries the World Economic Forum has covered since the first edition of its report (it now ranks 149 countries).[28] To measure the gap,

the WEF looks at four different aspects — economic participation, political empowerment, health and survival, and
educational attainment — and can, in doing so, unfortunately "mask important differences in performance."
Among the four categories, the economic participation and
political empowerment chasms — and they are chasms —
will be the most challenging to shrink, according to the
report, at a mind-bending 202 and 107 years respectively.
That's almost more frustrating when the education gap is
taken into account, which is set to close in a scant fourteen years. If women are just as qualified, then what the
hell is happening? The political gap, the report notes, looks
especially bad, representing a "particularly sporadic presence of women among heads of state." In the 149 countries
studied, the average tenure of a woman as head of state or
prime minister in the past half-century has been just over
two years. *Cool.*

For the record, as of 2018, Canada sat at number sixteen
on the global gender gap index; the United States was at fifty-
one. Before Canadians get too braggy, though, consider that
the political and economic gender gaps grow wider in Canada
the closer a woman gets to power, just as they do elsewhere.
And things don't always look so great beyond traditional
methods of measuring power, either. The #MeToo movement exposed the pervasive, pernicious sexual harassment
and violence women face every day. At the height of the
movement, in 2017, a record number of people in Canada,
the vast majority of them women, reported sexual assaults
to the police. While it's often assumed (or outright stated
by those leading the backlash against #MeToo) that most
complainants came forward to report old incidents, it's
simply not true. As was the case before #MeToo, the majority of complainants reported an assault that had taken place

recently, usually on the day of their report.[29] The uptick in complainants coming forward to police resulted in an average of seventy-four reports *per day* in 2017. But even that gut-churning number does not account for the sheer volume of assaults that are not reported, which, we know, is most of them.[30]

What's more, in Canada, half of all women have experienced at least one incident of either sexual assault or physical violence since age sixteen. Women of colour, women with disabilities, transgender women, and Indigenous women all face significantly higher rates of violence; Indigenous women are killed at six times the rate of non-Indigenous women. About every six days, a woman in Canada is killed by her intimate partner.[31] I could go on and on with the bad news; the statistics that catalogue the disparate experience of women in Canada and the general shittiness they face are both bleak and relentless. Cataloguing such numbers is exhausting and sickening—a reminder, if we even need it, that progress does not equal equality. We've been fighting forever and we still have a long way to go. No wonder women are fed up.

Which is all to say that the anger that rose up after the U.S. presidential election in 2016 built on decades of feminist rage; it has sometimes guttered but never been completely snuffed out. It did not come out of nowhere. The questions we're faced with now are *What makes it any different this time?* and, more pressing, *What do we do with all this anger?* In many ways, the response to both questions is the same. This new urge to act has a very specific target: a re-emergent and toxic brand of power that has the potential to rewrite an entire country's democracy—and send any progress we have made plunging back into history. So that's what feminists are doing. They're fighting *that*. To do so, women are attacking from all sides. They are changing the face and path of power, as they also change the judicial, political, social, and economic systems it governs. They're working outside those systems, forming new ones, not even bothering to play by the old rules. *We're done adapting*, I heard over and over again from the women I spoke with. *Let them adapt to us.*

It was no doubt this undercurrent that prompted a *Maclean's* writer to hypothesize what Trudeau must have thought as he watched the SNC-Lavalin controversy brewing: "Is Jody Wilson-Raybould going to burn my government to the ground?"[32] The answer is *yes*. And many women don't want to stop there.

We Don't Need Another *Ghostbusters*

Women have often imagined equality within the confines of a patriarchal structure in which we were never meant to succeed. We've been striving for victory in a game we were never meant to win, or even to play. Think of it this way: we've been stuck trying to make blockbuster gold with movies like *Ghostbusters* or *Ocean's 8*, with too little attention focused on figuring out which stories we might want to tell for ourselves. But what would happen if we stopped casting other people in roles written first for men? Burning it all down does not necessarily mean anarchy, or a future that's plunged into chaos. Burning it down means looking beyond parity as a simple solution for equality. It means looking at representation and why it isn't a blanket guarantee of power or change. It means asking how power really works for women, and how we interact with it, and why it seems so slippery for anyone who isn't an old white dude. It means asking if it's time to change the essential demands of feminism.

We have been told that we will all achieve equality when we have what affluent white men have. But maybe it's time to question whether that's what we really want. When it comes to women and power, nothing is simple or straightforward. There are the solutions researchers posit, and then there are the things we feel from experience to be true. There is the need for parity and gender balance in our governments, in our businesses and organizations, in our schools and museums, and in our everyday lives. But there's also a need to recognize that unless we overhaul the power structures of our institutions and our societies — unless we give women equal power and respect to go along with equal access — achieving parity might not fundamentally change a damn thing. Without deep change, women might be on the team, but they'll be sitting on the sidelines. Perhaps this volatile, angry time offers an opportunity, too: a chance to create a new definition of power, and with it, a new vision for equity.

Of course, it's one thing to say that and another to actually figure out what power would look like if it weren't, as Kingsley Malo described it, a man's game. If we decided to stop playing by the rules, or even playing altogether, what would we play instead?

If I wanted a model for a new way, perhaps I might actually find cues from the past. Or maybe I wouldn't have to look so far at all. Maybe it was just a matter of asking how two little words were able to upend the world.

CHAPTER 2

This Time It's Different

*#MeToo, social change, and the cyclical nature
of women's push for power*

TARANA BURKE WALKED ONTO the stage in Toronto and the crowd in front of her rose to their feet. Hundreds had gathered in the theatre to see the founder of #MeToo speak, and dozens more had waited outside, a line snaking into the March cold, hoping the box office would release more tickets. By now, plenty of women in the room knew the bones of Burke's story. How in 2006 Burke, a civil rights activist from the Bronx, started Me Too to help young women and girls of colour, as well as those from low-income communities, who had experienced sexual violence. How in 2017 that movement went viral, extending far past anything Burke had initially expected. And they knew that what she said mattered, because she, like so many of them, spoke from a survivor-informed perspective. That she herself could say, "Me too."

But there was a time, Burke told the crowd, when those

two words stuck in her throat. "People often accuse me of bravery," she said. "But when I think about bravery, I think about Heaven." Heaven is the pseudonym Burke has given to a young girl she met long before #MeToo went viral, and long before Burke founded her movement in 2006. It's a story Burke has told often, and it's a story that deserves to be told over and over again.

When Burke was younger, then also working as an activist and community organizer, she was at a girls' camp in Alabama when the thirteen-year-old asked to speak to her privately. Burke looked into the girl's eyes and knew, in her gut, that Heaven wanted to disclose something horrible to her. She avoided the girl all day. When she finally sat with Heaven, the girl told her she was being sexually abused by her stepfather. Burke interrupted her and sent her to another worker.[1]

"In my heart, I was thinking, *This happened to me too*," Burke told the Toronto crowd. "I wish I could have said that to this child. I wish I could have given her the gift nobody gave me." But she could not get the words out. Could not face them and all that they meant.

She kept thinking about that day, just as she kept trying to understand what healing looked like. Over time, she realized that what had helped her most was having others who'd experienced sexual violence empathize with her. It was having them believe her. It was as simple and as infinitely difficult as hearing the words "me too" from their own lips. And even though she hadn't been able to say it then, she could start saying it now.

In the first year after Twitter set fire to the movement Burke had sparked, the #MeToo hashtag was used roughly 19 million times, according to the Pew Research Center.[2] Put another way, that's about 55,319 uses of the hashtag per day. It's worth noting that the centre compiled only English-language tweets and those that were in the public domain; during high-volume use periods, only about 70 percent of tweets were in English. Use of the hashtag peaked on September 9, 2018, the day that Leslie Moonves resigned. Moonves was at that time chairman and CEO of CBS, and he stepped down following numerous allegations of sexual assault and harassment, dating from the 1980s to the early 2000s.[3] (Moonves denied the allegations; he was initially set to receive $120 million in severance pay, but, following plenty of backlash, CBS withheld it.)[4] Other spikes included the day Harvey Weinstein resigned from the board of his entertainment company, and the day Christine Blasey Ford testified in front of the Senate as part of the Supreme Court confirmation process for Justice Brett Kavanaugh. The #MeToo hashtag had become part of a powerful movement taking on powerful men.

Burke has said, more than once, that #MeToo is not a moment, it's a *movement*. And she said much the same thing that night at her Toronto talk. "There's nothing new about talking about sexual violence. There's nothing new about fighting against sexual violence. What's new is that we're doing it out loud." What's new is that auditoriums now fill with people who are interested in hearing about sexual violence, and in doing something about it. What's new is that so many more people can voice how sexual violence has affected their lives and not feel shame.

After making that point, Burke paused, and stressed that what she was about to say next should not be seen as discounting the work that came before #MeToo. "What we're doing with #MeToo is building something that doesn't exist. Literally. It's an international survivor-led and survivor-focused social justice movement." Cheers, applause, and loud whistles rose up through the crowd. She'd hit on exactly what was so different about #MeToo: who it put in power.

As I heard her speak, her voice like thunder, I thought back to something she'd said earlier. People dismantle power structures by telling the truth, she'd told media at the one-year anniversary of #MeToo. That's where the whole idea of "speaking truth to power" came from: "the more truth that you tell, the less power people have over you."[5] For Burke, the real world-changing strength of #MeToo wasn't in taking down powerful men—she saw that as a distraction—but in helping survivors to free themselves. To begin healing. And, in so many ways, even that was only the beginning of what #MeToo could do, has already done.

What Is Power, Exactly?

Power can be difficult to define. Questions of how it operates, and how the structures and hierarchies of power relate to individuals, groups, and societies, often require complex, and even equivocal, answers—when there are answers at all. Many sociologists have spent a lifetime studying power and are still unravelling it, perhaps only agreeing that it is, at best, ambiguous. A lot of academics rely on German sociologist Max Weber's classical definition (Weber is generally considered to be one of the founders of sociology itself). Weber wrote that power is "the ability of an actor or actors to realize his/her/their will in a social action, even against the will of others." Vincent Roscigno, a professor at Ohio State University and one of today's big thinkers on power and inequality, notes in his 2011 paper "Power, Revisited" that those same sociologists are very likely to also offer

"piecemeal caveats that render the original Weberian definition either useless or so complex that it becomes difficult
to imagine how one might go about actually observing or
studying it."[6] Oh, yay!

I know from asking the roughly one hundred people
interviewed for this book that even people who don't spend
their entire academic careers looking for a definition rarely
agree on what power means. Roscigno opens "Power,
Revisited" by observing that "There is perhaps no construct
in sociology as theoretically ambiguous yet simultaneously
appealing as power." Again, that word: *ambiguous*.

I decided to call Roscigno in hopes he might have more
to say on the subject—particularly about how social movements might disrupt power, and also about power and
inequity. As a historical sociologist, Roscigno has spent a
lot of time looking at how and why structures of inequality
shift. In poking at these long-term trends, he often comes
back to power. A question that lingers at the back of his
mind, he told me, is this: Why do structures of inequality
not change much over time, and if they do, why are they so
slow to change? Much of what we see as progress is really
only a blip—a moment, to borrow Tarana Burke's phrase in
reverse, and not a movement. Take for example the Women's
March on Washington, generally agreed to be the beginning
of today's resurgent feminism. To Roscigno, this was a blip.

He wasn't being intentionally dismissive. The march was
amazing, he said, and, like many others, he watched it thinking, *Oh, this is it*. But it hasn't yet moved past the first step
in making a movement: consciousness-raising. Yes, there's a
need to get people on board with the message, to give them
information about what's going on and why so many people
marched that day. Yet, he added, without a fundamental
structural or cultural shift, nothing will happen to actually

undermine inequality in meaningful, concrete ways. "The next step is to get politicians to do something about it," he added, "and I sort of scratch my head about whether or not we have social movement action now that generates that kind of reverberation or earthquake in the structure." The reverberation needs to be big enough, loud enough, *dangerous* enough that politicians must get involved, must change laws, must bow to pressure from the public.

Then again, he added, none of this is happening in a vacuum. Roscigno's research looks at what makes social movements successful in disrupting power, but also at why they dissipate. Good, powerful, world-shaking social movements are contentious by nature; they often provoke backlash. In terms of feminism, that backlash has been on the rise since women effected changes to the law in the 1960s and '70s. A lot of major, progressive legislative change, at least in the United States, added Roscigno, has flatlined, if not started a slippery backslide. That backlash has generated the same sort of unease and walls-crumbling-down feeling that's usually reserved for progressive social change. Roscigno would like to see progressive movements become more innovative, for them to stop playing by the rules and to create distress in the system. "The Women's March at least reinvigorated hope, but successful social movements only happen when they're durable," he said. "That is, when they last. When they last over time and can create actual organizational, political momentum and changes."

#MeToo, Public Opinion, and Social Change

So where does that leave #MeToo? At first glance, it seems as though the movement has caused massive change. On

further examination...well, everything is a bit more complicated at second glance.

Seen from Burke's point of view, #MeToo has already
done something remarkable: it has restored power to those
who have felt robbed of it. But when it comes to the type
of tangible, cultural change Roscigno talks about as being
central to a successful social movement, #MeToo has hit
some surprising roadblocks. For a movement that seems
to be everywhere, I'd expected — or maybe hoped — that
its ubiquity would have translated into measurable change,
whether in popular perceptions or in application of our
legislation. Not so much. After one year of #MeToo, numerous publications and research firms tried to capture that
exact shift I'd hoped for, offering us a plethora of data on
people's views toward sexual harassment and violence as
well as consent. The numbers did not tell a happy story. It
turned out that, if anything, people had become even more
skeptical about sexual harassment, more confused about
sexual assault, and even less inclined to do anything about it.

Men are more likely to feel this way, but such frustration isn't relegated to one gender — as we saw when French
actor Catherine Deneuve and one hundred other women
denounced #MeToo in an open letter, arguing that "insistent
or clumsy flirting is not a crime, nor is gallantry a chauvin-
ist aggression."[7] As one twenty-four-year-old woman put
it to me when I asked about her experience of harassment
at work: "As for verbal sexual harassment, personally I'm
confused [as] to what...that even mean[s] anymore considering it's 2019 and post #MeToo. Does that mean have I
been harassed in an extremely inappropriate manner? And
does that also include if someone has given me compliments
or tried to be insistent on expressing how attractive they
think I am?"

She went on to explain that some might think she'd been harassed at work, but she believed it wasn't so cut and dried. "Have men I worked with made comments on my appearance, suggesting I was attractive, sexy, etcetera?" she said. "Yes, but I did already have a great rapport with them and it did not make me uncomfortable." The same went for office humour that some might construe as not funny at all. "Have I worked with someone who made extremely inappropriate jokes with women around the office? Yes. Was he a bad guy? No, he was married, had kids, in his sixties, came from a Maritime culture where that was normal, and to be honest some of the jokes were funny. Some were just dumb." She continued: "Was I personally offended or uncomfortable? No, because I was friends with [him] and he was harmless." She was, he said, a nice guy. "Were some of the women offended by his jokes? Yes, some were, and when they voiced their feelings, he would apologize and refrain from doing those jokes around those women." She conceded that there were likely other women who did not speak up and may have been uncomfortable around him.

One Economist/YouGov poll found that, in the year since #MeToo went viral, a slight shift *against* the complainants had occurred.[8] More American adults felt that any men who'd sexually harassed women at work in the more distant past (say, two decades ago) should keep their jobs. More Americans thought that those who bring forward sexual harassment complaints cause more problems than they solve. And more Americans thought that so-called false accusations were a bigger problem than attacks that go unreported or unpunished — a result that was replicated in a different poll completed by HuffPost/YouGov.[9] Only 17 percent of those surveyed for the HuffPost poll felt the movement hadn't gone far enough; 28 percent felt that it had gone too far. Less than half of Americans held a favourable view of the movement. Lest we think this is a problem singular to our frenemies in the south, the Canadian Women's Foundation also found that, in the year after #MeToo, understanding of consent actually dropped.[10] Half of the women surveyed said they'd felt pressured to consent at some point in their lives.

This mixed public sentiment, unsurprisingly, hasn't done much to move policy. University of Massachusetts Amherst researchers released a report in December 2018 that looked at how the federal Equal Employment Opportunity Commission dealt with sexual harassment complaints over a five-year period. Researchers estimated that 5 million people experience sexual harassment at work every year in the United States, but only 9,200 of them, on average, file a charge with the EEOC or their state's Fair Employment Practice agencies. In other words, noted the researchers, 99.8 percent of people who experience sexual harassment at work never file a charge.

Perhaps those 99.8 percent of people know what kind of bullshit is heading for them if they do. Of those who filed, only 1,800 received any kind of redress, even though the EEOC judged almost 90 percent of the charges plausibly legally actionable on intake. Almost three-quarters of those who reported workplace sexual harassment received no benefit from the EEOC, a scant 15 percent received monetary bene-fit, 8 percent received monetary and workplace change, and 4 percent saw only change at work. The majority of those who filed were, in fact, subject to punitive measures from their employers. Because of course they were. About two-thirds of those who filed were either fired or faced retaliation at work.[11] But, yeah, sure, people must be lying if they don't file charges right away. There could be no other plausible reason!

At the same time, there's a deliberate diminishment that comes with characterizing #MeToo as a movement that focuses only on sexual harassment. The movement is very much about those who've faced sexual violence — including rape — the vast majority of which did not happen in the workplace at all. If we're going to talk about public response to women speaking out, en masse, about the sexual violence they experience, we'd be remiss not to mention the arguably corresponding astronomical rise in calls to Canada's rape crisis centres. The first noted rise happened during one of the first "blips," as Roscigno might say, of the new movement to end sexual violence: the national conversation around former Q host Jian Ghomeshi, who was charged with several counts of sexual assault and one count of overcoming resistance by choking in 2014. In one pre-#MeToo year, for instance, Ontario's centres responded to 50,000 crisis-line calls — up from 30,000 in 2009. Centres only became more inundated with #MeToo. One Toronto clinic, for example, reported an 83 percent increase in requests for counselling in 2017. Yet some centres have not seen changes in their staffing levels since the early 1990s. No wonder centres have seen a devastating surge in wait times for counselling, with some waitlist times stretching as long as eighteen months.

In Ontario, where Canada's most populist-macho leader, Doug Ford, governs, political will has turned chilly toward #MeToo's aims. In early 2018, the Ontario government, then headed by Liberal Party leader Kathleen Wynne, pledged a 33 percent increase over three years to Ontario's nearly forty rape crisis centres as part of its gender-based-violence strategy, "It's Never Okay." In many centres, that money would have gone to hire additional counsellors, which, in turn, would have helped to alleviate increasingly long wait times as centres struggle to keep up with skyrocketing demand. Ford's government has repeatedly refused to honour the promise. Considering all this, it becomes easier to understand why Roscigno isn't so quick to bless the change-making potential of the current iteration of the women's movement. Then again, maybe it really is more ambiguous than all that.

The Power of Speaking Up

There is an iconic photograph of Christine Blasey Ford taken on the day she testified before the Senate Judiciary Committee in September 2018.[12] Snapped at the moment of her swearing-in, the much-circulated image shows Blasey Ford with her palm raised, head tilted up, eyes closed, shoulders squared. She is somehow bathed in light. Like many others, when I look at that photo I see someone who appears to be taking a deep breath, steeling herself before the expected onslaught, an emblem of grace and courage.

She was there to recount how Brett Kavanaugh had raped her nearly four decades earlier (a charge he has denied). I watched that testimony streaming online, as did so many of the women I knew, texting each other notes of rage and reassurance, filling each other's phones with *Are you okay?* and *I am here for you.* We could see ourselves in Blasey Ford. We could relate when she opened her testimony by saying, "I am here today not because I want to be. I am terrified." We were terrified for her.

Blasey Ford had already experienced death threats. Her email had been hacked, and she'd been impersonated online. She'd even had to relocate her family—and would eventually go on to move at least four times and be forced to hire private security.[13] Watching her testify, it was hard not to think of her initial reservation about coming forward: "Why suffer through the annihilation if it's not going to matter?" The question became even more heartbreaking when senators voted to confirm Kavanaugh to the Supreme Court in October that year. Blasey Ford had challenged a powerful man, in a powerful institution, and she had not, it seemed, shifted any of that power. Many people asked if she came forward for nothing, the silent "Yes" hanging after their question mark. But, then again, how does that saying go? Vast patriarchal institutions that support, and even elevate, sexual violence against women weren't un-built in a day? In testifying, Blasey Ford showed us a different type of power, one that resonated with women in particular.

"In her courage, many Americans saw the opposite of everything they think is wrong with Washington. Politicians spin, fudge the truth, grasp at power. Ford appeared guileless," wrote *Time* journalist Haley Sweetland Edwards, adding that Blasey Ford spoke up even though she knew she was unlikely to gain from it. "That kind of courage is rare, especially in Washington today. And Ford showed how powerful it can be."[14]

From one angle, her testimony confirmed the fortress-like hold men have on power. From another, her decision to speak up, and people's reactions to it, proved that power can wear many faces—likely one reason why it's so difficult to define. It doesn't always look like a person (usually a man) sitting at the top of a company or government, looking down. Power can also look like speaking your truth, forcing inconvenient questions into the mainstream, and inspiring countless others to do the same. Power doesn't always have to *win*; it isn't always a triumph *over* someone else. Sometimes it's what happens when a person breaks the silence. It's what happens when a person acknowledges to others, and to themselves, that their experiences matter. Sometimes, it's just for you.

Media and researchers alike have gravitated toward evaluating #MeToo based on what people *think* about it, as if we need a consensus for rebellion. We ask if people agree with it. If people #BelieveHer. If people were surprised at the sheer magnitude of it. If he — any he — should be punished, and if it matters if the alleged assault happened so many years ago. (Incidentally, people were significantly more inclined to support Kavanaugh's confirmation once they learned the alleged assault happened more than thirty-five years ago, as if there's an expiry date on being a horrible human being.) These are all worthwhile questions, and it's important for us to consider them. They help us gauge the likelihood of institutional change, as Roscigno rightly noted, which is necessary for a movement's success. But I have to wonder if Burke struck closer to the real change-making potential of #MeToo when she spoke about its power to heal. Because these methods and measurements do little to help us evaluate the movement's power *outside* of an institution and the dominant culture that influences it.

Blasey Ford made her first public statement since the testimony in December 2018 when she presented the *Sports Illustrated* Inspiration of the Year Award to Rachael Denhollander, the first woman who spoke up to publicly accuse Larry Nassar, the former U.S. gymnastics team doctor, of sexual abuse. Eventually more than 150 women and girls publicly accused him; their victim impact statements took a full seven days to be read in court. One, from gold medallist Aly Raisman, spoke to what many have taken to calling an "army of survivors." "We, this group of women you so heartlessly abused over such a long period of time, are now a force, and you are nothing," Raisman said. "The tables have turned, Larry. We are here. We have our voices, and we are not going anywhere."[15] And while it should be lost on nobody that it took 150 women to take down *one* powerful man, it should also not be lost on us that these women did come together, for the first time in their lives. In many ways, their speaking up was also about reclaiming their own power: power over their own narratives, power over their own voices, power over their own truths.

In her award presentation, Blasey Ford herself acknowledged the risk Denhollander took in speaking out, and also how her actions galvanized others. "The lasting lesson," she added, "is that we all have the power to create real change and we cannot allow ourselves to be defined by the acts of others."[16] In another context, that statement would sound like a platitude. Except we know that the tide of #MeToo has washed over far more men than Nassar — despite the generally lukewarm attitude toward it (itself arguably a product of that change). In the year after media broke the Harvey Weinstein story, #MeToo brought down a total of 201 once-powerful men, according to a *New York Times* report.[17] In contrast, the year before, only thirty high-profile people made the news for losing their jobs following public reports of sexual misconduct. More interestingly, though, in the 124 cases in which companies hired replacements to fill the big (ass)hole at the top, a total of fifty-four women were chosen. (Presumably still in turmoil, some companies had yet to hire anyone at all.)

That's far from a guarantee of deeper power shifts. As we'll see later, in chapter 4, just as parity is not always synonymous with equality, having a woman CEO does not necessarily guarantee her, or any other woman in the company, power. But disrupting the default-male-CEO tradition is a start — evidence that, as *The New York Times* put it, the

#MeToo movement is shaking the most *visible* power structures. "We've never seen something like this before," Joan Williams, a professor who studies work, gender, and class at the University of California, Hastings College of the Law, told the paper. "Women have always been seen as risky, because they might do something like have a baby. But men are now being seen as more risky hires."

And yet it's more than that. There's a reason Burke — and others — calls focusing on the number of downed men a distraction. What about those of us who've experienced violence at the hands of strangers, casual acquaintances, or people we thought we loved or trusted? Threaded through all of this is one constant, and it isn't bad bosses. It's how #MeToo has given those who've experienced sexual violence a way to talk to each other, unfiltered and without any interference from the systems they are typically forced to navigate. Some have used that power to cut the head off the monster. Good for them. Others have used it to do something that is Burke's goal for the movement, something that is perhaps far more radical: to begin healing. I cannot think of a more anti-patriarchal vision of power than thousands of women coming together to heal one of the deepest wounds that system can inflict.

Survivors to the Front

As someone who has experienced sexual violence as a child and as an adult, I know first-hand how shame, guilt, and silence can eat away at your sense of self, your own sense of power, and even the belief that anything *can* change. I know that sexual violence is itself not an act of passion-gone-wrong, as it's so often portrayed, but a particular exertion — and abuse—of power. Those who benefit from traditional power structures should fear #MeToo not because they could be the next target, but because it facilitates a way for us to validate each other and our experiences, to share knowledge and compassion, to be vulnerable and honest, and to land in the open arms of a thousand hugs, real and virtual. It tells us we can cry and rage and stumble. It tells us we deserve to talk about these things, and in the way that we want to. Ultimately, in speaking up and being listened to, we become more whole again. #MeToo helps us to imagine what we can do when we're not being systematically, intentionally broken down; to dream of all that can happen when the systems that break us are themselves broken, torn down, set on fire. And it invites us to believe that such a future is, at last, possible. Hope. It gives us hope.

In so many ways, then, #MeToo not only allows survivors to reclaim their narratives, it also enables them to reclaim power itself. Maybe it won't yet stop assault, maybe it won't yet punish everyone who's at fault, maybe it won't get every bad man fired, but #MeToo sure as hell lets us know we're not alone. And that none of what happened to us is our fault. Nobody can demand our damned silence anymore. In reclaiming power, we're also forcing systems to change the way they deal with survivors. Consider all the women who have asked for their publication bans to be lifted in the #MeToo era so that they can speak out, connect with other women—and criticize the system. In March 2019, one thirty-one-year-old woman, Bekah D'Aoust, who lives in a small town outside of Ottawa, petitioned the court to lift the publication ban on her name after meeting many other women who'd also experienced sexual violence. She told the *Ottawa Citizen* that those women found strength in each other, and that she wanted to offer that strength to other women. The best way to do that, she thought, was by releasing her identity.[18]

Another woman, twenty-year-old Vancouver-based Sam Fazio, had the publication ban on her name lifted after her rapist, then nineteen, served only two weeks in a detention centre for assaulting her and another woman; the rest of his three-year sentence would be served at home, under supervision. Part of the judge's reasoning? That even though the second assault occurred *after* the first, he deemed the teen unlikely to reoffend. Fazio told the CBC she wanted to come forward, with her name, so she could publicly question why anybody would report their assault when the system still treats them like this. Her story inspired two women, who didn't know her, to organize a protest on the steps of Vancouver's provincial courthouse.[19]

Then there is the group of women who in early 2019 petitioned to have their names heard in the case against Canada's former national ski coach, Bertrand Charest. One said she wanted to come forward because hearing so many women share their #MeToo stories had helped her, and she wanted to help others in the same way.[20] Another said that restoring her name to the public record was important for her to continue on her path toward healing. In many cases, it's as simple, and as difficult, as that: the decision to reclaim an identity that feels stolen. "For eight years part of my identity has been taken away from me. You have all known me as a victim, but today I am more than that. I am a wife, I am a daughter, I am a sister," D'Aoust said in a statement posted online. "I am extremely proud to say I am also a survivor, and I hope in the future that I become an advocate."[21]

It was almost as if, pre-#MeToo, people saw women who'd experienced sexual violence as machines, as Sarah Sharma, an associate professor at the University of Toronto and the director of the McLuhan Centre for Culture and Technology, told me one day over coffee. Those who enacted the violence certainly did not treat them as human, and nor did much of wider society and the systems that maintain it. The women were seen as unfeeling objects, not dissimilar to a computer or, perhaps more accurately, a toaster. When I spoke to her, Sharma had recently spent a lot of her time looking at common contemporary gender struggles through a technological lens. Suddenly, with #MeToo, she said, it was as if the machines were talking to each other, forming this powerful mass of *people*—and that really freaked out men.

When you're talking about the elements of #MeToo that should be harnessed for future change, she added, it's exactly that. "You can name any space in this city, you can name any company, you can name any university—women are sexually harassed in it," she said. "The more interesting thing about #MeToo is the fact that women were talking to each other without regular institutional help, without doctors, without lawyers." She paused. "That's what was so great about it: it was rogue."

We should ask ourselves something else, though, too, she contended: What was going on? What was happening in all these places—a person's everyday workplace, their domestic arrangement, their university or high school classroom—that these thousands of people initially felt safer turning to the internet, land of Reddit and misogynistic trolls?

Pressure from Both Sides

Mandalena Lewis would know the answer to that question all too well. After a pilot assaulted the then WestJet flight attendant during a layover in Maui in 2010, she did all the "right things." The next morning, Lewis messaged her then partner, disclosing right away. Then, she told her first officer. When she got home to Vancouver, she told the company itself what had happened. The next day, she reported her assault to the police. None of it was easy, she told me, and she immediately understood why more women don't report. She waited and waited and waited for something to happen. But, she said, WestJet did very little.

Eventually, the company called her into a meeting where she recounted everything that had happened, again. She was asked never to speak the pilot's name. She was asked to sign a non-disclosure agreement. And, at the end of the meeting, throughout which Lewis said she was "crying, yelling, screaming at how unjust this all was," a woman pulled her aside and asked why she didn't just leave WestJet.

Lewis walked out of that meeting with the clear message that she was the problem. And while she was never scheduled to work with the pilot again, she saw him all the time: at the airport, at the hotel gym, constantly. Every time it happened, WestJet representatives gave her one answer, she said. *Write it up.* She sent email after email. Finally, years later in April 2015, her complaint still unresolved, she attended a career resource management class, and at the end of it she asked about what she felt was the company's inadequate (or non-existent) sexual harassment training. It was so quiet, she said, you could have heard a pin drop in the room. Somebody reminded her that men can be assaulted too. Several months later, though, she received a Facebook message from a woman who had also been at the seminar and wanted to share a story with her. Lewis was on a layover in Toronto and it was 1:00 a.m. Still, she told the woman she could call her, and she did. Over the next two hours, the woman shared her own story of rape. It didn't take long for the women to realize they were talking about the same man.

"I had my first panic attack on my plane back to Vancouver that morning," said Lewis. Somebody made a "that's what she said" joke and she just "snapped." When she returned home, this time she asked for a copy of her employee file to see what, if anything, WestJet had done in the five years since her complaint. Company policy, she said, guarantees the file within thirty days. By day 125, after many follow-ups, Lewis lost her patience and sent a terse email: "Where the fuck is my file?" She was fired, over email, shortly after. She decided to sue the company, and eventually she launched a class-action suit that accused WestJet of fostering a workplace culture that fails to keep women employees safe and, in fact, tolerates harassment. Over a period of two years, WestJet twice tried to quash that suit but failed. Lewis has regained some of her power by speaking out, by not letting a giant corporation silence her, and by starting a very loud conversation that is making that corporation *very worried*.

While waiting for her lawsuit to make its way through the system, Lewis co-founded a website called You, Crew, and #MeToo. The website is dedicated to providing information and community-building to support other flight crew who are experiencing sexual harassment at work. Lewis told me that she wanted to see #MeToo move off the screen and into action. She seemed skeptical that this was happening, or that it was happening fast enough. It certainly must have felt that way when women routinely reached out to her and just as routinely demurred when it came to the point of speaking out. Right when she was reclaiming some of her power, the system—and the corporations that benefit from it—were reaching back for some of their own. But I wondered how many of the women who refused to join Lewis in speaking out publicly were perhaps acting in other ways, how many had started to work on shifting things in their own way, without her even knowing it. Because the more I delved into the nature of #MeToo, its reverberations, and its potential, the more I realized one thing: those who've experienced sexual violence are everywhere, including in the system.

Past movements have often relied on outside pressure to force change within a system. We need that pressure; it works. (And, as we have already discussed, it's hard to push from the inside when you're not represented at all within most institutions.) But, in so many ways, *we* are now the change. Groups that seek equality are pushing their way into spaces of traditional power with the explicit mission to overturn that power—not easily, and not yet en masse, but it is happening. We're seeing this push in ways both big and small. It could be as microscale as employees successfully banding together for gender-neutral washrooms or to get an updated, more equitable, harassment policy. It could be the newspaper or magazine editor who prioritizes bylines from people of colour, or the director who hires transgender actors. And it could be the politicians who, after fighting their way into the system, extend a hand to others.

In February 2019, for instance, uber-popular (and uber-loathed) U.S. Congress representative Alexandria Ocasio-Cortez literally brought a survivor into the halls of power as her guest to the State of the Union Address. That day, she and Ana Maria Archila, one of the two women who confronted Arizona senator Jeff Flake in an elevator after he said he'd vote to confirm Kavanaugh, both arrived in white, part of a tribute to the suffragist movement. Archila told media at the time, "I just feel particularly moved that in her first participation in the State of the Union, she is inviting me to join and inviting that moment of the elevator, my confrontation with the men who do not understand the life of women and the lives of people who are not in power, that she's inviting that into the imagination of people again."[22]

Ocasio-Cortez's tweet announcing Archila as her guest was "liked" 42,000 times. Some people might be tempted to remark, "Sure, yes, but it's just Twitter." They'd do well to remember that not only did #MeToo gain much of its present power through Twitter, it's the primary method of communication for America's 45th president. (Twitter is also where, months later, he would attack Ocasio-Cortez and three other congresswomen, saying they should "go back" to where they came from and that he did not believe they were "capable of loving our Country.")[23] The support Ocasio-Cortez's tweet received was a signal to survivors that, perhaps for the first time ever, there exists a mass of other people, like us, who are saying *yes, yes, yes, this is a priority for me too.* Which is a good thing, because to crush anything, even vast misogynistic systems of power, you need to exert pressure from both sides...*pop!* Just like cracking a nut.

Law Needs Feminism Because

Still, we'd need more than disruptive party guests to truly reimagine a system that works for women. One of the many flaws in the system that #MeToo has revealed is that the legal establishment seems to fail those who have experienced sexual violence the most often and the most gravely. But if those inside the system weren't just bowing to pressure, if they truly believed in the goals of a movement like #MeToo — healing, survivor-first, radical power shifts — what new system would they create? If these new systems wanted to centre women and survivors, what would they actually look like? How would they restore power to those who'd been denied it or robbed of it? To find out, I boarded a plane to Halifax in February 2019 to attend the annual Law Needs Feminism Because forum — a gathering of, as the name suggests, hundreds of lawyers, lawmakers, and others in the establishment who believe in a feminist legal system. That year's theme: the power of grassroots movements. The power, essentially, of #MeToo.

The organizers — students from law schools across Canada — wanted to highlight the idea that groundswell change can lead to bigger change. The organization itself was born when a group of students started a photo campaign asking people to take and share pictures of themselves holding up signs that completed the phrase, "Law needs feminism because . . ." They soon realized that the potential conversations were much too big to fit on bristol board. The previous year's conference was held in Ottawa, with only those in the legal profession invited to attend. But if they were going to highlight grassroots movements, thought the 2019 organizers, maybe a better location was *away* from Canada's symbolic centre of power. They also opened up the event to those outside the profession, including activists, social workers, and staff at rape crisis centres. Most (but certainly not all) of the attendees the year I went were young, either still students or in the early stages of their careers, those years when they will decide their governing values in the workplace and in their lives.

To one co-organizer, Kathleen Kontak Adams, the idea behind the event was the same as the one behind the organization itself. "Small movements just pick up speed and pick up speed and pick up speed," she told me. "But those little cracks in the marble start with one little person [speaking up]." I thought of what she said as I walked down the hallway to the main conference room, passing "Law

Needs Feminism Because" posters, stark against the white hallways. One, written by a man, said, "If law isn't feminist, it's just power." Another said, "If you don't have a seat at the table, you're probably on the menu." A third showed a black woman who'd inserted "intersectional" into the tagline, writing below: "No Supreme Court Justice looks like me." I thought again about all these steps we must take, fast and slow, as I looked out the window of Halifax's Pier 21 Immigration Museum, where the conference was held, and gazed at the vast expanse of cobalt water that was working over the stones, turning them to sand.

The day's workshops included sessions that, rightly, stretched far beyond #MeToo, including ones on women and wrongful convictions, how to use social media for advocacy and activism, and reproductive justice for criminalized women and transgender people. At one session I attended, focusing on grassroots organizing "by survivors for survivors," the speaker system from the adjoining room blared such loud, repeated feedback that the presenter, the Dandelion Initiative's Larissa Donovan, couldn't be heard. Every time she opened her mouth to suggest how anti–workplace harassment policies might better serve complainants by becoming survivor- and trauma-informed, the system screeched at jaw-clenchingly loud volumes. Eventually, the group huddled into one of the museum's common areas, a few young women in blazers and "Je Parle Féministe" T-shirts joking, "They're trying to silence us!" I laughed, but as the day wore on, it seemed less and less funny.

In another session, we learned how sexual assault centres, including the Nova Scotia–based one that led the discussion, were fighting the use of counselling records in sexual assault trials. Those counselling records are often used by defence lawyers to, unsurprisingly, undermine the complainant. Their use is also on the rise across Canada, with courts granting 51 percent of applications to obtain the records from 2011–17, up from 30 percent in 2007–11. The reasons for granting said applications has also shifted, with judges most often allowing that the accused needs those records to make a full answer of defence. As a result, shared the presenter, they are seeing women opt out of treatment, knowing that treatment might one day be used against them.[24] In fact, I only had to open up Dalhousie University law professor Elaine Craig's most recent book, *Putting Trials on Trial: Sexual Assault and the Failure of the Legal Profession*, which I'd started reading shortly before my trip, for a flood of examples of just how brutal the system can be for survivors.

To wit, Craig quotes from the transcript of one 2013 trial, *R v. Adepoju*, held in Red Deer, Alberta:

Q: And—and then eventually you stopped saying no, and you opened up your legs and the sex act occurred; correct?

A: Yes.

Q: You didn't scream?

A. No.

Q: You didn't cry?

A. No.

Q: You didn't go lock yourself in the bathroom?

A. No.

. . .

Q: Well you did let him have sex with you; right?

A. Eventually, yes.

Q. Yes. You stopped saying no.

A. But I didn't say yes.

Q. You stopped saying no, and you used body language, um, complying with the sexual act; correct?

A. I—I guess I'd [sic] did.[25]

One of the other presenters, Grace Cleveland, had a very simple but very revolutionary idea to stop exchanges like that from happening: make every law student take a course on feminist jurisprudence as a requirement for graduation. "Feminist legal methods combine to show that neutral rules and procedures are not so neutral, that the decision-making process is always inflected with 'the ideologies of the decision-maker,'" she wrote in a handout for her talk, "and that much work remains to be done in order for women to be supported through, rather than subordinated by, the Canadian legal system." Under this paradigm, lawyers and judges might "unmask the patriarchy"—that is, confront the idea of a neutral law—and they might also use a feminist framework to reach decisions. If survivors' voices were centred in the legal system, for instance, we might see more cases of restorative, not punitive, justice.

While over half of Canadians still report limited familiarity with the concept,[26] restorative justice has gained ground in recent years among those searching for alternatives to a system that often works against, not for, survivors. Restorative justice holds offenders accountable, and while it can include punishment, that isn't the primary goal of the process. Instead, it provides an opportunity for those affected—the survivor, the offender, and their communities—to talk about their needs and to find a solution that puts healing first and focuses on reparation, reintegration into communities, and solutions against future harm. Essentially, it seeks to treat everybody as a human being.[27] And although only 5 percent of those who've been sexually assaulted in Canada report it to the police, as many as one in four survivors are interested in restorative justice; in some studies that number is over 50 percent.[28] There's good reason for this: research suggests that restorative justice can help reduce symptoms of PTSD and post-assault stress. Participants in one pilot project in Arizona agreed that, in comparison to other justice options, it helped them "tak[e] back their power." Yet those who choose restorative justice often face backlash from a public that is more focused on equating punishment with justice.

If we reimagine a legal system that operates according to feminist values, we might also see a legal system that is anti-colonial and anti-racist. After all, a feminism that successfully disrupts power is not just about helping white women who've experienced sexual violence. It's about (or it should be about) making everyone's lives more equitable. Canadian law has long been wielded to disempower Indigenous people—this is what I was told by Naiomi Metallic, a member of the Listuguj Mi'gmaq First Nation, an assistant professor of law at Dalhousie University, and the school's Chancellor's Chair in Aboriginal Law and Policy. But the law is also more flexible than we often imagine, and it can be used as a tool for reconciliation as well. That's particularly true if the face of those who practise the law also changes. She pointed to the Indigenous Blacks & Mi'kmaq Initiative at Dalhousie's Schulich School of Law, which acts as an affirmative action access program for the school, and which celebrated its thirtieth anniversary in September 2019.

As Metallic noted, Nova Scotia is not alone in its long history of racism, but it is one of the few provinces in Canada to put that history under the spotlight via a public inquiry. That inquiry, eventually dubbed the Marshall Report, was made public in 1989. At that time, none of the province's 1,200 lawyers were Mi'kmaq and only about a dozen were Black. Today, three decades after the launch of the affirmative action initiative, crafted in part as a response to the report, 2.2 percent of the lawyers in the province are Indigenous and another 2.7 percent are Black. That still isn't enough, but it's a whole lot better than zero. In increasing the number of Black and Indigenous lawyers in the province, the initiative gives more power to those individuals but also to the communities they represent — and power, after all, said Metallic, is really about the ability to affect lives and effect change. "Diversity is important because we're important," she told me. "The law permeates everything."

Back at the conference, discussing those possibilities for change involved getting the lawyers to engage in "feminist practical reasoning." In one scenario, they were asked to consider what to do when a white foster family and the biological parents of an Indigenous child are both seeking custody. Questions they were encouraged to ask poked at biases, social conditioning, and facts beyond those traditionally considered "legally relevant." My own group was asked to look at consciousness-raising, which is the practice of sharing personal experiences to illuminate deeper truths and build both empathy and community. In this context, though, it was also presented as a tool to help other lawyers (i.e., the grizzled white dudes who still hold all the power) to "get it." We were asked to share what barriers or harm we'd experienced during our careers and then discuss how we might use the narrative around those experiences to help build empathy.

As we went around the table, it became clear that we all had alarmingly similar stories to share, despite our differences. One older woman, one of the few lawyers there, told us about standing before a male judge, along with a group of male lawyers. The judge asked the others about their cases, but when he got to her he only remarked on how nice she looked that day. A younger woman, still a student, who'd driven all the way from Fredericton, New Brunswick, that morning, was there to see if she might go into law after completing her environmental sciences degree. She told us about a job interview she'd had in Alberta in which the interviewer had asked at the end how she'd handle the mostly male staff, who were known to be fairly crude, especially in the field. She declined to take her callback interview. One of the presenters was also at our table. She shared how impossible it was to find a clerking position with her impressive feminist legal organizing on her CV; she'd been baldly told it would be easier for her if she deleted it.

I told a story, which I've shared elsewhere, about a writer-in-residence who, not realizing he'd written for the magazine I was editor of at the time, spent an inordinate amount of time commenting on my skirt and then told me my career would pick up after I'd written my first magazine article. I'd just won a gold medal at the National Magazine Awards.

Hearing the stories shared around the table, so easily recalled, I felt furious and I felt sick, as if an army of bees were blinking in my stomach, across my skin, my vision. Forget stopping with law. Every field needs a mandatory feminist course.

Too Far and Not Far Enough

A couple of days later, I called Lady Drive Her, a female-drivers-only cab service, to take me to the Halifax airport. Crissy McDow launched the company after several high-profile sexual assault accusations in the city involving taxi drivers, or those posing as them. When I called, the service was still restricted to doing airport drop-offs and pickups, with a proposal before city council to become fully licensed to operate throughout Halifax. Perhaps predictably, the proposal had raised some controversy, including debate over the risk female passengers actually faced.[29] I thought about that backlash as my driver picked me up from my hotel, wind whipping a slushy, freezing rain into my face. I thought about how one of the Law Needs Feminism Because co-organizers had told me that she'd joined the group after seeing its posters vandalized all across the Dalhousie campus. Her own poster soon said "...Because this isn't Don Draper's 1961." When my driver told me she was going slowly that morning because the rain had caused blackout puddles, it seemed symbolic.

The emerging lessons of #MeToo seem both simple and impossible. First, break the imbalance by breaking the silence. Second, show women and other equity-seeking groups a new version of power by also showing them a way to start healing. Third, take that tenderly healing nation and that thunderous chorus of voices and use it to squeeze out the rotten power, putting pressure on systems from within and without, grinding down like a vice. Fourth, build something new and feminist in its place. A practical step-by-step guide to remaking the world!

Except that, as much as #MeToo has started to give women new ways to think about power, and to enact it, it has also generated enormous backlash. And that backlash is popularizing a regressive, violent form of power, one that operates with a not-so-hidden goal of silencing women. Thinking of the roadblocks ahead, it seems as though we face the same thing we always have: patriarchal power. Except on steroids.

CHAPTER 3

Would It Kill You to Smile?

How racism and sexism fuelled a new toxic masculinity — and galvanized a whole generation of women

IN 2014, THE UNIVERSITY of British Columbia's Sauder School of Business announced Jennifer Berdahl as its first-ever Montalbano Professor in Leadership Studies: Women and Diversity, heaping expected praise on her academic research. While the title was a mouthful, her goal was more straightforward, although not exactly simple. In the words of UBC, Berdahl's hiring would make the school "a centre of excellence for the study of equity in the upper echelons of the corporate world" with a mandate to explore how "business leadership can be made stronger through greater gender equity and increased diversity."[1] In other words, whoever held the professorship was to make a business case for diversity. Or, put even more bluntly: undo all the white-dude domination.

UBC had picked the right person for the job. Before joining the school, Berdahl had spent more than twenty years researching workplace equity, working at both the University of Toronto's Rotman School of Management and the Haas School of Business at the University of California, Berkeley. Her research, UBC gushed, had helped form the spine of Sheryl Sandberg's arguments in *Lean In*. She had been an adviser to the Canadian Parliament and a court-room expert witness. For Berdahl, the hiring was a *woohoo!* moment. Business schools had not always supported her research, particularly when it delved deeply into sexual harassment, power dynamics, and workplace cultures, but the Sauder School wanted to be at the forefront of change. They were even open to turning the focus back on the school itself. Or so Berdahl thought.

First, she flagged some problematic comments made by a male professor within the department. Then she flagged some student behaviour. Each, she thought, was indicative of the type of work environments that undermine success for women and people of colour. Each instance was dismissed. Berdahl began to feel as if she'd been hired to do the "corporate feminist dog-and-pony show" and nothing more. Then, a year into Berdahl's professorship at UBC, the president of the university, Arvind Gupta, abruptly resigned after less than a year in office. Berdahl heard the news as the conference she'd been at all day came to a close. That conference, incidentally, was a gathering of interdisciplinary scholars focused on studying work as a masculinity contest — that is, workplace environments which, belying what appear to be neutral practices, pressure men into proving manhood on the job to get ahead.[2]

It seemed to Berdahl that Gupta was yet another real-life example of her research. She decided to write a post on her blog, titled "Did President Arvind Gupta Lose the Masculinity Contest?," analyzing his resignation through her decades-long scholarship.[3] She was careful to open the post by stating that she wasn't privy to the detailed information that might explain the "unfortunate outcome" of his resignation. UBC had failed in either selecting or supporting him, she wrote, and while she didn't know which it was, she did know that women and people of colour, including men, rarely won the masculinity contest at white-dominated institutions like UBC. (At the time of her writing, eleven of the twelve deans at the school's Vancouver campus were white, and ten of them were men.) It wasn't just that Gupta was not a physically imposing white man — both considered gold-medal qualities in the masculinity contest — but that he also advocated for more diversity in leadership. From Berdahl's experience with Gupta, she knew him to be a leader who listened, encouraged the less powerful to speak first in group settings, felt confident in expressing his own uncertainty, and never encouraged others to fall in line.

"He exhibited all the traits of a humble leader: one who listens to arguments and weighs their logic and information, instead of displaying and rewarding bravado as a proxy for competence," Berdahl wrote. Unfortunately, she added, none of those things are valued when work is a masculinity contest — in fact, they're likely to cost a leader. "Instead, those who rise to positions of leadership have won the contest of who can seem most certain and overrule or ignore divergent opinions. Risk-taking, harassment, and bullying are common. Against men this usually takes the form of 'not man enough' harassment, with accusations of being a wimp, lacking a spine, and other attacks on their fortitude as 'real men.'" She continued, presciently describing a leadership style that has permeated world politics, "'Frat-boy' behavior sets the tone, like encouraging heavy drinking, bragging about financial, athletic, or other forms of prowess, and telling sexual jokes."

University leadership reacted swiftly, and brashly, to Berdahl's post.[4] Or, as Berdahl put it to me, "All hell broke loose." Though she had named no one in her short blog post, evidently some men thought it was about them. She received a call from John Montalbano, who, at the time, had an extensive list of titles to his name: chair of the UBC board of governors; member of the faculty advisory board for the Sauder School; and, as CEO of RBC Global Asset Management, the man behind the $2-million gift that had created the Montalbano Professorship in Leadership Studies: Women and Diversity. Montalbano was not happy. He felt the blog post was directed at him (and, indeed, while Berdahl told me she did not have him in mind when she wrote the post, documents later leaked showed Montalbano had a rocky relationship with Gupta, to say the least).[5]

Montalbano told Berdahl that her blog was hurtful, inaccurate, unfair, and grossly embarrassing to the board. According to Berdahl, he worried it made him look like a hypocrite. He mentioned talking to the dean of the Sauder School about it, and repeatedly brought up RBC, which funded Berdahl's research. Her academic credibility, Berdahl recalls him telling her, was now shit. Shortly after that call, the dean's office reached Berdahl, relaying concerns about future fundraising prospects and the school's reputation. That evening, at a Sauder reception, said Berdahl, two more administrators pulled her aside at the party and chastised her again. To Berdahl, the message was clear: you should have kept silent. She had never felt more institutional pressure in her life. She had never felt more as though her academic freedom had been curtailed. And she had also perhaps never been more trapped inside a losing masculinity contest of her own.

It's Only Smart When a Man Says It

In the end, after Berdahl spoke about the fallout on her blog[6] and in the media, UBC and the Faculty Association of the University of British Columbia launched an investigation into whether her academic freedom had, in fact, been violated. Perhaps unsurprisingly to anyone following the facts, former B.C. Supreme Court justice Lynn Smith concluded that UBC had failed in its duty to protect and support that freedom.[7] "Dr. Berdahl reasonably felt reprimanded, silenced and isolated," wrote Smith in her October 2015 decision. Yet she added that the interference was unintentional—a result of a series of "several relatively small mistakes" as well as "some unlucky circumstances." Not exactly a sound victory. That apparent win becomes even murkier considering the details of Berdahl's subsequent mediation with the school. Montalbano eventually resigned from the board. But Berdahl herself lost her position, was put on a two-year academic leave, and was also moved from the business school to the department of sociology, effective upon her return to the school. It was as if she, and the once-lauded equity goals of her original professorship, had never existed at all.

Revealingly, in the weeks following the whole debacle, much of Canada's powerful mainstream media sided with the status quo. Some argued that Berdahl's blog post wasn't grounded in academic research at all, it was pure feminist conjecture—erasing her and others' entire field of deeply considered study. *The Globe and Mail* dedicated not one, but two opinion pieces to undermining the concept of her academic freedom, and, in turn, Berdahl's voice. First, it published a piece by James Tansey, the executive director for the Centre for Social Innovation and Impact Investing

at the Sauder School, that seemed to almost wilfully mis-
interpret Berdahl's blog. Tansey wrote that, "Just because
an academic is speaking, it doesn't mean that what they are
saying is scholarly or academic."[8] And then, in a later editorial, The Globe described Montalbano's actions as those of
someone who "may or may not have let off some needless
steam," adding that "[Berdahl's] post was one remark about
one unexplained kerfuffle in a university's administration,
not a piece of data in a social research program."[9]

In contrast, two years later, when the director of McGill
University's Institute for the Study of Canada, Andrew
Potter, came under fire for writing an article about what
he described as Quebec's "essential malaise"—a topic not
even remotely grounded in decades of academic research,
but rather an anecdote about being stranded in a snow-
storm—The Globe, and other media, bemoaned the supposed
violation of his academic freedom. "Did Mr. Potter, a professor of philosophy and former newspaper editor, truly resign
voluntarily from his 'dream job,' as he described it? Or did
someone inside or outside the school apply undue pressure?
Why didn't the university defend his academic freedom?"
the Globe editorial board wrote. "We need to know. The
right of university professors to speak their minds without
fear of sanction is critical in a free society. It matters not a
whit that the online Maclean's column that got Mr. Potter
in trouble was poorly thought out . . ."[10]

Because of course it doesn't. Why would it? It only matters whose power was, supposedly, being violated. When I
spoke to Berdahl, she was in the final months of her leave.
She didn't regret speaking up, but she still seemed ambivalent about the whole thing. On the one hand, she felt as
though it set a bad precedent to take away a named professorship from a professor because they wrote something that

upset the donors. That they made the work environment so poisonous that she couldn't return to her department was also wrong. Clearly. And yet, "On the other hand, I don't want to work there at all anymore," she told me. "I can still do my scholarship, still do my speaking and still be who I am — maybe even more who I am — in sociology." She would no longer be under any pressure to win the masculinity contest, she added. She'd been released from the game.

Berdahl's case has an element of the absurd. She was punished for doing her job, and the very research that she was once celebrated for was suddenly minimized as feminist mudslinging. *Lady gossip.* The case itself, as well as the reaction to it, exposed how reluctant old institutions are to change, no matter the cloying lip service paid to fostering diversity and equal treatment. But while Berdahl's case might win for the most ironic, it is not singular, and it is far from the most jarring example of a woman, trans or cis, clashing against, or being felled by, toxic male leadership. Things have only become worse in the past five years. We still witness the type of bumbling interference seen at UBC, of course, but we've also seen an escalation to full-out harassment and, often, violence that has become almost surreal in its ordinariness. It's like we're stuck in a global masculinity contest — one that more and more men keep joining. Eagerly.

A Global Masculinity Contest

If the push for equality is experiencing a renaissance, and arguably it is, this galvanizing moment cannot be divorced from a new sort of leadership, one that is grounded in *inequality*. While the emergence of that leadership is often pinned on Donald Trump, he is — likely much to his dismay — only one part of the depressing equation. Democracy has been in an alarming decline for thirteen consecutive years, according to Freedom House's 2019 Freedom in the World report, which examined 195 countries and 14 territories over the 2018 calendar year. The organization has conducted its annual survey of global political rights and civil liberties since 1973, and in that time it has seen a dramatic reversal in democratic values.[11] After the fall of the Berlin Wall in 1989 and the collapse of the Soviet Union a few years later, democracy rose around the world. That surge of progress, however, warned the Freedom in the World report, has now begun to roll back. In 2018 alone, 68 countries saw a weakening in democracy.

"So far it has been anti-liberal populist movements of the far right — those that emphasize national sovereignty, are hostile to immigration, and reject constitutional checks on the will of the majority — that have been most effective at seizing the open political space," wrote researchers in the 2019 report. The ascent of such far-right groups into the political sphere has led to a successful, emboldened backlash against democratic liberal ideas, in both expected and unexpected places. "In countries from Italy to Sweden," added the researchers, "anti-liberal politicians have shifted the terms of debate and won elections by promoting an exclusionary national identity as a means for frustrated majorities to gird themselves against a changing global and domestic order." In those countries, groups have attacked institutions designed to protect minorities against abuse, dismissed core civil and political rights, and polarized the press — enabling a globally used blanket cry of "fake news" any time a leader wants to silence and discredit criticism. And while Trump does not bear sole responsibility for the slipping democracy in the United States, the report stressed, he has certainly been greasing the path there, and for countries far beyond his own.

The report's assessment of Trump at the midpoint of his presidency reads like a how-to primer in the newly popular, ultra-toxic, ultra-masculine power: "[He] has assailed essential institutions and traditions including the separation of powers, a free press, an independent judiciary, the impartial delivery of justice, safeguards against corruption, and most disturbingly, the legitimacy of elections." Trump's unwavering commitment to "America First," his reluctance to talk democracy abroad, and his belligerent praise for some of the world's most repugnant dictators and, dare I say, *fellow* strongmen has only cemented his place as one of the world's new power icons — like a sort of Lady Gaga for bigots. This type of power, which extends far past politics, is not only spreading, not only being emulated, it's being celebrated. At its core, it disregards individual rights, embraces extreme hierarchies, promotes an almost radical self-interest, ignores limits, and seems chiefly concerned with expanding its own reach. Oh, and it's naturally misogynistic, homophobic, transphobic, anti-immigrant, and racist. Just for starters.

Canada has not escaped its oily reach. Much ink has been spilled debating whether or not Ontario premier Doug Ford, in particular, is a sort of Trump Lite.[12] That, unfortunately, distracts from the larger reality, which is that Trump's brand of power and leadership does not begin and end with him; it's worldwide. Whether Ford is Trump Lite is almost beside the point. He employs the same type of power, to the benefit of himself and others like him.

The Identity Politics of Lonely, Angry Men

Ford, Trump, and their ilk are fond of reminding every-body that they were democratically elected. People — many people — chose them. And it is important to remember this; it is a reminder that this type of power does not exist without support. Their power is sustained, even in its chaos, even in dissent, because it's seen as restoring a particular world order. It's a power that constituents hope will also trickle power down to them, elevating them to whatever place — in society, in the workplace, and in their own homes — they believe they have a natural right to occupy. It's perhaps no wonder, then, that expressions of this power are seen in movements, and public figures, beyond politics.

Online, misogyny flourishes in the so-called mano-sphere, a loose network of anti-feminists, traditionalists, and men-first men that includes members of the men's rights movement, the Red Pill movement, Trump supporters, Gamergaters, the Incel movement, and, also, just general jerks. In the past, there's been a tendency to dismiss such digital hate as "not real," as if the digital space confines rampant misogyny to a series of magical bubbles spread across the dark, lonely basements of losers everywhere. But nearly a quarter of women experience online abuse or harassment, according to a 2017 Amnesty International poll that surveyed women in eight countries. Most of it comes from complete strangers. A lot of it is unsettling, terrify-ing, demeaning — meant to undermine, diminish, and exert power, just the same as offline abuse. "Online abuse began for me when I started the Everyday Sexism Project — before it had become particularly high-profile or I received many entries," UK women's rights activist Laura Bates told Amnesty International. Her project, as the name suggests, catalogues everyday sexism through submissions to her site. "You could be sitting at home in your living room, outside of working hours, and suddenly someone is able to send you a graphic rape threat right into the palm of your hand."[13]

Not all digital violence is directed at specific women. On the extreme and murkiest end of the manosphere is the Incel movement, which is not unlike a mass temper tantrum of men kicking and screaming for the power they believe they're owed. The term "incel" is a slang identifier for those who describe themselves as "involuntarily celibate." For a movement that, on the surface, seems primarily focused on getting laid, it would almost be laughable, if it weren't also so dangerous. As I've written elsewhere, in *The Walrus*, it would be a mistake to underestimate the Incels.[14] When Reddit banned its Incel subreddit in November 2017, the online community had 40,000 members.[15] Though the sub claimed to be a "support group" for those navigating a "normie" world, Reddit said the Incel community violated its then-new policy prohibiting any group that "encourages, glorifies, incites or calls for violence or physical harm against an individual or group of people" — in this case, women.

Though many Incel members have said they were merely commiserating, not preaching violence, on the Reddit channel, the misogyny threaded through the group's rhetoric is undeniable. Incels often refer to women as both "femoids" (a portmanteau of "female" and "humanoid") and "roasties" (a term that's meant to liken a woman's genitals to a roast beef sandwich). Women are "sluts" by nature, "nothing but trash that use men," and "genetically hardwired to exchange sex for money, status, power, shelter and material — things that they presumably cannot earn or make for themselves."[16] The deeper one goes into the archives of the community's messages, the more disturbing it gets.

Unsurprisingly, scrubbing the Incel subreddit did not succeed in silencing them — on Reddit, or elsewhere. A new community, called Braincels, was more than 17,000 Reddit members strong in April 2018; it remains accessible, but because of its dedication to "shocking or highly offensive content" it is now "quarantined," which means those who want to access it have to actively opt in to see it. Incels have a presence on 4Chan, as well. Beyond that, the dedicated website Incels.me has over 5,000 members. Conversation threads there happen under stomach-churning subject lines such as: "[Serious]Can you talk to a girl knowing that her mouth has been filled with semen?" (answer, from one user, whose profile photo is of Bill Cosby: "They weren't made to talk. I have no reason to listen to them talk"); "The END GAME is women losing their rights" (initiated by a user who was later banned); and, in reference to then-recent events, "Honestly, reading all the comments that people on news articles and Facebook [write] about us only JUSTIFIES what the van killer did."

That "van killer" is a former Seneca College student from Richmond Hill, Ontario, whose name is Alek Minassian. On April 23, 2018, the twenty-five-year-old allegedly rammed his white rental van into Toronto pedestrians on a northern stretch of Yonge Street, killing ten and injuring fourteen. Before doing so, Minassian reportedly posted a single message on a since-deleted Facebook page, widely circulated in the aftermath of the attack.[17] "The Incel Rebellion has already begun!" it read, in part. "All hail the Supreme Gentleman Elliot Rodger."

In 2014, Elliot Rodger committed a mass shooting that killed six and injured fourteen students at the University of California, Santa Barbara, including two sorority girls. Before the shooting, Rodger uploaded his 140-page "manifesto," in which he freely called himself an "incel."[18] After the mass shooting, the "Supreme Gentleman" achieved a cult-like status within the Incel movement, with certain members later calling him, and others they believe to be like him, a hERo — with intentional emphasis on his initials. Other "ER" homages include "winnER," "altERnative," and "bettER."[19]

The movement also adopted Nikolas Cruz, the nineteen-year-old who in 2018 killed seventeen students at Marjory Stoneman Douglas High School in Parkland, Florida, as a hERo after discovering a YouTube comment the school shooter had apparently made, promising "Elliot rodger will not be forgotten."[20] That Cruz chose Valentine's Day for the massacre only added to his mythos. And in November 2018, Scott Paul Beierle became a winnER in the community when he walked into a yoga studio in Tallahassee, Florida, and shot six people, killing two. The forty-year-old was a self-described misogynist who likened his adolescent self to Rodger, had twice been arrested for groping young women, and often posted women-hating screeds on YouTube and SoundCloud, including a song called "Handful of Bare Ass."[21] The list of men who have committed mass violence and claim allegiance to the Incel movement doesn't stop there, either.

Men like Trump and Ford may not condone this type of violence, but they have helped establish the culture in which it now flourishes. They benefit from it. It's the same type of culture that allowed Trump to mock Christine Blasey Ford at a rally in Mississippi, to roars of delighted laughter.[22] The same culture that helped elect Ford on a promise to scrap the sex-ed curriculum — a curriculum that focused on things like consent and gender identity. And it's the same type of culture that helped Canada's own

Jordan Peterson become world-famous. The University of Toronto psychology professor rose to fame by, essentially, refusing to refer to students by their preferred pronouns and then creating YouTube videos to explain why (among other things). Once the second-highest-funded creator on Patreon (he claimed), Peterson left the platform, a crowd-funded subscription content service, in January 2019, citing growing discomfort with censorship after another user was banned for using the N-word and for other hate speech.[23] Still, Peterson's internationally bestselling book, *12 Rules for Life: An Antidote to Chaos*, is marketed not as some alt-right screed, as it's often portrayed, but as a self-help book. Marketing material promises the "renowned" psychologist's answer to an almost laughably huge question: What does everyone in the modern world need to know?[24]

Well, apparently, it's that boys will be boys.

Examples of Peterson's twelve rules include both the friendly "Do not bother children while they are skateboarding," and the fair "Set your house in perfect order before you criticize the world." That this advice is coming from a man who once mused to a *Vice* reporter that he didn't know whether men and women could ever coexist in the workplace without sexual harassment—but that one way to help would be to ban makeup in the workplace because it's "sexually provocative"—is exactly the point.[25] Peterson does not advocate for violence against women or for the Incel movement, but, as with Ford and Trump and many others, that hasn't stopped those with violent views from mimicking and even co-opting his rhetoric, or from seeing him as a champion.

For those who want to use his views to justify their own, Peterson and the men presumed to be like him personify reason and natural order; feminists, and their allies, are illogical, hysterical fascists, grasping at power they don't need or can't use. In *12 Rules For Life*, Peterson allows that girls can win by winning their own hierarchy, "by being good at what girls value, as girls" (I'm going out on a very twig-like limb here to guess he means being attractive, like-able, nurturing, wearing pink, and also able to find a "good man"), and they can "add to this victory" by winning in the boys' hierarchy (we will soon learn how untrue that is, but let's let him have it for now).[26] Boys, on the other hand, he contends, can only win by winning the male hierarchy — the masculinity contest, if you will, painted in a positive light. Men must be men, so that they can look after their women and children, and women must only look after their children. Forget equal partnerships! And definitely forget same-sex partnerships!

Predictably, Peterson's self-help book has some things to say about power, too, as it pertains to oppression. Namely, that one doesn't at all influence the other, at least not in any way that people couldn't overcome if they were talented or dedicated enough. "Any hierarchy," he writes, "creates winners and losers. The winners are, of course, more likely to justify the hierarchy and the losers to criticize it." Sure, fine. But Peterson also believes that the collective pursuit of any valued goal produces a hierarchy, and it is the pursuit of those goals that gives life meaning. To him, "Absolute equal-ity would therefore require the sacrifice of value itself—and then there would be nothing worth living for."[27] Peterson posits that competence, not power, is the prime determiner of status in any hierarchy. This, he stated, is obvious. (And obviously not true for women; see chapter 1, and also your own life.) In fact, Peterson's belief that hierarchies are not socially or culturally constructed, but are instead instinc-tual, has become something of a trademark. In early 2019, he started selling lobster merchandise in a reference to his oft-repeated claim that lobsters naturally develop hierarchies so ... science? Anyway, the leggings are $60.[28]

By pretending neither power nor privilege has anything to do with social status, and that neither can be passed down through systems of elitism, Peterson and his disciples exalt a sort of modern, gender-infused social Darwinism. Those who have less just can't hack it, and those who have more are simply better. Life is viewed as a simple binary. Men and women are miserable, unsuccessful creatures when they break the conventions of their genders; they are happy in their hierarchy when they do not. At the same time, because the manosphere is nothing if not contradictory, for all the talk of individual responsibility and improvement, many of those who follow the sphere's various creeds often blame others for their inability to achieve personal fulfill-ment, usually pointing toward Peterson's so-called chaos, the corruption of traditional roles, and, of course, women themselves. In other words, if you're great and exemplify the traits of a straight, white man, congrats, that's on you. If you can't get ahead, and you're a woman, that's on you, too — you're where you're meant to be. But if you can't get ahead and you're a man? That's on feminism and greedy, whiny, not-nice women who want too much. That's on the world that is struggling to diminish the power structures under which you're meant to thrive.

I saw some of this thinking on display in person near the end of April 2019 when I joined more than 3,000 other people in Toronto to see Peterson debate Slovenian philosopher Slavoj Žižek on "happiness," capitalism, and Marxism. The square-off between the two pop-intellectuals was billed as the "debate of the century," and, to be fair, the audience did seem incredibly pumped to be there; the tickets, which topped out at over $500, sold out quickly, and Peterson later boasted that people were reportedly scalping them outside the venue, charging more than they do for Toronto Maple Leafs games. At first glance, when I arrived outside, the crowd seemed exactly as I had expected it to be: a sea of young men—not all white, but mostly. Inside, it was more diverse: a Black man and a woman wearing hijab and clutching an autographed copy of *12 Rules* were seated in front of me; well-coiffed older couples wandered the venue with wine glasses in hand; and somewhere in the crowd, judging by the jeers made during the actual debate, there were haters. The venue warned that everyone who attended, even children, must have a ticket—a fact I found eye-rollingly funny until I saw some people show up with babies strapped to their chests.

As media who covered the event noted, the two men, who were supposed to be mortal enemies (at least, according to their Twitter spats), had more in common than most expected.[29] For starters, both men were largely boring. Onstage, neither presented as blatantly sexist, racist, or xenophobic. In fact, they both bemoaned the perceived injustice of being described as too Eurocentric, too colonial, too high on Judeo-Christian values, too anti-transgender, too anti-feminist, too anti—well, you get the idea. Each seemed supposedly tortured by the misunderstanding, as well as the apparent weight of his own intellectual burden. *Only they could see the truth!* Peterson expressed his anguish by hunching over and splaying his hands, as if he were playing an invisible, miserable piano; Žižek plucked and brushed at his shirt. Each agreed upon a shared enemy: the so-called "academic left," a cadre of progressives whose apparent political over-correctness will send the world into chaos. And each man received voracious applause with every jab at the thusly defined other side.

By the end of the night, perhaps the most shocking part of the whole exchange was that anyone could have thought they were that different in the first place. Both men are the traditional benefactors of an academic system that grants them automatic power, rewarding their way of thinking, their way of research, their approach to how the world is studied and seen — and establishing who deserves to study and see it. Neither Žižek nor Peterson is the absolute monster their enemies have made them out to be. But that hardly matters. They're willingly mouldable symbols, seemingly loath to condemn the legions of fans who have adopted them, made them, given them power. It isn't the men who should scare us so much as the culture that groomed them for the pedestal. The same culture that's given us academics and philosophers who preach a natural order has also given us volatile internet communities, violent shooters, politicians and world leaders who bulldoze over democracy, and bosses who insist the best person has won — all of them engaged in a renascent battle for hyper-masculinity. To win that battle is to become the best said-with-a-grunt *man*, rewarded with all the status-quo checkmarks such a man supposedly deserves: women, stature, money, physical prowess, and the admiration of other people.

Welcome, in other words, to the angst-ridden identity politics of mediocre men.

Women Are Wonderful!

Most men in this New (Old) World Order will protest that they don't hate women. They will hold their sexism and their misogyny clenched tightly in their fists as they tell you that they love women. Worship them! Lay chocolate and flowers at their feet like a fleet of Aphrodites! Researchers dub this popular shield against criticism the "women are wonderful" defence. In examining the disadvantages and inequities women and others continue to face in society, feminists often tend to look at what researchers Peter Glick and Susan Fiske called "hostile sexism" in their much-cited *American Psychologist* article, "An Ambivalent Alliance."[30] That's the kind of obvious sexism that causes men to lash out and, for example, refer to somebody as a "nasty woman" when they perceive them to be usurping their power. Then there's what the researchers termed "benevolent sexism." Such sexism rewards women for conforming to conventional roles, gifting them with both protection and affection.

Glick and Fiske surveyed more than 15,000 participants across nineteen countries using what they called The Ambivalent Sexism Inventory to measure the connection between the two types of sexism. They discovered a troublingly tandem relationship. Taken together, hostile and benevolent sexism become even more potent, with the latter working to pacify women's resistance to gender inequality. It's the type of sexism that creates, and then elevates, Pampered Princesses and Daddy's Little Girls, but is less celebratory of women's leadership and independence.

"Ideologies of benevolent paternalism allow members of dominant groups to characterize their privileges as well-deserved, even as a heavy responsibility they must bear," wrote Glick and Fiske. "On its own, this ideology may seem unobjectionable, even laudable, but what if... it is a crucial complement to hostile sexism, helping to justify men's greater privilege and power? If men's power is popularly viewed as a burden gallantly assumed, as legitimated by their greater responsibility and self-sacrifice, then their privileged role seems justified."

Women who seek their own power are then seen as ungrateful, deserving of whatever harsh treatment they get. (Ahem, Peterson. Ahem, Trump.) But the thing about benevolent sexism, noted the researchers, is that it's also seductive. Women are wooed into waiting for a Prince Charming, a mythical man who promises to use his power for her benefit — be it at home, at work, or in the political system.

Women are granted power, then, but only so long as it upholds restrictions on rigid gender roles. It's the same bind as it ever was: those who are the nicest, the prettiest, the most communal, the most motherly, the most likeable, and the most *feminine* are also the most rewarded. These same women are sometimes allowed to succeed in other ventures, too, but they must succeed most in being a good woman. Trump once ran a PSA, for instance, in which his daughter Ivanka, who is an arguably savvy businessperson, whatever one may think of her, said, "The most important job any woman can have is being a mother."[31]

And while much has been made of Trump's "pussy-grabbing" comment, it's perhaps the comments both he and his wife Melania have made about their relationship that are the most revealing of how today's power imbalances have cemented themselves on the wider stage. "Now, I know Melania, I'm not going to be doing the diapers, I'm not going to be making the food, I may never even see the kids," Trump told Larry King in an interview after he and Melania were married in 2005. "She'll be an unbelievable mother. I'll be a good father."[32] Melania, on a press junket to promote a new jewellery line she'd ostensibly designed, offered an echo of that sentiment to Parenting.com in 2016, after that once-dreamed-of child was born. "It's very important to know the person you're with. And we know our roles," she told the reporter. "I didn't want [Trump] to change the diapers or put Barron to bed."[33]

When it comes to power, often it's not just about who has access to it, it's about how the world values (and undervalues) different types of power—and about all the trappings that go with it, including knowledge and leadership. Sociologists, and the rest of the world, may not be able to agree on a precise definition of power, but that is, in large part, because there are so many different kinds. Traditional power structures and systems, mostly dominated by men, have sought to maintain those gendered views of power, in good part by limiting the socio-cultural capital of traditionally feminine pursuits. Mainstream society has doled out a certain kind of power to motherhood, for instance, but it isn't on par with the perceived power that comes with C-suite status. All genders are encouraged, and even expected, to succeed in their socially defined roles. That is, in many ways, the trade-off of benevolent sexism: women and other equity-seeking groups (because, of course, there's also benevolent racism and benevolent colonialism) get protection from the imbalanced world, usually in the form of financial stability, and in return are granted a smidge of power, always within the confines of their prescribed roles. (See: *Being a mother is the most important job!*) Those in power—or those who believe they ought to be in power—are less enthused, however, when women break from that benevolence. They especially don't like it when that break shakes the very power hierarchy they've come to rely on.

Consider what happened after Radio-Canada announced Manon Bergeron as its 2018 Scientist of the Year. Bergeron is a professor within the sexology department at the Université du Québec à Montréal (UQAM), as well as lead researcher in an influential study, l'Enquête Sexualité, Sécurité et

Interactions en Milieu Universitaire — or, in English, the Sexuality, Security, and Academic Interaction Survey. She is also the first person from the social sciences and humanities to win in the prize's thirty-year history. Which is point one against her. Point two: her research area. For her seminal study, Bergeron led a team in surveying more than 9,200 people who worked or studied at six of Quebec's French-speaking universities.[34] They found that roughly 37 percent of those surveyed reported experiencing a form of sexual violence in which the perpetrator was somehow linked to their university, whether it was a professor, a TA, or another student.[35] Point three: she and her team went on to host the first-ever bilingual and multidisciplinary Canadian symposium on sexual violence in higher education.[36] And point four: her research also played an integral part in developing Bill 151, which passed in late 2017 and requires all CEGEPs and universities in the province to create a stand-alone policy on sexual violence, harassment, and misconduct, as well as to report on its implementation. And, really, point five, the most egregious of them all: her motivations were grounded in feminism.

In announcing her win, Radio-Canada's senior vice-president, Michel Bissonnette, noted that, in the time of #MeToo, Bergeron's research provided important context for action — something that people could no longer close their eyes against.[37] But many men sure wanted to. The backlash against her win was swift and brashly dismissive of her work. La Presse journalist Yves Boisvert led the charge with a January 24, 2019 column headlined "Pauvre Science."[38] Writing in French, Boisvert called Bergeron's survey sample "worthless," snidely concluding that, logically, the results of her study must therefore be worthless as well.

When Radio-Canada later streamed an interview on

Facebook with Bergeron about her work, the page was flooded with comments before the video even started. Most of those comments criticized her win, reducing it to pure activism, and therefore bad science—an apparent affront to real scientists everywhere. Let's look at some of the translated comments. "In 2018, Dr. Daniel Borsuk was the first surgeon to succeed in a face transplant in Canada," wrote one Facebook user who did not watch Bergeron's interview. "But she's a feminist activist who deserves the scientific prize of the year for putting a biased poll online. Does that make sense?" Another wrote, "Nothing against Mrs. Bergeron whose cause and action is noble" —*women are wonderful!*— "But it is an insult to all scientists who have contributed to the advancement of knowledge this year." The more Radio-Canada tried to explain its choice, the more people retaliated: "Stop justifying yourself and recognize your mistake, it's a matter of respect for real rigorous scientists."[39]

It wasn't lost on other social scientists that the poisonous reaction was connected to a bigger backlash, one that did not like the changing parameters of the game. Shortly after the public outburst, *University Affairs* published an opinion piece signed by more than a hundred members of the Quebec Network of Feminist Studies—professors, course instructors, graduate students, and researchers.[40] "We are not surprised that this recognition provokes controversy: feminist researchers, especially in the humanities and social sciences, are used to seeing their knowledge production work questioned, if not disqualified by the yardstick of a positivist and one-dimensional vision of science," wrote the article's two lead authors, Francine Descarries and Sandrine Ricci. "Like the current controversy over what constitutes or does not constitute 'science' this vision appears obsolete and untrue." Untrue, they added, because it was also at odds with the United Nations' new definition of science, outlined in its 2017 "Recommendation concerning science and scientific researchers." In it, the UN clearly states that the term "science" "signifies a complex of knowledge, fact and hypothesis, in which the theoretical element is capable of being validated in the short or long term, and to that extent includes the sciences concerned with social facts and phenomena."[41]

In fact, if we shifted the definition of science — and, by extension, the power — away from its masculine-skewed roots (that is, a definition limited to the STEM fields) and instead used the more inclusive vision the UN outlines (that is, one grounded not in stereotypes but in worldwide expertise), we'd see how far women have come, how much they already lead and influence. Women are gaining in the medical field and they are gaining when it comes to life sciences.[42] Women often lead in the non-profit sector.[43] Not enough women head colleges and universities in Canada, but there are certainly more of them represented there than as CEOs.[44] For that matter, women also fare better when it comes to entrepreneurship and small-business ownership.[45]

I'm not advocating that it's time to stop shaking up these heavily male-dominated spaces. It's essential that feminists do not stop. Even in the arenas where we're doing better, we're still suffering from pay gaps and a general lack of representation in leadership, particularly in larger and higher-earning organizations. I *am* saying we need to end the narrative that women's pursuits and expertise don't measure up to an arbitrary standard we had no say in creating. I'm saying, yes, maybe men should be scared, just a little, because *here we come.*

Men Against Toxic Masculinity

Then again, maybe it would be nice if, instead of being scared, men helped change the game. Much debate has been stirred over whether men can truly be allied to feminism—and, if so, how they can help. For all that feminists insist feminism will rewrite gender roles and power structures so that the world is better for everyone, the movement is hesitant to bring men on board, and is even more reluctant to give them a vested reason—beyond support—for joining Team Feminist Killjoy. This is understandable. Feminists don't need another bro telling them what's best. Studies have even shown that when men take action to support women's rights, people often react in surprise, but also anger. Like, what's the catch here? (There's so often a catch.) But also, returning to the masculinity contest: helping the losing team makes you a loser, too. This, in turn, makes men reluctant to act.[46]

Yet as tempting as it may be to put the responsibility for finding solutions in the hands of women and other equity-seeking minorities, I wondered how much faster change would happen if men were included in the process. And more than that, I worried that any solutions that excluded them would only further entrench the idea of us-versus-them—a binary division that seemed ultimately unhelpful and also utterly beside the point. What if men also had a stake in reimagining power?

In search of an answer, I found myself seated among nearly a dozen men gathered in a top-floor studio of a downtown Toronto Lululemon in late August 2018. Hunched into Japanese meditation chairs, their long legs arranged before them in various geometric shapes, the men faced each other in a circle. Two of the facilitators had decided to sit on plywood boxes, which were usually used for the work-out classes hosted in the space; rows of medicine balls and yoga mats were stacked against the exposed brick walls. Age aside—most of the men looked to be in their twenties or thirties—the group was diverse, and most of them were strangers to each other. They were all here, quite simply, to talk: about themselves, about their insecurities, their challenges, and how these things were all entangled in their perception, and expression, of what it means to be a man.

Organized by Next Gen Men, a national non-profit that focuses on "building better men," the gathering was part of a monthly meet-up held under the moniker Wolf Pack—a cheeky gesture to the idea of men as lone wolves. That night, the group was there to tackle the subject of competition. But, as one participant put it, "The subject is not as important as looking at the basic problematic parts of masculine stereotypes." He had never attended Wolf Pack before, he added, and characterized the night as his "first step into the community," which I soon learned could basically be described as something like a club of IRL Peter Kavinskys—your favourite internet boyfriend, but better.

The evening opened with a land acknowledgement, then an invitation from one of the facilitators, a psychotherapist, to share names and preferred pronouns. One of the first questions the group tackled was: What comes to mind when you hear the word "competition"? In response, one of the men next to me wondered whether competition was gendered, and, if so, how. Another man mused that, for men, competition—winning—was tied to social capital, how men present, and the pressure to show a perfectly curated version of themselves, without weakness. Others talked about zero-sum mentalities, self-confidence, and setting achievable goals. There was a lot of discussion about failure, and how men are never, ever supposed to feel its heartbreak, how it can make them angry and bring out unhealthy competition.

Throughout the discussion, the men remained respectful. They waited their turn and *appreciated* what each had to say—nodding, murmuring agreement, telling each other a point hit home. If they challenged a thought, it wasn't meant as a dig, but as a means of digging deeper. Take one exchange, in which a young man returned to something another man had said earlier, in reference to competition in sports.

"You said when you lose, when you fail, you're *pissed*." He looked pointedly at the other man, whose first name was Jermal. "Why?"

Jermal considered this for a second, then answered, "I think it's a lack of my own value." If he loses, he added, he begins to think he's a bad guy—and the negative self-talk will roll on from there. *How can my mother possibly love me? Will I ever amount to anything?* A few heads bobbed in recognition. *Yeah, yeah, yeah.* They'd been there.

Wolf Pack preached a style of open vulnerability among men that was rare—and frankly stunning to watch. It was only later, walking alone in the pitch-black to the subway station, that it hit me: I'd never felt that comfortable before in a room full of men. Not that the gathering had anything to do with me. The central idea behind Wolf Pack, after all, was to encourage men to have conversations they wouldn't traditionally have in other spaces. The lessons learned there were universal ones of humility and humanity, of figuring out what being decent means, not because someone (your girlfriend, your wife, your sister) demands it, but because *you* want it. Nobody was there handing out woke-man cookies; nobody was gathering to mansplain feminism. These men were part of the wider reckoning on whose voices were loudest and what power balances needed to shift, but they also contended it wouldn't help anybody if people kept telling men to just shut up. That's because, they believed, toxic, restrictive masculinity harmed them, too — and the only way to break its power was for men to start talking about it.

Bro, We Gotta Talk about the Patriarchy

Next Gen Men launched in late 2014 in Calgary, after co-founder Jake Stika decided boys needed a better outlet to discuss sexual health and romantic relationships. But he also recognized that before most boys could have in-depth macro-conversations about those things, they needed to talk about how to establish their sense of self, their identities as growing men, what masculinity looked like for them, and how to have healthy, respectful relationships, period. Then, as Stika entered his thirties, he started to constantly think about, and question, what it meant for him to be a man, particularly at this point in history. He thought about it again when he recently celebrated his father's sixtieth birthday. Each generation of masculinity imprints itself on the next. What would his generation pass on? Would it be something new, or more of the same? Wolf Pack kicked off in 2016 when the co-founders realized such conversations weren't vital just for boys but for adult men, too. For Stika and Next Gen Men, it's all a process of learning and unlearning — debugging the complex software of patriarchy.

But to do that, men need to step up. Toronto-based Jeff Perera has spent much of his adult life exploring healthy masculinity. Perera is now in his forties, and some of his earliest memories are of his father being physically violent toward his mother, who, he recalls, was often covered in bruises. His parents immigrated from Sri Lanka, and had an arranged marriage. The abuse stopped when Perera was about seven, but it took him a lot longer to see that his father — whom he describes as a "physical monster" — was also, at his core, just a broken man, someone who faced immense discrimination as a man of colour and as an immigrant in a less-woke Canada. Perera also mentions the kids in his neighbourhood — those born in Canada as well as refugees and immigrants from all over the world — who, similarly, postured a hyper-violent model of masculinity. Growing up, that meant not admitting to watching *Strawberry Shortcake*; later on, that brand of masculinity translated into violence, a pressure to be hard and invulnerable.

Perera now makes it his work to create space for men to have conversations in which they can talk freely about their own experiences, their experiences with women, and all the good and the bad in between, without being completely dismissed or vilified. "It's not about us-versus-them," he told me. "It's about working together toward a common goal." When men start openly talking to each other, they hit the sweet spot that Perera calls the "learning zone." Outside of that zone is the "comfort zone" — eating chips and watching Netflix, assuming you're a nice guy who doesn't need to think about masculinity — and the "panic zone" — waging war on a Twitter feed that calls you out for being sexist, denying any culpability. Most men, said Perera, are not in the learning zone. Well, yes. Men need to be called out, he added, but they also need to find a place where they can admit they've "done some shit," and then process what that means accountability-wise, growth-wise. Those seeds of being better, of being *good*, won't grow in the panic zone. So that's what he and others are doing right now: creating the right environment, where the seeds of healthy masculinity can flourish.

But how exactly to reframe the "toxic masculinity" conversation so that men see how restrictive visions of manhood harm them, too? Humberto Carolo is the executive director of White Ribbon, a male-driven organization that launched in Toronto in 1991 and has since gone global, working to end violence against women and promote "a new vision of masculinity." He describes toxic masculinity as the belief that it's okay for men to exert control and dominance — particularly through violence. Those things are toxic to other people's lives, he says, but those modes of behaviour are also very toxic to men, personally. If the only emotions men feel they're able to express are anger, frustration, dominance, and control, he points out, then what about all the other human emotions? What happens to empathy, concern, sadness? "When we give that up, our lives become very limited," Carolo says. "If men are not able to express those emotions, then how do we deal with our own challenges in our own lives?"

The answer, as we have seen, is that too many men do not. Still, it is one thing to encourage men to have a conversation; it is another to cut through a potentially appealing buffet of "let men be men" offerings on today's menu. But Lisa Hickey, the publisher of the U.S.-based website The Good Men Project, founded in 2009 by two men, is one of many people who insisted to me that there are many men who want to have these conversations. The site runs articles that challenge perceptions of masculinity and manliness, striking a tone somewhere between *Esquire* and Goop: "Understanding My Purpose"; "How 'Can I Kiss You' Changed My Life for the Better"; "The Little Ways We're Sexist (and Why It Matters so Much)." Hickey stressed that she looks forward to the day when the site's tagline — "The Conversation No One Else is Having" — becomes obsolete.

The Good Men Project hosts daily group calls for men

all over the world, she told me. On Mondays, the men talk about sex, relationships, and sexism; on Tuesdays, it's racism; on Wednesdays, it's environmental activism; on Thursdays, it's mental health. On a recent call, there were men from Pakistan, Canada, France. It's easy to be skeptical of all this — a kneejerk reaction to men, again, being centred in the conversation. But, honestly, groups of men gathering around the world to talk about how to become better men sounded, to me, a whole lot better than them gathering on the internet to call women "roasties," or to suggest a new nation of Stepford Wives.

"I don't know how to describe it," Hickey told me. "The conversations are game-changing." I hoped she was right. Because as much as it seems like a cliché, the game does need changing. Of all the traps this new hyper-masculine power lays, perhaps the most insidious of them all is that it keeps forcing everyone else to keep playing the game by its (totally damaging) rules. And I don't think we, any of us, know how much that is truly costing us.

CHAPTER 4

This Is What Equality Looks Like

For women, power often comes
with a very heavy price

I F YOU DECIDE TO follow conventional wisdom, there is a clear recipe for women's equality on the job in male-dominated fields — and, by extension, in women's lives. First, take one job, office-variety or otherwise, and add one cup of goals and a pinch of best intentions (optional). Then, work hard (the spoken-on-repeat rule) and eat shit (the quietly assumed one). Study more than everyone around you, put in longer hours, prove yourself over and over, and, if you want to keep advancing, figure out the fine balance of when to play nice and when to be firm. Know when to let the sexist joke roll off your shoulders, learn to laugh when you really want to say *fuck you*, somehow stop making the office cupcakes, do not crumble under the weight of your emotional labour, and always, always be excellent. If they see you crying or yelling, you're dead. Then, at the end of it all, reach your hand down, wield your hard-won power, and help the next woman up to do the same. Repeat until an equal number of individuals of all genders exist at the top of said field, whether it's politics, corporate North America, or STEM. Once that happens, we are done cooking. *Voilà!* You have made equality. Enjoy.

We stake a lot on workplace and economic equality, often making it the yardstick by which we measure women's progress more generally. In North America, Europe, and elsewhere around the world, money plays a huge role in defining power. It's no wonder that both capitalism, the all-powerful system by which we structure our societies, and the desire to break into everything that all-powerful system spawns heavily influence our ideas of equality. For women to be equal, we believe, they have to earn as much as men, own as much as men, be in the same decision-making rooms as men; the women's rights movement has fought hard — *is* fighting hard — for these things. And so, when we take the measure of how far women have come, we know there is still a long way to go in Canada, because while women represented an average of almost 38 percent of MBA students in North America and Europe in 2018,[1] they held just under 10 percent of executive positions at Canada's largest 100 publicly traded companies that same year.[2] We know this because while nearly half of practising lawyers in Canada are women,[3] they make up less than 30 percent of equity partners at law firms and 25 percent of senior leaders,[4] and only 39.6 percent of judges.[5] And we know this because while 60 percent of university graduates are women (discounting STEM, *sigh*),[6] only about 28 percent of them were tenured professors as of 2017.[7] If we ever forget, we really know this because while women make up half the voting population, at the start of 2018 they accounted for only 26 percent of Canada's MPs, 29 percent of MPPs, and 18 percent of mayors.[8] Canada has had only eleven female premiers in its entire 150-plus-year history; the first was elected in 1991.

If that weren't depressing enough, there's also the problem of us getting the solution all wrong. There's an assumption that, in making it to the top of any particular field, women are, well, at the top. Things are better there. They've achieved power, and with it, some taste of equality. They can effect change, enact a vision, control their own lives and the lives of people around them. They have resources and organizational influence, and positions that effectively halt the need to grin and bear it. They do not have to suffer men grabbing their asses, making crude sexual jokes, or masturbating into office plants—or whatever it is men do that day to show dominance and control, or just because they feel like it. At the top, those days are gone. Except, they're not—that is, at least by every standard that we use to measure equality: equal pay, equal opportunity, a work life free from sexual violence and discrimination, and fair treatment and evaluation. As awful as things are for women at the bottom, they're just as awful for women at the top. Actually, they're worse.

For an example of how the fantasy stacks up against reality, let's look at "glass ceiling pioneer" Ann Hopkins.[9] By 1982, Hopkins was a rising star at Price Waterhouse (now PricewaterhouseCoopers). She had billed more hours than any of her colleagues, all of whom were men. And she had recently secured a $25-million contract with the Department of State, historically one of the firm's biggest deals. Some of the partners sang her praises. And how could they not? She'd only been at the firm for five years, and look at what she'd already done. In their joint statement, evaluators called Hopkins "an outstanding professional" who had a "deft touch" and "strong character, independence and

integrity." One major client called her "extremely competent, intelligent," as well as "strong and forthright, very
productive, energetic and creative." Her bosses put her up
for partnership. (It's worth mentioning at this point that
there were then 622 other partners at the firm, only 7 of
whom were women.)[10] Other partners were less impressed.
Not only was Hopkins too good, she wasn't ladylike. One
man called her "macho," another remarked that she "over-
compensated for being a woman," and a third quipped that
she needed "a course at charm school."[11] They denied her
the partnership. Twice.

So she sued, and won, and went on to work as a partner
at the firm for two decades.[12]

Generally, though, the story of the double standard
for women at the top does not have such a happy ending.
Consider what happened to former Yahoo! CEO Carol Bartz,
one of the few women to speak openly about her firing. (On
the whole, executives and the companies they work for are
unlikely to admit to firing, preferring to cloak the decision
in euphemisms; one study found just 5 percent of CEOs are
openly dismissed.)[13] Bartz was hired in 2009 to help the ailing
company right itself against the onslaught of Google, and
also the lingering tidal waves of the 2008 recession. At the
time of her hiring, the company's chairperson, Roy Bostock,
enthused that she was "the exact combination of seasoned
technology executive and savvy leader that the board was
looking for," and that he was "thrilled to have attracted such
a world-class talent to Yahoo."[14] Two years later, Bostock
called Bartz on her cellphone, the day before she was set to
appear at a huge conference in New York City, to fire her. He
was only blocks away, but he did not give her the courtesy of
a face-to-face.[15] Speaking to reporters the next day, she put
it bluntly: "These people fucked me over."[16]

These people, it seems, are always fucking someone over. Consider also that the first high-profile person—not company—blamed for the financial crisis of 2008 was a woman.[17] Or that, in the wake of JPMorgan's 2013 "London Whale" trading scandal, which cost the company at least $6 billion and launched a Senate investigation, it was not the company's CEO, a man, who stepped down, but its chief investment officer, a woman (she was replaced by two men).[18] Or maybe just consider a December 2018 headline from an *Inc.* magazine column looking at the latest scandal for Tesla's CEO: "If Elon Musk Were a Woman, He'd Have Been Fired Already."[19] *Yes.* In fact, when things go wrong and there is no woman to blame, sometimes men will even *invent* one. Or several, as happened with a particularly sticky rumour that circulated online after a pedestrian bridge collapsed at Florida International University in 2018, killing six people.[20] A murky corner of the internet published a so-called article claiming an all-women engineering team built the bridge, cribbing photos from the company's International Women's Day posts on social media.[21] That's all it took. I heard the rumour again almost a year later when a friend met me after work one day and told me a "weird" story about a colleague—one who had totally bought it. Maybe that wasn't so surprising; we're primed to believe stories that scapegoat women.

It's a depressing, enraging reality that women can be reminded of our unequal rights and poor representation anywhere: on the street, on our screens, in our homes, and at work. But it's at work where we find some of the most measurable, glaring, and unexpected examples of the power gap. It's also where we see most clearly how male conceptions of power often work *against* us—pushing to keep us in last place, even when it looks like we're winning. This chapter is not about inviting us all to feel sorry for women whose shoes likely cost more than my rent. It is not about crying "poor little rich girl." It is about asking: If the game doesn't work for women and people of colour at the top, then what is it we are all striving for? And who really benefits from keeping us stuck in the game?

Better than Perfect

If the world generally expects women to be perfect, it expects women in leadership to be superhuman. More than once in my interviews, I heard a variation on the same half-truth, half-joke: *We'll know we've achieved something special once there are as many mediocre and flawed women in politics as there are men.* Most days, that future seems very far off indeed. We can point out that the high expectations suffocating the success of women politicians has everything to do with sexism, until we, ourselves, are out of breath. But what comes next?

Part of the challenge right now, one long-time feminist, Amy Richards, told me, is that so many people are still stuck in that "pointing out what's wrong" stage. Richards and Jennifer Baumgardner are co-authors of the seminal book *Manifesta: Young Women, Feminism, and the Future* (published in 2000 and reissued in an anniversary edition in 2010) and co-founders of Soapbox, the world's largest feminist speakers' bureau. I spoke to them both shortly after several women put their bids in for the 2020 U.S. presidential race. People, they contended, are too busy looking at the individuals within power structures instead of changing the structures themselves. When women are in the disempowered zone, added Baumgardner, it's too easy for them to believe they're not part of the problem — after all, they're not in power. "After we have exposed all of these corrupt systems and corrupt individuals and the depths of the injustices, we have to be willing to step into that power," Richards said. "I don't fully believe that women are there yet."

When I asked Richards what, exactly, she meant by that, she replied, "We don't make it easy on women." She knows people who are sad, now, that Hillary Clinton lost the 2016 election; at the time, though, they hated her. She was a bitch and a liar. "We have a hard time really supporting women in power," said Richards, referring to all genders. "We need to get over that if that's really what we're claiming right now, that that's what we want. We have to realize that women are flawed, but we have to support them anyway." Baumgardner jumped in: "In the same way we do with men." People in her world, she added, still blame Clinton for losing. She ran a terrible campaign. She wasn't likeable. Now, there were four women candidates for the presidential nomination (by March 2019 two more would toss in their hats) that people "loved five minutes ago," said Baumgardner, drawling out the "o" in "love," turning the vowel into a virtual eye roll. But would any of them make it? "Will we do anything that we can to make sure that men are looked up [to] instead of women?" she asked. "Maybe." *Maybe.*

Institutional and systemic factors have held women back from leadership, Baumgardner agreed. But there is something else, too. "There's this deep-seated misogyny that we've all been soaking in for a long time," she said. "And on the surface maybe we don't feel it, but deep in there, there's this sense of, 'Well, when somebody is harmed, or when Hillary didn't make it, or when that girl got raped, it's her problem.' There's something about *her.*"

I spent a great deal of time talking with actual avowed

anti-feminists for my first book, *F-Bomb: Dispatches from the War on Feminism*, and I don't believe it's inherently anti-feminist to question a woman's behaviour or track record. We know women do heinous things, too. Still, Baumgardner and Richards are not wrong. We tend to blame women for their own hardships, just as we also fail to credit them for their accomplishments. As Deborah L. Rhode noted in her book *Women and Leadership*, women's work is held to a higher standard than men's—sometimes with no apparent value assigned to the work itself. Meaning, it doesn't matter what the work is, or how well a woman performs it; so long as said work or experience is attributed to a woman, people will be less impressed. (If she even gets credit at all.) Rhode referenced one study in which participants evaluated the resumés of fictional job-seekers. One half of the group looked at the resumés of a female applicant with more education and a male applicant with more work experience. The other half of the group evaluated the reverse: a male applicant with more education and a female applicant with more work experience. Participants in both groups gave less weight to whatever advantage the female applicant had.[22] "The last half century has witnessed a transformation in gender roles," Rhode notes elsewhere in her book, "but expectations of equality outrun experience." Many of those obstacles, she adds, involve gender bias. Clearly. That bias plays out in myriad ways. Women's workplace mistakes are less tolerated and more often recalled than those of white men. See: Trump's Teflon-like performance during the 2016 election race.

Beyond that, all of us, regardless of gender, are too often predisposed to simply not see women as leaders. Take one study, in which researchers showed college students photographs of five people seated at a table, telling the students the people were working together on a project. The groups were varied: some all men, some all women, and some a mixture of both. In groups where either all men or all women sat around the table, students identified whoever was sitting at the head of the table as the leader. In mixed groups, if a man sat at the head of a table, he was still identified as the leader. Okay, fine. But if a woman sat at the head, she was no more likely to be identified as the leader than a man seated elsewhere at the table.[23]

On the rare occasion that a woman's success is acknowledged, it's also likely to be undercut by some implication that chance played a role. Researchers call this the "he's skilled, she's lucky" phenomenon.[24] Women of colour are especially likely to have both their credentials and their competence questioned. One much-referenced study, "Are Emily and Greg More Employable than Lakisha and Jamal?" (published in the *American Economic Review*) answered what was really perhaps a rhetorical question with a resounding "Yes."[25] The researchers answered 1,500 job ads in Boston and Chicago by sending out nearly 5,000 resumés, attributing identical qualifications to names like, for example, Emily and Lakisha. Anyone named something like Emily, Carrie, or Kristen received 50 percent more callbacks than someone named Lakisha, Aisha, or Tamika. A so-called white name, they determined, yields as many more callbacks as an additional eight years of experience on a resumé. What's more, the researchers also sent out resumés showing varying levels of experience. If Emily and Lakisha both had a high-quality resumé, their callback gap did not shrink, as one might reasonably expect, but instead notably widened.

But racism and sexism are only partly to blame for the gap in "positions of greatest status and power," argued Rhode. The other challenge is that women are self-selecting out—or, as Sheryl Sandberg has stated, they aren't leaning in. There's certainly some truth to this. When I was interviewing women for this book, I lost count of the number who told me that they simply didn't try to get (fill in the blank with whatever opportunity you like) because they assumed they weren't qualified and would not get it anyway.

One experience in particular stood out. In 2018, on the International Day of Women and Girls in Science, I called France Légaré, a professor in the department of family medicine and emergency medicine at Laval University and also a Tier 1 Canada Research Chair, to talk about the leaky pipeline for women in science and technology. That morning, she'd had a recruitment interview with a woman who'd received her Ph.D. in 2010. Légaré told her that, with her CV and her research profile, she could apply for a job more senior than she had. The woman responded with something like, "Oh, that's true. Everybody tells me that I'm better than what I apply for." And then she told Légaré that she knew it, too; her career had hit the next stage. But she was afraid she wasn't good enough.

Because Légaré didn't know the woman well, she did nothing more than reassure her. Yes, there will be a learning curve. Yes, you should still think about applying at a higher level. Take a week to think it over. However, for people whom Légaré does know well—those friends and colleagues who come to her for advice about their work or professional life—there is another, more direct answer. "I tell them, 'Okay, stop talking like a woman. Stop talking like a woman who says, *I'm not good enough. I don't know enough. And, and, and . . .*'" The list could go on forever. Stop internalizing that negative attitude, Légaré wanted women to know. Stop that dismissal of your skills and experience. Instead, tell yourself the truth. Reflect on your own accomplishments and see them objectively, as they are, not what you fear. "You don't need to be so severe on yourself," she added. "Because everybody else will be severe on you."

She has a point. I don't know many women who haven't felt the chokehold of Imposter Syndrome at some point in their lives. That voice telling you that you don't belong, or that you're not good enough, can be both seductive and damaging. In 2017, the *Harvard Business Review* asked fifty-seven female CEOs for advice on how more women can make it to the top.[26] Of them all, only five said they always wanted to be a CEO. Two-thirds said they never realized it was an option until another person suggested it to them. They described themselves as being focused on improving their results, rather than advancement and success. "It wasn't until that conversation," one woman told researchers, "that I even imagined anything past manager, forget CEO. I really just wanted a good job with a good company. That conversation was a bit of a wake-up call."

It can be difficult to interrupt that story, too, and be your own wake-up call. One friend told me that she often faces anxiety when she feels she hasn't answered a co-worker's question in enough detail. That detail usually, she said, "goes far beyond what their original question was." So, she went on, "If someone asks me 'Who do I contact in XYZ scenario?' I will feel like my response was inadequate if I only tell them the contact's name and their email, instead of their name, plus their email, plus the reason why contacting them for this scenario is important." She feels constantly worried that she isn't doing enough, even though she is a valued, skilled member of her team.

Another friend told me about a vow she made with a colleague to stop saying "I'm bad at math" as a joke to male colleagues in workplace settings, because, really, when she thought about it, she wasn't. I've had my own bad-at-math moment. Often feeling like a fraud at public events, blooming red with embarrassment as presenters read my bio, I started supplying a short, ten-word version instead. It took hearing several onerous, paragraphs-long introductions for male fellow panellists before I finally stopped underselling myself. Even so, I still shift uncomfortably in my seat.

The Confidence Industry

If only a little bit of swagger was all it took.

It seems clear to me that women's self-diminishment often creates a feedback loop, with society's dismissal of our accomplishments feeding into our own derision, feeding back out into the perception that women aren't ready for X, eating itself over and over again like a sort of ouroboros of negativity. And I also understand why it is alluring to tell women they most need to change their own perceptions (hard, but not impossibly so), versus rewriting the system (incredibly daunting, seemingly impossible), in order to achieve power. But there is a danger in proposing confidence and its sister-solution, empowerment, as the best answer to women's equality and advancement. In 2018, the *Harvard Business Review* conducted another study, this time using text from *Lean In*, as well audio from Sheryl Sandberg's TED Talks, to look at whether the DIY approach of "women can solve this" risked leading people to an unintended conclusion: "that women have caused their own under-representation."[27]

The researchers chose *Lean In* because, as they rightly noted, the language of the book has come to dominate discussions on women and leadership since it was published in

2013. For the experiment, one group of participants read or listened to messaging that emphasized everything women could do to help themselves: be more ambitious, speak with confidence, demand a seat at the table, take more risks. The other group read or listened to messaging that highlighted structural and societal factors, including discrimination. Those who consumed the DIY narratives were more likely to believe women have the power to solve the problem, wrote researchers — which, they acknowledged, is probably good news, in isolation. More on the bad news side: those same participants were also more likely to believe that women were accountable for *all* aspects of workplace inequality.

"These findings should worry anyone who believes we need structural and societal change to achieve gender equality in the workplace," the researchers wrote. "They suggest that the more we talk about women leaning in, the more likely people are to hold women responsible, both for causing inequality, and for fixing it."

This is how we get things like *#GirlBoss* — Sophia Amoruso's autobiographical book was published the year after *Lean In*, and it was then adapted by Netflix as a TV series that premiered in 2017. The #GirlBoss brand is a glossier, more Instagram-ready version of *Lean In* that heavily relies on the same type of messaging: the only thing standing between you and success is you. Amoruso, who rose to fame after founding the fashion retailer Nasty Gal, also launched a conference in New York City in 2017 called Girlboss Rally. Half "experiential inspiration wonderland," the conference has called itself "A Noah's Ark of Ambitious Women," and also an "empowering" space for "women taking their careers, side hustles, and small businesses seriously."[28] A pillar in what can be thought of as the new confidence industry, the idea of #GirlBoss — and all of its various, contemporary iterations, pushing us to slay, hustle, and kill it like a "boss bitch"—is girl power grown up. It tells us we only need to believe in ourselves (and also perhaps buy various items, usually pink) to help us achieve our #goals. "I have three pieces of advice that I want you to remember," Amoruso wrote in the introduction to her book. "Don't ever grow up. Don't become a bore. Don't ever let the Man get to you? Okay? Cool." Then let's do this, she hyped. "#GIRLBOSS for life."[29]

It's easy to see why this kind of messaging connected with millennial women, and it's easy to see why it has persisted into Gen Z. Following it, women are largely excused from worrying over the larger structural and societal inequities that can hold them back. More than that: they are told that they are *stronger* than those inequities. The empowerment creed relies heavily on endorsing the belief that if women just go for it and never give up, they will triumph. It confirms their ambition, but bottles it within a contained, achievable space. Things like the pay gap, racial inequality, and sexual harassment are not ignored, exactly, but they are branded—usually into shirts that say things like "Cats Against Catcalls," "My Favourite Position? CEO," and "Pay Me"—along with the message that any individual can overcome them just by being excellent enough. The secondary, less-spoken message in all this is that while women deserve both power and equality, they will get it piecemeal, in dribs and drabs, as soon as they stop putting up their own roadblocks. Underneath it all, the dual mantras of "hustling" and "killing it" are not much more than a dressed-up version of something we all know already: that women have to work harder, better, and longer to reap even close to the same rewards as men. Only, this time, we're doing it to ourselves and calling it power.

The patriarchy likes this type of power, too, because it can be sold to women. Take, for example, the much-lauded Nike commercial "Dream Crazier,"[30] which debuted during the 2019 Oscars. Vox called it "moving," adding that Nike was "pushing the envelope and making a statement."[31] *CR Fashion Book*, run by the former editor-in-chief of *Vogue Paris*, called the ad "inspiring."[32] Hello Giggles said it was "secretly the best part of the 2019 Oscars."[33] Admittedly, the first time I watched the commercial, which is narrated by Serena Williams, I felt a swell of recognition in my chest, a visceral response of *yes, exactly.* I wasn't the only one. In its first month online, the YouTube video racked up more than 8.6 million views.

The video opens with a montage of women athletes showing the types of emotion we don't usually see women show—at least not on mainstream commercials. It feels both rebellious and good. "If we show emotion, we're called dramatic," says Williams. "If we want to play against men, we're 'nuts.' And if we dream of equal opportunity, 'delusional.' When we stand for something, we're 'unhinged.'" She continues, "And if we get angry, we're 'hysterical,' 'irrational,' or just being 'crazy.'" And then comes the empowerment twist. "But a woman running a marathon was crazy. A woman boxing was crazy. A woman dunking? Crazy." And so she continues until the expected rallying cry at the end. "So if they want to call you crazy? Fine. Show them what crazy can do." The implicit answer is: anything. But it's also: buy some Nike shoes.

Divorced from corporate interests, it isn't that this messaging isn't, well, empowering. It absolutely can feel uplifting. It can remind us that we can achieve, even as it simultaneously reminds us that nobody thinks we can. Not that the victor–victim dichotomy matters much, so long as you *go get it, girl.* (Bring your Nike shoes!) In my research for this book, I found myself at one particularly energetic "no excuses" empowerment session in New York City, in January 2019. The facilitator, Natasha Nurse, had one jaw-droppingly impressive resumé and a true find-yourself story: she left a career in law to pursue her dream—fashion and writing—and she founded Dressing Room 8, a web-based resource that offers consultation and coaching services. Nurse herself radiated confidence and, while she acknowledged "we live in a very exclusionary world," her answer to that was a message of ultimate self-empowerment: "If you're not finding what you need, create your own." She also had little patience for anybody in her workshop who bemoaned their circumstances or outside challenges. "The answer to everything," she said, "is confidence."

I began to fill up my notebook with Nurse-isms, all of which could have, quite honestly, become slogans on a (best-selling) confidence merchandise line. She doled them out as soon as a participant hit the "but" mode. As in, "But what about...?" or "But I can't because..." A short list: "Why won't you move the Earth for you?" "Is it enough to stop you from doing what you want?" "Stop blocking your blessings. Why are you doing that? Stop. It's 2019." "What are you doing to achieve that? That's the question of the day." And, of course, the hustle: "Be ferocious about your goals. You have to be hungry. Hungry. Hungry. Hungry." None of this is meant to single Nurse out; it's refreshing to completely disregard the crushing influence of power structures and systemic inequalities. But the problem is that we're also completely disregarding the crushing influence of power structures and systemic inequalities.

As the *Harvard Business Review* researchers noted, the (often) inadvertent consequence of all this is that it implies blame. I have no doubt that people like Nurse *do* care about righting wider systemic issues. Frankly speaking, though, neither confidence, individual empowerment, nor being a #GirlBoss will solve all of them — at least not on a wide scale, and not for more than a very successful few. Insisting that they can, and on a mass level, not only mirrors the blame back on women, it too often punctuates the conversation with easy answers, or ends it altogether.

Instead of looking at why women might lack confidence, those in power can deflect blame, saying that poor representation in corporations, academia, science, the law, and politics has nothing to do with them. We've all heard the routine excuses. Women and other equity-seeking groups haven't pushed hard enough to be there. They don't want to be there. Women are not CEOs or judges because they don't ask to be. They would rather be doing something else (presumably being a mother, or some other typically feminine job). The problem is that even for those of us who care about equality, such messaging often deploys a same-coin, different-side effect. It can look like asking: *How can women be more confident? How can we make them feel like they're a #GirlBoss? How can we get women to speak up about their ambitions?* Feminists have better intentions on their side, no doubt, and they may desire more equitable outcomes. But buying shares in the confidence industry still forces all of us to keep playing by the rules of someone else's game. Beyond that, it also lets companies, quite literally, profit from our sustained inequality.

So yes, sure, there's nothing wrong with wanting women to be more confident, but as a popular message and often-proposed panacea, it obscures some deeply urgent questions. For one, women do not start out less confident; something happens to steadily chip away at their self-assurance.

Research shows this undermining of confidence begins in adolescence (a sad fact to which we'll return later on) and continues right on into adulthood. In one 2014 study of 1,000 men and women in the United States,[34] researchers found that early-stage career women were actually more ambitious than men, with 43 percent of them aspiring to top management, compared to 34 percent of men at the same stage. Both men and women were equally confident that they would reach their goal. Those numbers drop dramatically, however, as women advance (or don't) in their careers. As men and women each gain more experience in the workplace, researchers found, the number of women who aspired to top management plunged to a dismal 16 percent, while the men's percentage remained the same. Likewise, men's confidence in reaching their goals sticks, whereas women's drops by half. Evidently, not only does the journey suck, the destination looks much less attractive the closer it gets.

It's (Not) Nice Up Here

When it comes to positions of power, women are often set up to fail. If the glass ceiling has come to dominate conversations on women and leadership, the idea of the "glass cliff" has made a forceful play to replace it as a more pertinent metaphor. Researchers Michelle Ryan and Alexander Haslam coined the term in the mid-2000s after reading an article in the *Times* headlined "Women on Board: Help or Hindrance?" written by journalist Elizabeth Judge. In it, Judge bemoaned women's advancement to leadership, arguing that the "triumphant" march of women into Britain's boardrooms had actually sunk companies' share prices.[35] "So much for smashing the glass ceiling and using their unique skills to enhance the performance of Britain's biggest companies," Judge wrote. "Analysis . . . shows that companies that decline to embrace political correctness by installing women on the board perform better than those that actively promote sexual equality at the very top."

Ryan and Haslam doubted that analysis told the whole story. What, they wondered, did the financial health of those companies look like *before* women stepped up? The short answer is: not good. "Women are more likely than men to find themselves on a 'glass cliff,' such that their positions of leadership are associated with greater risk of failure," they wrote in one paper. "If and when that failure occurs, it is then women (rather than men) who must face the consequences and who are singled out for criticism and blame."[36] Examples of this ostensible hiring strategy include women like Carol Bartz, but also Marissa Meyer, another Yahoo! CEO; as well as Meg Whitman, brought in to help a struggling Hewlett-Packard; Ursula Burns, brought in to help a struggling Xerox; Indra Nooyi, brought in to help a struggling PepsiCo; and, most recently, Mary Barra, who took over a struggling General Motors in 2014 and was subsequently named "Crisis Manager of the Year."[37] And, if a woman does become the next American president, she will almost certainly be stepping into crisis.

Sometimes, as evidenced by the successful leadership of women like Nooyi, women CEOs do not plunge off the glass cliff (although their tenure can tend to be significantly shorter). When they do, however, they might find that the news of their replacement makes them want to punch something. (Okay, or, less violently, sigh *really* loudly.) A 2013 study published in *Strategic Management Journal* by researchers Alison Cook and Christy Glass reiterated the findings of previous "glass cliff" papers, affirming that women and people of colour were far likelier to be appointed CEO when a firm was already performing poorly.[38] In particular, more than 40 percent of women CEOs were appointed during times of crisis, compared to just over 20 percent of men. What's more, in a sort of power-lite move, only 13 percent of women were concurrently appointed as the company's chairperson, as opposed to half of the men, who got that extra bump of influence.[39] But Cook and Glass also wanted to know what happened *after* said promotion, when a woman inevitably left or was fired.

Using a data set of CEO transitions in Fortune 500 companies over a fifteen-year period, they discovered that if a company continued to perform poorly, which it often did, since companies are big and difficult to turn around, women and people of colour were almost always replaced by white men — a pattern they dubbed the "saviour effect," a really depressing echo of the larger relational narratives-slash-fantasies we build around women, people of colour, and white men. "These findings suggest that occupational minorities face greater challenges when appointed CEO," wrote the researchers, "and are provided few degrees of freedom with which to establish their leadership capabilities." In other words, they never even get a chance to succeed; the game is often rigged from the start. Even knowing this, women and people of colour tend to take the job anyway, largely because, as other research has repeatedly shown, they (sadly, correctly) believe it might be the only opportunity they'll ever get to advance.[40]

The way we talk about women in leadership does little to counteract these narratives. One 2016 survey, commissioned by the Rockefeller Foundation, examined media coverage of America's top CEOs.[41] As its authors, perhaps naively, stated, "The skills and performance of a CEO should matter most in a crisis." Meaning: media coverage of a company that was doing badly would, a person might reasonably assume, focus on the performance and strategy of its CEO. Except that's not exactly what happened. Framing of such stories instead relied heavily on the gender of the CEO, whether the journalist was conscious of it or not.

In cases where the company's CEO was a woman, 80 percent of the stories blamed her as the source of the crisis. But when a man was the CEO, only 31 percent of the articles named him as the source of the calamity. To add to the "you don't belong" line, articles focusing on women CEOs were also more likely to mention their personal lives, and when they did, the vast majority of them discussed family. None of the articles cited mentioned a man's children or his family. If any article did delve into a man's personal life, it was to focus on his retirement plans, his post-career life, or his social relationships. All of which is to say that discrimination can choke especially tightly at the top of the hierarchy.

This is undeniably discouraging, but here's the real gut punch: if women are more likely to be hired when a company is tanking, they're also significantly more likely than men to get fired *when their company is doing well*. One 2018 paper published in the *Journal of Management*, cheekily titled "You're Fired! Gender Disparities in CEO Dismissal," found that women are about 45 percent more likely to be dismissed than male CEOs.[42] When the company was performing poorly, rates of dismissal were about the same, which is moderately encouraging. However, women were found to be significantly more likely to be dismissed when the firm had high performance. "Higher levels of firm performance protects male, but not female, CEOs from dismissal," wrote the researchers, adding that their results challenged an age-old nugget of conventional wisdom: that how well a person does a job corresponds to their job retention. That gender plays a role in firing is inescapable. And all of it feeds into the idea that women just aren't cut out for leadership.

Speaking of: women CEOs are also more likely to face pressure from activist shareholders (so dubbed because they try to get firms to change strategic direction).[43] Using an eighteen-year data set, one team of researchers found that activist investors were more likely to tell women how to manage the firm, even if, statistically, their company was performing as well as a man's. (Sound familiar?) Such findings, they added, show that power is not enough to overcome bias. That isn't exactly encouraging for those without power, either. "If prejudice based on gender role incongruity occurs for such visible roles," they added, "it suggests there may be even more prejudice against women in less visible high-level positions." Meaning: if men are annoyingly confident enough to publicly correct the CEO of a high-profile company, can you imagine what they say in private? You probably can.

High Power, Low Reward

So, the paradox of female power, thus far, in a nutshell: women are held to a higher standard than men, but it ultimately doesn't matter how good they are because neither their purported power nor their stellar performance shields them from the effects of sexism. Yet it's even more complicated than that. Women who play the game too well can often pay a steep price. For as much as we force power-seeking women to be exceptional, that very extraordinariness is usually what men perceive to be most threatening. That's the kind of fun world we live in! This fact becomes particularly devastating when considered in tandem with girls' and women's rising advancement and achievement in educational systems, particularly in North America and Europe, a statistic that's often meant to soothe worries about the advance of equality. And maybe it would if we weren't living in a backlash against women's perceived power grab. Or, as Natasha Quadlin asks in a 2018 study published in the *American Sociological Review*: "Women earn better grades than men across levels of education—but to what end?"[44]

Quadlin sent out more than 2,000 job applications, varying her fictional candidates' GPA, gender, and major. She discovered that women benefited from moderate achievement, but not high achievement. Indeed, high-achieving men were called back at a rate of almost two to one compared to high-achieving women. And when those high-achieving fictional applicants specialized in traditionally male-dominated fields, such as math, the callback gap leapt to three to one. This is partly because employers greatly value likeability in women, a characteristic that they assign to mediocre women but not high-achieving women, whose personalities, as Quadlin wrote, "are viewed with more skepticism." They are simply not "supposed" to do well in those fields; if they do, they're assumed to be uptight. High-achieving women, it should be noted, also lost out in relation to moderate-achieving women. Quadlin called it an inverted-U shape for achievement, in which the women with the best grades were disproportionately penalized, most starkly in STEM. That disadvantage is likely to be even worse for women of colour, Quadlin theorized, as they are often held to an even stricter standard when it comes to demonstrating warmth.

Often, when we say we want women to be confident, what we really mean is that we want them to be *feminine* and confident. Warm and confident. Charming, full of acquiescence, and confident. Consider what one retail manager of a major chain told me about how both staff and customers respond to her leadership style. "People do not like hearing 'No,' but they really don't like hearing it from a tiny woman, with conviction," she said. Unless she feels she should be apologizing, she added, she refuses to inflect her voice with "sorry." People don't like it when she factually, calmly explains rules; they really don't like it when she enforces those rules. Men especially don't like it, she told me. Her staff also don't like that she can say no to them with confidence. They call her authoritarian "because I consistently ask them to adhere to company rules, without empathetic inflections in my voice." But when she tried being empathetic they didn't respond at all. "When I have to constantly remind them to do their job I'm a 'nag,'" she said. "But worst of all, they call me 'moody.' If a man emotionlessly told them to do something—not a problem."

In fact, women reap few of the rewards we've come to expect from power, achievement, and success. As we first examined in the introduction, the pay gap becomes chasmlike once women make it to the top executive positions. In January 2019, the Canadian Centre for Policy Alternatives released a report that examined the compensation of all the top executives—including the CEO and the chief financial officer (CFO) positions, as well as the three next highest-paid ones—on the S&P/TSX Composite index, which accounts for roughly 250 companies.[45] Among full-time workers, women make eighty-three cents for every dollar men make, a gap that widens for women of colour, Indigenous women, and women with disabilities.

Yet while the gap narrows slightly among senior managers, it stretches to what the report called "an abysmal" sixty-eight cents among top executives. For women supposedly at the top of the hierarchy, that amounts to nearly $1 million less a year. There are three main factors that account for the disparity: position type, company size, and sector. That is, considering that there were more CEOs in Canada named "Paul" or "Brian" in 2018 than there were women CEOs, women who are top executives are more likely to be in HR positions, not CEO ones. They're also more likely to work at smaller companies, which pay less; and be less represented at larger ones, which just pay *them* less. Plus, company sectors that do hire many women are likely to have bigger pay gaps.

Bonus salary, as opposed to base salary, drives much of the compensation gap, according to the CCPA report. At the top level, a person's base salary accounts for only 27 percent of their compensation, with bonus pay accounting for the rest. Personal performance often has little to do with it. Bonus pay is mainly (theoretically) based on a company's share price and is usually awarded through stock options to everyone who occupies the C-suite. Nevertheless, women at the C-suite level get substantially less bonus pay even at the same company, based on the same stock performance. It's also worth mentioning that, when looking at base salary alone, the pay gap is the same as it is elsewhere. It's the system of rewards that, in the end, rewards men. "The lack of female executives and their substantial pay gap is an issue of fairness in its own right," wrote the report's author, CCPA senior economist David Macdonald, "but it also lays bare the cumulative impact of corporate culture on women's working lives."

Of course, corporate culture is only the surface-level problem at work. Misogyny has helped to define that culture, filtering it through a history of treating women as office lackeys, workplace subordinates, and colleagues who need to be "put in their place." It's presumably the same attitude that led one of my first bosses, a man who owned several stores in a Toronto mall, to one day tell me I was hired to "pretty up" the place. Whether he meant by virtue of my face or my presumed workplace decorating skills I'll never know; I was too enraged and embarrassed to ever speak to him again. I had no workplace power then, but even if I had, it might not have saved me from such a comment. Just as women might expect workplace power and authority to result in better pay — respect, even! — they might also reasonably expect that no subordinate would ever make inappropriate comments about how pretty they are, grab their ass, or make a "joke" that involves an eggplant emoji. Not so. In fact, a woman's power and authority at work seem to *attract* bad behaviour, like flies to honey. While those who are most vulnerable in the workplace — including women in junior positions, people of colour, and LGBTQ+ workers — certainly face sexual harassment, and often feel powerless to stop it, there is a growing body of research showing that women in positions of authority are just as, if not *more*, frequently targeted. Researchers call this the "power-threat" model, referring to men's discomfort with women's authority over them as the driving motivation for harassment.

It makes a sick kind of sense. Sexual violence is, at its core, about asserting control and domination. And what is more threatening to a man's control and domination than a woman who has achieved more power than him? This is why sexual harassment has been shown to increase at the promotion stage for women, and it's also why studies have found that men (and particularly men who identify as strongly masculine) are more likely to harass women who identify as feminists than they are women who adhere to traditional values.[46] What's worse is that researchers have also discovered that men believe this works: those who engaged in harassment essentially felt a boost to their perceived manliness following the action. Which also makes a sick kind of sense: there's a reason the larger manosphere and the anti-feminists within it target women with violence and derision.

"When women's power is viewed as illegitimate or easily undermined, co-workers, clients, and supervisors appear to employ harassment as an 'equalizer' against women supervisors," concluded a team of researchers who completed the first longitudinal study that clearly revealed the power-threat pattern. That study, published in 2012 in the *American Sociological Review*, found that women experience a power paradox, in which their authority counterintuitively seems to invite more bad behaviour instead of protecting them from it. This can be exacerbated when a woman or person of colour is the only person in a room with high-powered people, as she so often is.

The researchers shared the experience of a woman they called Holly, the first woman in upper management at her manufacturing firm. Her subordinates would joke, "If we had somebody with balls in this position, we'd be getting things done." Then, one evening, a client—the vice-president of an influential firm—sexually harassed her at a company dinner, trying to put his arm around her, groping her leg, repeatedly remarking, "Oh, I love her. She's beautiful." She was the only woman there. After co-workers finally saw what was happening, one suggested *she* leave. She did. They then stayed behind for drinks at the bar with the client.

Reading this, I thought of the comments and behaviour I was subjected to back when I helmed one of Canada's oldest, most progressive political magazines: "Oh, you must be the intern" (countless times); "What a cute little blog you run" (not a blog, and you know it); "Are you on Tinder? Will you show me how to use it?" (just no); "You're so beautiful" (silence, silence, nothing else); "I think he has a crush on you" (not an appropriate response to a meeting wrap-up with an outside consultant); a note telling me that "a bit of slap and tickle can be a good contrast to the serious side of sexism" (really?); an unsolicited, lingering backrub and a literal "Good job" from a professor after I gave a presentation to his class on being a successful woman in journalism (patronizing and gross!); an older industry professional who rested a hand on my forearm throughout an entire conversation he was having with *another* person, then suddenly turned to me and suggested coffee (thank u, next). Yes, I could see how the power-threat paradox could play out, over and over into monotony, grinding down someone's will, sort of like a *Friends* rerun marathon.

I called the lead researcher on the paper, Heather McLaughlin, an assistant professor in Oklahoma State University's sociology department, to see how the power-threat model might clash against the increased push to see women advance in the workplace. One of the biggest mistakes people make, she told me, is conflating a woman's supervisory authority at work with an automatic increase in workplace power, and not accounting for the social hierarchies that exist outside the workplace. She referenced Holly's case. Too often, a woman who occupies any top executive or supervisory role is the only woman at that level—a token nod to diversity or progress that doesn't necessarily mesh with the wider company culture (or world culture). "To what level are they able to effect change?" McLaughlin asked, imagining the solitary woman at the top. "And what is their role there? Are you hiring this person because you value their voice and you want to make changes? Or are you hiring this person simply to assuage concerns that you're sexist?" And if those questions are answered honestly, how much voice and agency does a person really have?

No wonder women at the top aren't helping other women rise, or at least not in the numbers we expected. They're too busy fending off everything, and everyone, around them.

Queen Bees

Several years ago, a photo of me popped up on an older colleague's Facebook page. Taken the night of our national industry awards, it showed me in a neon floral dress, standing next to the colleague and beaming. I was holding up an envelope that contained the certificate marking my gold-medal win from that night. Underneath the photo were a couple of comments from his friends, older women in the industry, women to whom I'd looked up. One was to the effect of, "Is she even old enough to drink?" And the other said something like, "I didn't realize they let children into the event now." I blinked red. Then I blinked tears. Not only was I old enough to drink—*thirty!*—it was only a few weeks after my then husband had unceremoniously announced he wanted out of our marriage. I'd revelled in the win that night. I'd needed it. To face the kind of behaviour I usually expected from men coming from women jarred me. And it wasn't the first (or last) time a woman with more experience cut me down or behaved coldly toward me.

Researchers coined the (super-sexist) term "Queen Bee" in the 1970s to describe this kind of behaviour in workplace settings: women who've achieved high positions, particularly in male-dominated organizations, by distancing themselves from other women, and also by essentially emulating the behaviours of the types of men whose positions they wanted. Think of it as the power-achieving equivalent of the "cool girl" who "prefers to hang out with the guys." In organizational settings, the Queen Bee may act in a derogatory manner toward other women — de-emphasizing their career commitment, achievements, and goals, as well as generally underscoring other qualities, like their family life, their looks, their personality, in a way we have come to expect more generally from macho men.[47] Perhaps predictably, plenty of media articles have used the idea of the Queen Bee to feed into stereotypes of catty women and bad female bosses; others have insisted there's more to it.[48]

And, of course, there is. Research has shown that, rather than a simple *Mean Girl*-ing trait among successful women, the Queen Bee phenomenon is also a *consequence* of gender discrimination in the workplace. Put another way, stressing how much they differ from other women has been the main method by which women traditionally get ahead, acutely so when everyone else in power is a dude.[49] They have no inherent predisposition to battle other women; it's more that they, rightly, view mirroring masculine traits, and denouncing feminine ones, as a way to advance. It's much easier, however, to fall back on the trope that women are bitches. This lazy thinking is only aggravated by the gendered expectations placed upon women. Women are expected to help lift each other up in the workplace — consider the famous quote by former secretary of state Madeleine Albright, "There's a special place in hell for women who don't help each other" — while men are not only allowed, but expected, to compete among each other for the best jobs. Women who do try to compete up the hierarchy in organizations are then seen as unnatural, cold, and even shameful. They are not nice girls.

This isn't to say the Queen Bee phenomenon doesn't harm women; it does. One ground-breaking study published in 2018 discovered that the Queen Bee effect can be just as damaging to women workers as sexism; although, unlike sexism, other women are unlikely to attribute it to ill intent—a factor that can make it harder to name and address.[50] Study participants who were exposed to Queen Bee behaviour were more sad, angry, and anxious than those who weren't.

None of this means that women are toxic banshees who should be banned from power. Nor does it mean that women make terrible mentors. Rather, it recalls McLaughlin's point about what it means to be the solitary woman at the top. She contended that hiring a single woman CEO was unlikely to hugely shift a company's larger culture, but employing more women who can more collectively make changes—without experiencing backlash—could. The authors of the above study concluded much the same thing. "Only placing a few more minorities and women in the higher echelons of the organizations is not sufficient without also targeting the organizational diversity climate," they wrote, "or at least not if this increase in women and/or minorities does not lead to a critical mass."

So, no. One woman alone cannot entirely change the deeply disadvantageous power structures that have been built over centuries. However much power she has, so long as she's still playing the game, the game has more power. Faced with this messy reality, many trans and cis women, as well as people living beyond the traditional gender binary, have given the middle finger to traditional power structures—and the rules that govern them. Think of it as the ultimate "boy, bye" move: reimagining a world without men in it at all.

CHAPTER 5

No Boys Allowed

The revolutionary resurgence of
women-only spaces

Toronto co-working space Make Lemonade is what the phrase "You Got This" would look like if it came to life in the form of a 3,000-square-foot office. Walking in, the first thing I noticed about the space, which is geared toward both trans and cis women, as well as women-identified people, was a bulletin board covered in members' business cards. I picked out one for a graphic designer who has created a product line and brand called Mantone in response to a certain other brand's oft-irrelevant "colour of the year" picks; her business card was a dark green swatch in "wage gap." Another card promoted a member's company that makes "the first bra that adapts to your breast size," available in more than ninety (!!!) sizes. I saw a business card that advertised a comprehensive online mental health service called Inkblot, which offers video counselling to clients. Many other cards belonged to writers, social media and brand consultants, women offering diverse beauty and fitness services, and business coaches.

A person could not even pee without being assured of their excellence. Inside the washroom, members had covered the walls, mirrors, and stalls with handwritten inspirational messages to each other. *Be True to U. No Bad Vibes. Love Yourself The Most. You are Beautiful. You are So Worthy. Seek Magic. Life is Tough and So Are You. It's Okay To Pivot. Who Run the World? Girls.* Little hearts and smiley faces popped through where there was no room left to write. If it weren't for all the colleagues and friends who'd told me stories over the years about escaping their office to cry in the bathroom, it might have almost seemed cheesy. As it stood, it felt more like a refuge. Women sat at both the shared tables and individual desks, typing, scrolling, and softly chatting to each other. Looping back to the front of the space, I saw a soft-pink wall filled with another affirming motto, this one giant-sized: "She believes she can so she does."

"We're changing that," Rachel Kelly, the space's founder and owner, told me. On reflection, she'd come to see the phrase as exclusive. "Our wall will become, 'We believe we can so we do.'" Make Lemonade, she stressed, is advertised as women-identified, a description that is meant to be inclusive of both trans women and non-binary people. With steaming mugs of tea from a woman-owned social enterprise in hand, Kelly and I settled into the space's indoor patio—a whole area outfitted in AstroTurf, designed to mimic a chic outdoors—as she explained to me how she devised Make Lemonade. She had been working as a freelancer in her mid-twenties and life had handed her a lemon when a full-time, in-office job suddenly fell through, days before she was supposed to start. Tired of working alone in coffee shops, she started studying communities and spaces from around the world that she wished were *her* communities and spaces. She posted the images on Instagram, created polls on Facebook. What she was really doing, bit by bit, she said, was creating a new version of reality, realizing it could be possible, and sharing that vision with everybody else. She knew that she wanted a bricks-and-mortar place for women to make the same sort of connections in real life that she saw happening online. So she built one.

Make Lemonade opened its doors in fall 2017, right as #MeToo was breaking the internet. Experiencing the collective power of the movement, as well as the feminist furor over 2017 in general, combined with being around so many other amazing women, pushed Kelly's feminism in a new direction. She went from thinking *Let's figure out a way to work within the system* to *Let's disrupt the system*. For the longest time, she said, she had focused on having the right chairs, achieving the perfect lighting, getting fast Wi-Fi—all good things, but not, she realized, what actually made people come to the space. The epiphany: members came to Make Lemonade because they, like her, thought it felt like the future. Just a little taste of it: a place where women could form inclusive, encouraging communities in which they would feel welcome. The point wasn't to sit around and diss men, as some might assume, or to have 24/7 conversations about feminism (obviously while simultaneously burning one's bra and making an altar to Supreme Being Gloria Steinem). The point was to not be part of the game at all. "There's a lot of healing that goes on in here," said Kelly. "Just by coming in here, you're choosing to have a space for you, to come in and do your work in a supported way."

We chatted a bit more about the idea of having a space "for you." While Kelly hadn't explicitly called it such, her workspace, and others like it, embraces a sort of modern separatism: a callback to century-old feminist solutions that proposed that the answer to being kept out of male-dominant spaces was simply to create new, better ones.

Make Lemonade also hosts regular "master classes," Kelly told me, to help women "get their shit done," whether that's learning more about social media or how to earn a steady income as a freelancer. Such things sound so simple and small on their own, but they are monumental when contrasted against the trenches women can find themselves in at traditional workplaces—trenches they may not even realize they've been waging war from until they step out of them. Kelly mused that Make Lemonade members are surely working on a lot of feelings, whether they know it or not. Radical things can happen when women feel safe—not to mention when they feel it's safe, and even necessary, to help other women. When they don't have to worry so much about power because everyone has it, at least while they are there.

It isn't utopia. I'm sure some potential (and even current) members don't respond to the space's ethos, which hews more closely to empowerment messaging than it does to outright disruption. Personally, I'd rather have a never-ending lunch with Will Ferrell and Seth Rogen while *Family Guy* plays in the background than adopt the princess-aligned "mood" of that day: sparkle. Still, it beats the de facto all-day, every-day moods of many other workplaces: harassment, exclusion, aggression. Just look at what was going on at some of the world's highest-profile companies around the time Make Lemonade, and many other women's co-working spaces like it, launched. Over at Google, one male employee named James Damore sent out a now infamous ten-page screed that went viral inside the company, and then around the entire internet. Titled "Google's Ideological

Echo Chamber," the memo attacked the company's (honestly, not very effective) diversity initiatives, arguing, in a very Peterson-esque way, that under-representation in the workplace exists because men and women are inherently different. Because women's personalities are different, wrote Damore, they have a "harder time negotiating salary, asking for raises, speaking up, and leading. . . . This leads to exclusory programs . . . and swaths of men without support."[1]

After the memo was leaked, numerous women came forward to say they had left Google because of racial and gender discrimination.[2] One woman, Qichen Zhang, a technical specialist, told media that she was in the middle of a bustling Google office when a white man started "joking" about her hiring. "He said, 'It must've been really easy for you to get your job because you're an Asian woman and people assume you're good at math,'" Zhang said. "I didn't see a lot of women, especially Asian women, Black women or other women of color in the executive ranks. I didn't see any opportunities for myself." Another woman, who is Black and asked the *Guardian* not to name her for fear of retaliation, told the paper that she faced discrimination every day she worked for the company as a specialist: "I felt like I didn't belong nor did anybody want me to belong." We know this awful behaviour is pervasive, too — happening anywhere women are not traditionally represented in power, which is mostly everywhere.

On second thought, I'd take the damn sparkles.

The New Girls' Club

Gender separatism has long been a recurrent — and a recurrently controversial — solution to a misogynistic world.

Women's clubs began their rise in the late nineteenth century, in direct response to women's exclusion from the male-dominated public sphere. One of the most famous, and most influential, of the early clubs originated after journalist Jane Cunningham Croly and several other women were barred from entering a New York City all-male press club dinner honouring Charles Dickens. The men refused them tickets on the grounds that it would supposedly make the event "promiscuous."[3] In response, Croly decided women needed their own club.[4] She called it Sorosis. While technically that means "aggregation" and refers to a grouping of plants that bear fruit, let's be honest: it also sounds like it could be the name of a badass Marvel villain who threatens to end the world with equal rights. And the club did adopt an unabashedly feminist outlook, bent on reforming women's roles in and influence on the wider society.

On the twenty-first anniversary of Sorosis, Croly called on women's clubs throughout the United States to band together. (In my head, she's on a parapet yelling, "Feminists Unite!" cape blazing behind her, but in reality she hosted a convention in New York City, drawing considerable, if less fantastical, attention.) Sixty-three clubs did so, officially forming the General Federation of Women's Clubs.[5] Croly later wrote of her motives, referring to herself in third person: "Many women, she herself among the rest, were hungry for the society of women, that is, for the society of those whose deeper natures had been roused to activity, who had been seized by the divine spirit of inquiry and aspiration, who were interested in the thought and progress of the age, and in what other women were thinking and doing."[6]

Much of the early work of the Federation and other women's clubs focused on, as one researcher put it, "seeking to wrest some social, political and economic power from the men who dominated public life." Still without the vote, or any high position within influential institutions, women decided to instead work outside of male systems (which were, at the time, basically all of them) and to exercise their collective power to effect the type of social change they wanted to see.[7] They secured significant victories against child labour, expanded opportunities for public education, and joined the abolitionist movement, speaking out against lynchings in the Southern states.[8] In doing so, these women gained experience in types of activity usually reserved for men: organizing public speakers, raising money, writing publicity materials, lobbying politicians, circulating petitions, and so on — all useful strategies to broaden women's power in society. Needless to say, that freaked out a lot of men, including former U.S. president Grover Cleveland, who wrote an article in *Ladies Home Journal* in which he discussed the "danger of the club habit." Maintaining women already had enough power in the nation because they, he suggested, essentially influenced their husbands and sons, Grover wrote, "I believe that it should be boldly declared that the best and safest club for a woman to patronize is her home."[9]

Luckily, it didn't matter what one former president thought. In gathering, women began to realize they had a whole host of needs; and if the men wouldn't let them into their established structures, they'd meet those needs themselves. Soon, they had established women-only professional associations for doctors and lawyers, and women-only unions for factory workers. They even started a secret society or two, including the Eastern Star (mirroring Freemasonry, minus the blockbuster movies and conspiracy theories). Women's clubs held operas and built libraries. One member, Alice Ames Winter, described the sheer breadth of them thusly, displaying both a contemporary snobbery and a tart dislike of women who chose to remain coddled: "Women's clubs are distinctly all-American in their constituency; ranging geographically from the big city organization with its thousands to the little body of isolated farm women or the ranchers' wives who drive sixty miles across the waste to attend a meeting, and sell one of the cows to get money to go to a convention; ranging intellectually from the Ph.D. to the shut-in woman who, in her middle age, is groping toward 'culture'; ranging socially from the wage earner to the anathematized parasitic wife — whom by the way we used to call by the kinder name of lady . . ."[10]

In both Canada[11] and the United States, women's clubs, in all their various forms, also became the backbone of the suffrage movement. The message was the same everywhere: having achieved critical mass, the clubs would work outside the system to change the system — and to change women themselves. As one Federation club member put it, looking back on the organization's first fifty years, only an anti-feminist could love a woman's formerly narrow life: "She wove and spun, baked and brewed, sewed, dripped candles, nursed and taught her children and stayed at home. What else could she do . . . ?"[12] The "New Woman" — a name they often called themselves — had a chance at a different purpose, especially as the Federation grew to astounding numbers, making their own influence impossible to ignore: "What if the social power of two million members of the General Federation of Women's clubs may become the determining force in the readjustment of our society?" What if, indeed?

After the First World War, during which many more women stepped into previously male-dominated spheres, another question grew thunderous: *Why budget the house and not the nation?* Once women did win the vote, that question only became heavier on their tongues.

"What *do* women want?" asked Winter. "The over-whelming majority of club women were suffragists. They wanted the vote. Having secured it, their major interest is how to use it." The answer to that question soon became clear: to effect *equality*. Throughout the 1930s and '40s, many women distanced themselves from the self-segregation movement in favour of integration. They believed, buoyed by the independence gained during both world wars and by their legal emancipation, that the need for separatism was behind them. Alas, not quite.

In the past century, the cresting backlash against that lurch toward equality has almost always triggered a sort of half-voluntary, half-forced exit from male power structures. Not every feminist exit (*Fexit?*) has been as well-mannered or gentle as the first. While early suffragists may have wanted the vote, they had little desire to overhaul the era's fundamental notions of gender, class, and race supremacy. Many early feminists also placed a high value on women's traditional roles, exalting both wifehood and motherhood. As feminism's priorities and will to challenge conventions shifted over time, however, so too did the idea of useful sep-aratism. In the twentieth century, the idea of a woman's exit from male-dominated spaces would go through many cycles of radicalism and mainstream softening, each approach shifting to match the feminist movement's rise and fall. Notably, during the 1970s and '80s an openly radical lesbian separatism movement rose — underscored by the belief that violence against women, and the hatred that pushes it, meant women should detach themselves from male society, ultimately seeking to abandon it entirely. These separatists themselves often viewed their goals as more sweeping than those of mainstream feminists. As one put it, writing about the movement years later, many feminists thought society could be corrected and that inequality was, essentially, a mistaken lapse in a system still committed to good. "The analyses of lesbian separatists, on the other hand," she wrote, "have defined such inequities not as moral lapses but rather as deliberate constructions signed to benefit one group at the expense of another and to maintain the supremacy of one group over another."[13]

Radical lesbian separatist beliefs filtered through to the mainstream, leading to a boost in the creation of women's studies programs in universities and colleges, as well as women-owned enterprises such as music festivals, music companies, academic journals, and feminist magazines.[14] Many of these ventures still exist today. Dorothy Pitman Hughes and Gloria Steinem founded *Ms.* magazine in 1971, for example, and Canada's own *Herizons* launched in 1979, beginning as the *Manitoba Women's Newspaper*. The Feminist Press kicked off in New York City in 1970 by publishing "lost" feminist classics, such as works by Zora Neale Hurston and Charlotte Perkins Gilman;[15] Gilman's novel *Herland*, released in 1915, is about a secret, peaceful civilization of women that is eventually infiltrated by men (kind of like *Wonder Woman* without all the punching). These projects and spaces were seen as essential for the advancement of equality — places where women could define their own goals and work toward them without the constant drain of men.[16]

Today's resurgence of clubs for women and people living beyond the traditional gender binary have the same flavour of defiance. Trump's win, the Women's March on Washington, and then #MeToo have all cascaded into a rise in the same sort of consciousness-raising groups and women's-first enterprises that ballooned in the early 1900s and again in the 1970s. From book clubs, travel clubs, and brunch clubs, to co-working spaces, music festivals, and curated shops — not to mention a whole realm of digital collectives — women are, once again, forming sites of resistance. These spaces celebrate non-male creators, and host conversations on everything from weed-smoking to emotional labour to sexual abuse.

I remember attending one packed event, run by the Bad Girls Book Club, that looked at Sheila Heti's novel *Motherhood*, with a panel of women discussing, in stark honesty, what the once-expected life goal meant for women today. "There are a million different ways to live the female experience," one of the speakers said. The problem is we have been too quiet about them.

Sure, a mass women-only book club is a whole lot tamer than advocating for a world sans men. However, in the context of creating space to work against a culture that's increasingly revealed as one steeped in male power, like so much bitter tea, it's downright revolutionary.

Which means, of course, these spaces are under attack.

(White) Bro Backlash

I learned from a fairly early age that some men simply do not like the idea of women gathering without them. They think it's silly, antiquated, too feminist — a relic of a time before our supposed equality. What need is there to prioritize other groups? The first concert I ever attended was 1999's Lilith Fair. At the time, I had just turned fifteen. My personal politics were still geared more toward girl power than riot grrrl, and I had no idea that Sarah McLachlan had founded the travelling music festival not just as a cool thing, but as an act of defiance. The 1990s had ushered in a travelling festival trend, with tours like Lollapalooza skyrocketing in popularity. Male-fronted acts dominated all of them; radio stations refused to play women artists back to back. Reportedly sick of it all, and inspired by other shows she'd played with all-women-fronted acts, McLachlan decided to start her own tour, highlighting women. Few thought it would succeed; it became one of the top-grossing festivals of the year.

Still, McLachlan was asked constantly why she wanted to exclude men — even though she clearly described the show as women-centric, not women only. "The other really awful question that we got often was, 'Why do you hate men?'" she told *Rolling Stone* in an interview celebrating the festival's twentieth anniversary. "And I said, 'What does celebrating women have to do with hating men? That says way more about you and your ego than anything else.'"

Of all the women-first spaces that now exist, the most prominent and empire-like of them all is U.S.-based co-working space The Wing. Co-founders Lauren Kassan (a former director at fitness titan ClassPass) and Audrey Gelman (who worked on Clinton's 2008 campaign and is one of Lena Dunham's best friends) opened The Wing's first location in Manhattan's Flatiron District in October 2016, three weeks before the presidential election. Part of their motivation, Gelman told *The Washington Post*, was to celebrate "the golden age of women in power." Well. Then, she gathered with three hundred members of the new space to watch that fateful night unfold. "The concept of The Wing went from something triumphant to something that felt more protective overnight," she told the paper. Women went from feeling elated to feeling afraid. They wanted safe spaces.[17] But as one legal student and scholar quipped two years later, as The Wing expanded: "Entrenched power structures don't act in good faith when they're threatened. 'Hey, men have nearly every public space in the world, maybe women could have a few' is unlikely to be the Fox News narrative."[18]

And, as much as it was very definitely a corporate enterprise from the start, The Wing gave (some) women the space for disruption. Vox interviewed one such member in early 2019.[19] A reproductive justice activist, she told the publication that working in public spaces can be difficult. She can get some uncomfortable reactions from those around her whenever she says "abortion," and she often says it repeatedly throughout the day. That doesn't happen at The Wing. She can work on a comfortable couch, say "abortion" whenever she needs to without any "side-eye," and never has to deal with men "asking me stupid questions and trying to hit on me while I'm trying to read and get my shit done." The Wing also extends its "women power" ethos to its (mostly) women employees. Everyone, including part-time workers, has health-care benefits — a huge thing in the United States — and also stock options. At many locations, they have access to child-care facilities. The company hires formerly incarcerated women and is upfront about also hiring women who've experienced domestic violence. Everyone makes a minimum of $16.50 an hour. (For reference, in New York City, where many of The Wing's locations operate, the minimum wage for a company of its size is $15 an hour.[20] And in Canada, as of April 2019, the highest minimum wage is $15 per hour, and the lowest is just over $11 per hour.[21])

I visited one of The Wing's New York City locations in January 2019 with a friend who is a member. The two-storey space I toured was feminine, definitely, but not in a painfully obnoxious way — I'm thinking of those spaces where it feels like a man has imagined what a woman would want. The décor is pastel and velvet, the effect calming, not saccharine, with pops of greenery accenting an "I'm chill" vibe throughout the open, lit-just-so space. There is a sky-high, colour-coded library as you walk in, filled with books by women authors. Although nine-to-five had already passed, the place was still bustling, projecting an atmosphere that felt more focused than anxious. Women chatted on the phone, chatted with each other, gestured animatedly, typed fast on their laptops, and scribbled in their notebooks. Past all the work space is a meditation room and a beauty room famously filled with luxe products. I grabbed a desperately needed bobby pin and took a selfie with my friend.

Looping back to the front, near the café, which serves free coffee, were stacks of The Wing's magazine, *No Man's Land*. I flipped through a few pages of the inaugural issue, reading a note from Gelman, its official publisher. "The institutions that have long defined what success, prestige, and prosperity are in American society typically have one thing in common: they were founded—and are largely still run—by men," she wrote. "At The Wing, we ask: Why not create organizations where men no longer write the rules?" Inside are profiles on working women, including Angela Dimayuga, chef at New York's Mission Chinese Food; rapper Remy Ma; and actor and model Hari Nef. Another woman profiled in the magazine wears a T-shirt that read "Raise Girls and Boys the Same Way." There is an article on emotional labour and another on dressing for power. Also, there are stickers. So, yes, The Wing is an explosion of aesthetics and politics—a perfectly tuned blend of everything that makes modern, commercial feminism popular—but it also clearly calls to a deeper yearning in women. It was one of the first places I'd ever been to that made me feel settled, as though it was, indeed, made for me. And that, according to many people, was the problem.

To be clear, there is much to criticize about The Wing's

marketing of itself as a haven for women. Among the legitimate, necessary questions we should ask of places like The Wing are: Which women are included and which are patently excluded? Who gets to define the term "woman"? And what about all the other groups who also suffer from the systems perpetuated by the patriarchy — do places like this leave them behind? (None of these questions is exclusive to The Wing, and all of them are addressed in greater depth later in this chapter.) The vital conversation that those questions spark is very different from the conversation that actually happened, though.

The first blow to The Wing and its No Man's Land domination came in spring 2018 when the popularity of the co-working space brought it to the attention of the New York City Commission on Human Rights. Initially, The Wing did not let men join the club or visit as guests, and the commission decided to open an investigation into its practices, specifically looking at whether this constituted a violation of the city's law forbidding any business to deny entrance on the basis of gender.[22] Then, a couple of months later, a (seemingly) incredibly entitled man named James E. Pietrangelo applied to The Wing's branch in Washington, D.C., and was effectively denied membership. A practising attorney, he launched a lawsuit in August 2018, claiming "The Wing has a policy, pattern, and practice of discrimination against men."[23]

The Wing isn't the only no-men venture to have faced such backlash in recent years. Dangerous things — like equity and a crumbling patriarchy — happen when oppressed people band together. Another lawyer, San Diego–based Alfred Rava, has apparently made it his life's mission to sue organizations that he believes discriminate against men. One, Women on Course, designed to help women enter and network in the male-dominated golf world, settled with Rava in 2013, couldn't stay afloat, was later sold, and then shut down.[24] Another, Ladies Get Paid, an initiative to help close the wage gap, was served on the day of the inaugural Women's March on Washington for barring men from its events. The organization settled, nearly went bankrupt, and had to launch a crowdfunding campaign—which raised more than $115,000[25]—to keep its doors open.[26] In San Diego, members of the country's oldest men's rights group sued a women's networking organization, Chic CEO, again for apparently barring their entry to an event. The organization's founder was forced to settle; she later significantly downsized.[27] Over in Germany, in 2019 a man launched a lawsuit against a town after it designated some well-lit spaces—close to the entrance/exit of a car park—for women, following a violent attack.[28]

I have my doubts about whether any of these men sincerely sought to join these organizations or use these spaces in the ways for which they were intended. Why would they? It seems far more likely that they saw something that was not for them, something that threatened their formerly impenetrable power structures, and wanted to destroy it, not unlike the men who see women's workplace authority as a reasonable motivator for harassment. Like, can you imagine men creating the same furor to join a sewing class exclusively for women and non-binary people?

Such backlash isn't limited to lawsuits, either. It can come in the form of dismissal, and it can come in the form of refusal. I spoke to one co-working and event space for women and non-binary members in Richmond, Virginia, called The Broad. This organization centres much of its mission on prioritizing purchasing from and working with the same demographic it serves. In its first year, nearly

40 percent of the space's discretionary spending went to women. So when the local paper asked to do a profile on the space, founder Ali Greenberg responded with what had become a routine request to media: please don't send a male journalist or photographer. The photo desk editor wouldn't acquiesce, despite having women photographers on staff; the profile languished and was never published.

In the case of The Wing, at least, the controversy has spurred some good. Although the company has maintained that the two events were not related, while still in the midst of both the lawsuit and the human rights investigation, The Wing released a new, clearer membership policy. It states more explicitly that the space welcomes members "who identify as transgender or beyond the gender binary," adding that it has adopted written "policies to ensure that our staff is trained not to make assumptions about someone's identity based on how they present, or to ask prospective members or guests to self-identify."[29] Around the same time, The Wing also released a copy of Pietrangelo's application to the court in Washington. Even under the new policy, the company argued, it was unlikely his application would have been approved. In response to one of the key questions on the form—"What do you think is the biggest challenge facing women today?"—Pietrangelo had written: "The same challenges facing men."[30]

Inclusive, Exclusive

Truth be told, not all women face the same challenges either. For as much as women's clubs and spaces have provided a radical refuge from the power structures that seek to dominate women's lives, they have also replicated those same power imbalances, whether consciously or not. In many ways, the women-only movement has mirrored the challenges of feminism itself: the centring of biological definitions at the expense of transgender women; the exclusion of Indigenous women and women of colour from its most visible and influential positions; claims of battling tokenism while institutionalizing that same philosophy in its own histories and organizations. Many women have claimed to me that feminism has always been deliberately intersectional, even if that's not the language past generations have used. Those women are usually white, usually able-bodied, and have usually benefited from feminism in a way that not everyone has. There's no other way to put it: those women are also wrong. And if we cannot engage honestly with past and current wrongs, then we have little hope of building better spaces now.

For all the true good the General Federation of Women's Clubs did, it was also riven by a fierce racism within its ranks. Despite a motto that claimed "Unity in Diversity," in 1900 Georgia's white club members rallied against Boston woman Josephine St. Pierre Ruffin, a Black activist who had formed the Woman's Era Club seven years earlier. When she attempted to take her seat at that year's national convention, the General Federation's president, Rebecca Douglas Lowe, refused to recognize her right to do so. Apparently, Lowe had accepted the Woman's Era Club's membership dues before she realized its members were primarily Black. Once she realized what she'd done, she asked Ruffin to return the club's credentials. Ruffin refused. The Federation then demanded that the Massachusetts State Federation, to which Ruffin's club belonged, revoke her club's membership. To its credit, those women also refused—and actively supported Ruffin in her fight against the General Federation, which then moved to make the national organization for white women only. But here's the thing: by the General Federation's own rules, Ruffin's club, and any other club with valid state membership, was a de facto member and therefore guaranteed a seat at the national convention's table. It had always been that way. "Therefore, it is important to note that in 1900 Georgia's white clubwomen set out not to preserve the status quo," wrote one historian, "but rather to change the rules." They won. Despite protests, their motion passed in 1902. At the national level, but not the state level, the Federation became for white women only.[31]

And such exclusionary mindsets have endured. The Michigan Womyn's Music Festival, which launched in 1976 and became a seminal women-only event until it folded in 2015, exposed the endemic transphobia within feminism and the huge potential pitfalls of women-only spaces. The world-reshaping power of the festival, which started essentially as a party in the woods, is evident in the many laudatory accounts of its celebrations. One regular attendee wrote in 2003 that "When [somebody] asked me when I feel I am most outside of the patriarchy, I immediately answered 'At Michigan.' ... The experience of the Festival is to me that quintessential experience that tells me that another world, a world outside the patriarchy, is possible." That particular account appears in a newsletter decorated with hand-drawn squares that detail "One hundred simple things you can do to end the patriarchy." One suggestion is to "Make love to yourself tenderly." Another is to "Grow flowers." A third is to "Assume your ethnic and cultural identity is not normative."[32]

And yet.

Promotional material for the festival itself reminded those who attended to "Look around. Womyn built this

city. We carried every box, board and speaker. We pipe
every shower, fix every truck and chop every vegetable."[33]
It all sounds so revolutionary, except for the festival's policy
of being intended for "womyn who were born womyn."
Even in the face of criticism, festival founder Lisa Vogel
has repeatedly stated there is nothing exclusionary about
the festival's policy. After the Indigo Girls bowed out of the
festival in 2013 — yes, there's not even the excuse of being "of
the time" — Vogel affirmed the policy the following year, as
she has done any time public criticisms are made. In a letter
to the community, she reiterated, practically verbatim, the
statements she'd made elsewhere, maintaining that "this
space, for this week, is intended to be for womyn who were
born female, raised as girls and who continue to identify as
womyn."[34] She went on to insist that it was not a ban. "We
do not 'restrict festival attendance to cisgendered womyn,
prohibiting trans women' as was recently claimed...We do
not and will not question anyone's gender. Rather, we trust
the greater queer community to respect this intention, leaving the onus on each individual to choose whether or how to
respect it."[35] Neither she nor her many defenders seemed to
understand that "leaving the onus on each individual" scape-
goats discrimination onto the target — *You chose this!* — while
simultaneously refusing to condemn transphobia. Saying
"we won't stop you" is entire continents away from saying
"we welcome you." Which, to be absolutely clear, is the bare
minimum any feminist space can say to trans women and
gender-nonconforming people.

Echoes of both racism and transphobia persist today in
both feminist and women-only spaces, even in those that
are trying to do better. Part of this is growing and learning;
that these conversations are happening, and with an apparent openness to reflection and change, is an essential part

of figuring out what new systems of power might look like. Although I understand why everyone is growing impatient waiting for cisgender, able-bodied white women to hurry up and figure out that they, too, wield considerable power, and to stop abusing it.

Kaitlyn Borysiewicz is the communications director and co-founder of The Melanin Collective, a social enterprise for women of colour, and she wrote in a blog post for the group that "the golden age of women in power" that The Wing trumpets often seems to include only a certain type of woman, relegating the rest to stick it out in the Middle Ages — particularly when annual membership for the space runs into the thousands.[36] "When the choice is between putting food on the table and saving towards retirement or paying the heating bill or buying membership into an exclusive women's club, I think the choice is pretty clear," she argues. "And yet, The Wing is being lauded as a radical injection into women's organizations? Interesting." She goes on to say, "I write all this not to crap on The Wing, but to complicate notions of white women creating seemingly inclusive spaces without a single nod to the experiences of women of color. Women of color face extraordinary barriers, not just in the workplace, but in their health and wellbeing, finances, relationships, education, and more." And, while The Wing is certainly one of the best known of the contemporary "no men k thx centred" spaces, it is certainly not the only one with membership dues high enough to put it in the realm of inclusive-exclusive.

The Wing is not even the most expensive club I visited. That honour goes to the Verity Club in Toronto, Canada's only high-end private social club for women. Although it does offer co-working space, its owner and founder, Mary Aitken, stressed to me that that isn't at all how she classifies the club. Unapologetically lush, the club features room after impeccably decorated room, each managing to attain a sort of quiet opulence, an oxymoron that can exist only among the truly, tastefully wealthy. There is a gym, a boutique hotel and gourmet restaurant that are both open to the public, a spa, a pool, a gorgeous flower shop, a small fairy-tale court-yard, a library space that hosts workshops, a selection of boardrooms, a bar, and space upon space for women to network, work, and close deals. Aitken gave me a tour in the early months of 2019, moving through the luxuriously sprawling club at an impossibly high-clipped pace, stopping to greet nearly everyone we saw by name. Though buoyed by the profits from the hotel and restaurant, the club itself, Aitken told me, is a money-losing enterprise, and has been for most of the years since its 2003 founding.

That does not mean that it is cheap. The Verity charges a sliding scale for its annual membership, depending on a potential member's age. Those under thirty pay a one-time initiation fee of $4,700 and yearly fees of $2,095; those over forty-five pay an initiation fee of $10,700 and then $3,195 every year after. Such fees would relegate most early- to mid-career professional women (including me) and aspiring entrepreneurs to a steady, possibly permanent diet of neon-orange Kraft Dinner. (Even then.) Aitken called the membership diverse, with members ranging in age from seventeen to ninety-three, and she proudly chatted about the club's work with teenage girls from lower-income neighbourhoods. Still, she doesn't mince words about who the club serves (and is also fairly careful not to call it a feminist enterprise). There are more than twenty Verity members who have been hon-oured with the Order of Canada. This is a place for women who are already at the top of their careers, or very much want to get there.

These tense patterns of inclusion and exclusion frequently play out in other feminist spaces as well. Sally Dimachki is a project co-ordinator with Ottawa's Refugee 613, an organization that acts as a hub for refugees in Canada's capital city, and I spoke with her one early morning in March 2019. Our conversation happened, by chance, to take place just hours after news of the massacre at two mosques in New Zealand, further underscoring the rise of a festering Islamophobia, and also the urgent concern that no part of that hate be replicated in feminist spaces. A Muslim, Dimachki had immigrated from Syria to France at a young age, eventually ending up in rural New Brunswick, where she was often the only Muslim in any given space. Those experiences made her feel as though she would never have access to power and would need to self-filter her ambitions. Now, she is keenly aware when those diminishing power dynamics are replicated in women-only spaces. It happens often.

"I've been in many decision-making rooms," she told me, where she's seen "an automatic power dynamic and a specific type of confidence that comes with being Canadian-born, not having an accent, and having an education." She recalled a diverse table where about half the women had immigrant, refugee backgrounds and the other half were Canadian-born white women. The white women were loud, confident, and sure of their points. Meanwhile, nobody else was speaking—a sign that the white women took to mean they agreed. Dimachki didn't believe it was that simple. Looking at the unspooling, smothering power dynamic, she decided, *No, I've had enough.* And so she verbally battled these white women, one against five, repeatedly trying to explain the many layers of feminism. One woman's background might mean her feminism looked different; that only meant it was even more important to account for her lived experience. At the end of that meeting, many of the silent women thanked her for being their voice. That was when she realized: sometimes it isn't about getting more women at the table. Even when women sit exclusively at the table, the power scale can still tilt into inequity. The real question is this: Who has the opportunity to speak?

Fight Like a Girl

I joined the Toronto Newsgirls Boxing Club in early 2017 after a jarring experience at a co-ed kickboxing club—the kind that almost completely suffocated my interest in the sport. I'd been a member of co-ed clubs off and on since I was fourteen. As a kid, the experience of being in a testosterone-charged environment initially registered as unremarkable. The club I grew up attending was strict, unwavering in its discipline, and not the sort of place where a beefed-up guy could do anything about not being as skilled as a teenage slip of a girl.

The older I got, the more I saw it, though—the thing that happens when you're a girl in a place built for men (there was quite literally no women's change room). As I watched some of the teen boys advance faster than me, even though I was better, I grew both puzzled and frustrated. When I was eighteen, the discipline of class no longer protected me, and comments about my looks filtered through the in-between times, before and after training, in social settings. I began to wear makeup to class, constantly making adjustments to my appearance in the mirrors that lined the wall, worrying incessantly over whether I was skinny enough. I look back on that time now, imagining that girl so expertly applying foundation to her hairline, and feel a pang.

The co-ed club I joined as an adult largely spared me from comments about my body — but it did not spare my body itself. The majority of instructors there were volunteers, donating their time once a week to teach a class. In one session, a male instructor advised the men to partner up with the women and practise grabbing us in the various ways somebody might, presumably, attack us if we were out dancing at a club. We were chastised if we did not hit hard enough, or yell loud enough, to fend off our would-be rapist. What a fun game of make-believe to have absolutely no warning about or choice to participate in! My unease cascaded straight into fear after another class in which I was paired with a much larger, almost gleefully aggressive man. Holding the punching and kicking strike pads against my body, which were meant to shield me from the bulk of the force behind his blows, I could feel my body struggling to absorb the impact. Every time I flinched in pain or struggled for a grip on the pads, he hit and kicked harder, yelling at me to keep up. It felt like every blow was tattooing *You. Do. Not. Belong. Here.* Back at home, it wasn't long before I saw bruises across my torso, my arms. Time stretched out like taffy before I ventured to another club. Something that had once felt like a haven now spiked anxiety through me.

I did not know to expect everything Newsgirls gave to me. It feels impossibly difficult to describe the value of implicit ease and safety unless you have spent most of your life without both, not even realizing how bankrupt you were. The club is open to all genders, but cisgender men are invited to come only to certain weekly classes. There is one washroom, and it is prominently marked as all-gender. Beyond gender, the club actively encourages the full breadth of diversity in its membership, including Indigenous women, women who are disabled, women of colour, immigrant women, those who belong to LGBTQ+ communities, and those of all different body sizes, incomes, and religions. There is both a food and a book bank, and the club itself is plastered with notices advertising women- and trans-led initiatives, marches, rallies, plays, and services.

It's a place where people learn to do all the things they've been told not to: yell, be aggressive, stand up for themselves. It's a space for everyone, but technically, presumably, so is every public space. This, however, is a space that was designed for everyone *else* first, and when it invited the men back in, it was into a culture totally reimagined on our terms, without them. It's a place where I never care if I haven't shaved for weeks. A place where we happily turned off the fans in the sweltering summer because it triggered one survivor. A place where everyone is asked for their pronoun when they sign up and no instructor will ever touch you without your clear consent. It's a place where you never have to pretend.

Every once in a while, I've seen men try to re-shift the power; it never works. More commonly, though, I see men who are grateful for the space just as it is. In the years since I've started there, I've volunteered to teach classes when the owner cannot make it to coach. Because I'm usually there on the co-ed nights, it's not unusual for me to get a few men dropping in when I do. These men are almost always gracious, taking in criticism without ego, asking for help, and understanding, without anyone having to tell them, that they are not in charge.

This is just the very tip of it. There are so many reasons to host clubs, events, co-working spaces, and more that shift the focus away from men. These reasons also go far beyond addressing the routine harassment the #MeToo movement exposed. The gender gap in the success of start-ups completely disappears, for example, when women fund other women (without that factor, it's gaping).[37] Women CEOS, and their companies, may be at a disadvantage when the power structures beneath them don't change, as we saw in the last chapter, but they both do significantly better as the percentage of women employees increases.[38] And, as has been much reported, in mixed settings women are interrupted more than men[39] and spend appreciably less time talking than men—one study showed it's by as much as 75 percent.[40] They can't change much of anything if they are routinely silenced.

Still, I struggled with the idea of exiting male power structures forever. Who would do the hard work of dismantling gender binaries and power structures *everywhere else* if we're all dancing naked in the forest or sipping kombucha at our pastel-pink desks? I wondered instead if it were possible to replicate the deliberate magic of my boxing club on a wider scale—to kick out the toxicity, but then invite the men back into a remade world, one built for everyone. I wasn't sure what that would look like, but a place that bucked beauty standards, nurtured power for the oppressed, and welcomed everyone in dignity seemed like a good place to start.

A Woman's Place

In December 2018, I attended a talk, hosted by the New Democratic Party, featuring feminist foremother Gloria Steinem. Full of humour and dry wit, Steinem surprised me when she contradicted many of the feminists of her generation and proclaimed, early in her remarks, that "There is no gender. It was invented and we can dis-invent it." This statement speaks to the thornier aspects of creating space without men, fundamentally defined without their input. To dis-invent gender would mean also abandoning things like binary restroom spaces and award shows that delineate skill by gender. Yes, please, I'm all for both. We need more washroom spaces, especially all-gender ones. And, like, is there really a difference between *lady* acting and *man* acting? Don't even.

But working toward those goals also means asking some uncomfortable questions about our wilful exit from the patriarchy: Can women-only spaces truly be defiant if they're also mirroring traditional patterns of segregation? Even more uncomfortably, do they underscore gender seg-regation as a thing women endorse? When we leave, are we sending the subconscious message that a woman's place is, in fact, outside of all the traditional systems of power? I thought about a piece of news that broke as I was writing this book: in March 2019, NASA cancelled its first all-female spacewalk outside the International Space Station because it could not find enough spacesuits to fit the women. Except that all-female team was only *two* women.[41] I want to live in a world where gender separation does not lead to ridiculous shit like this. (And I would also like to live in a world that doesn't report this depressing news with the quip, "Blame it on a wardrobe malfunction.")

Feminist philosopher Marilyn Frye has argued that there is a clear difference between intentional, feminist separa-tism (whereby women and others *choose* to build their own spaces) and an existence at the borders of power (whereby women and others are pushed out or kept at a distance from meaningful participation in whatever space they want to be in, be it a workspace, a sports club, or even their own homes and personal relationships). Frye wrote the 1980s book *Some Reflections on Separatism and Power*, in which she grappled with the unwieldy "kaleidoscopic" nature of separatism. The theme of separation, she wrote, can be interpreted into a multitude of variations, from divorce to women's shelters to the expansion of child care to witches' covens to abortion services, and on and on. Touching on the backlash to come, she also noted that the idea of sep-aratism is often "vigorously obscured, trivialized, mystified and outright denied," not just by men, but also by feminist apologists who are embarrassed to admit a need for a space of their own. The difference in effectiveness—and whether women gain or lose power—lies in intent.[42]

A purposeful separation, she wrote, is one "from men and from institutions, relationships, roles and activities which are male-defined, male-dominated and operating for the benefit of males and the maintenance of male priv-ilege—this separation being initiated or maintained at will *by women*."[43] It depends, as always, on who has the power.

For Rachel Kelly, the ultimate success of her company Make Lemonade is rooted in its future redundancy. Like many of the modern separatists, she believes a true utopia isn't a world that draws a line between straight, cisgender white men and everyone else, but one that uses the lessons and healing and reimaginings learned in the self-imposed break to make things better for everybody. "Right now, this is wonderful. This is beautiful," she told me. "The point where we're at right now. But I think we all agree that in 150 to 200 years, the need for spaces like these won't... exist. This is the part that I'm coming to peace with. We can use this space and this movement and everything that we're doing right now to push us toward the future. We also need to understand this will be a part of history." On reflection, she added that such discrete environments have an important function: "to celebrate women and our history together."

Yes, but, *two hundred years*? What a bleak timeline. I wanted to know what women were doing right now to cut through the bullshit. And, after hearing about how the workplace had failed so many women, I especially wanted to know if we could ever upend one of the oldest adages around: money is power.

CHAPTER 6

More Women, More Money
Why an equitable economy is good news for everybody

IN APRIL 2018, SIXTY feminist leaders from around the world gathered in Ottawa to reimagine the global economy. Both the timing and location were strategic. That same week, leaders of the world's seven most economically advanced countries were set to convene in nearby Quebec for the annual two-day G7 meeting. Under Prime Minister Trudeau's direction, the G7 would, for the first time, include a Gender Equity Advisory Council meant to infuse feminism into the high-powered gathering. Trudeau had assured women's rights activists that the council would guarantee that "gender equality and gender-based analysis [were] integrated across all themes, activities, and outcomes" of the G7.[1] But for those sixty feminists meeting "on the sidelines" of the G7, Trudeau's promises weren't enough. Instead of relying on the Gender Equity Advisory Council to push a feminist agenda, they decided to create their own high-powered meeting—outside of, but in tandem with, the official G7 meeting. Dubbed the W7, the shadow gathering wanted to confront G7 leaders with a new way of envisioning the economy—one that placed women first.

In discussing motivations for launching the W7, Diana Sarosi, Oxfam Canada's policy manager and one of several W7 organizers, recounted her participation in numerous other economic equality initiatives gone wrong. Such initiatives often put rich businesswomen at the table, she said, and repeatedly offered policy recommendations that centred on women's entrepreneurship and their representation in big business. That was fine, but it also captured only a small, specific slice of the population. Such women could not have the answers for *all* women engaged in the economy, stressed Sarosi, and they were particularly ill-equipped to address the issues non-privileged women face every day. In contrast, those invited to participate in the W7's discussion of a better economy were chosen for their diversity of identities and lived experience. Without centring such diversity, Sarosi and the other organizers believed, any solutions put forward wouldn't change the economy at all. "We wanted to make sure the agenda was much broader than just getting women into business," said Sarosi of the W7, "or shoehorning them into an economy that doesn't work for them." In other words, unless the scope of who was at the table widened, neither economic opportunity nor the economy itself would ever change.

The kind of change that could lead to an economy meant to facilitate women's advancement, the participants at the W7 underscored, *must* be based on intersectional feminism. Hours of discussion envisioned an economy that would be less concerned with profit, entrepreneurship, and business grants, for example, and more concerned with building a more peaceful world for survivors of violence and conflict. If leaders of our future feminist economy truly wanted women to prosper, the W7 noted, they must think differently. They must work to eradicate violence against women, period. They must realize that the climate crisis is also holding back women's prosperity, and work to negate it. They would know that for women to get ahead in business, world leaders must adopt a feminist approach to reproductive rights and sexual health. They must support and build feminist movements, especially through funding. Simply put, stressed W7 participants, a feminist approach to the economy is one that moves away from policies that fuel conflict, inequality, poverty, discrimination, and destruction. Ultimately, it's an "economy based not on unchecked and rampant growth, but on sustainability and social, economic and cultural rights for all, in both the formal and informal economies."[2]

To his credit, Trudeau agreed to sit down with the W7 so participants could present him with their "feminist visions for the G7." In turn, Trudeau presented the Gender Equality Advisory Council with the W7's recommendations, which it immediately adopted, in turn forcing the narrative into the G7—exactly as the W7 leaders wanted. While Sarosi was quick to acknowledge that the inaugural W7 summit was only a first, small step, it was also a groundbreaking one. In explicitly injecting its feminist vision into a gathering of the world's most powerful leaders, the W7 had changed the terms of the economic conversation. (I mean, Trump stuck in a room that forced him to engage with the f-word? Yes, please!) Still, those in power deftly managed to avoid getting into truly messy territory. The resulting pledges from G7 countries—namely, a $3.8-billion commitment to support education for women and girls in crisis and conflict situations—will undeniably help push for women's economic progress.[3] It's exactly the type of move that everyone can champion and nobody will get mad about, a practised balance of bland empowerment and necessary action, designed to appease all quarters. But, bluntly, the point of revolutionizing the economy is not simply to feel good about ourselves. If we're doing it right, those in power should feel uncomfortable. They should absolutely worry for their bottom line. Because with every step women take away from the sidelines, they are saying, "There is another way to do this thing." We don't have to damage the planet. We don't have to embrace unbalanced work cultures and unethical companies. We can push boundaries, prioritize equity, and make feminist products. If the economy won't open itself to make room for us, that's cool. We'll make a new one. And here's the thing, patriarchy: it will generate more wealth than yours.

Put Your Money Where Your Feminism Is

Before Toronto-based entrepreneur Ali Ogston had even decided what her second start-up would be, she knew one thing: it would have to help other women, in a real way, or she wouldn't do it. One day, while discussing the latest deluge of #MeToo news with an entrepreneur friend, she decided that it was "kind of BS—actually, it's kind of *bullshit*"—that companies and brands weren't doing more to stand behind the social and political issues facing women. She'd seen a lot of companies touting female empowerment with little more than token gestures—such as, say, donating one percent of their sales to a women-focused organization. To Ogston, that was appealing from a public branding standpoint, but it wasn't committing to an issue. If she was going to spend another decade of her life building a company, she wanted it to matter. Sure, she cared about creating a profitable venture, but she also cared deeply about feminism. "Activists are working on the legislative front to change the way we look at equality," she said. Her question became: What do entrepreneurs do?

Ogston thought about what would have meant the most to her when she was in the early stages of her first company, a tech start-up. It would have been someone telling her they were interested in investing in that company — looking her straight in the eye and saying, "I believe in you, keep doing this. Here is what I can give you to show my faith: capital, resources, a network." Anything that meant, *Yes, keep going.* So she decided that's what she would do with whatever business she started next. As an integral part of the main business model itself, she'd incorporate an investment fund for women and non-binary people. So, if her business sold and produced cosmetics or cars or candy, for example, it would also invest in women.

More than that, she decided that, when considering who to invest in, she wasn't going to look for the next Bumble or Glossier CEO (Whitney Wolfe and Emily Weiss, respectively). She was not about to buy into the "boss bitch" ethos, which she called an unattainable archetype of success for many women. Instead, she'd focus on the full breadth of women's pursuits. If someone wanted to fly down to the next Women's March on Washington, but didn't have the cash for it? Yes, she should be able to invest in that. If somebody wanted to explore conversations around gender, race, and sexuality through Instagram art? Check. "Because women's pursuits are not just about starting businesses," she told me. "There's a million other things and places that we need to be helping with as well." Her business wouldn't just help women start other businesses; it would help them pursue whatever dream they had, from self-care to activism.

I spoke with Ogston three weeks into the launch of her new enterprise — Bon Temps, a beverage company — which she co-founded with another feminist. (*A man!* she stressed.) With a female ethos in mind, Bon Temps sells teas that are "clean," packaged in bags free from pesticide and bleach, and named after feminist icons such as Gloria Steinem and Maya Angelou. The tea isn't for women only, but it also doesn't default to male, either, like so many other products and amenities: air conditioning, power tools, beer, cannabis, sports gear, game consoles, comic books, superhero movies, trucks, sports cars, public washroom design and availability, and so on, into near infinity (until we hit cleaning products, anti-ageing products, and weight-loss tools). Ideally, Ogston said, the proceeds from the sales of tea products would eventually fund the small, no-strings-attached $1,000 grants — the investment end of the business — that she would award every month. Less than a month in, though, there wasn't much profit yet. That didn't deter Ogston; she would fund the grants from her own pocket until Bon Temps became sustainable enough to do it. If her business was going to commit to women, it would do so from the start. She'd already spent a lot of time talking to the people who'd applied for grants — which they could do on Instagram, in less time than it takes to brew a cup of tea — a process that she seemed to genuinely believe was the best part of her day. There would be no anonymous grant-giving here; if she were to invest, she'd be truly invested.

Ogston readily acknowledged that her investment fund is a small-scale enterprise. Yet, she added, it is also part of a larger movement: one where women look around them, say "what the hell," and then choose to help make a change. For many of them, that change doesn't mean marching or running for office, it means investing in other women. In theory, ventures like this are not selling empowerment to women; they are actively working to empower other women.

Feminism and capitalism do not often go hand in hand, for good reason. As feminist essayist Jia Tolentino wrote for *The New York Times Magazine* at the fever pitch of empowerment's rise, the concept has become "a series of objects and experiences you can purchase while the conditions determining who can access and accumulate power stay the same."[4] If you're a #GirlBoss, then it's also because you can afford the right clothes, the right hair, the right stationery, even; you can go to the right conferences and clubs, and so on. You can buy your way closer to power and success. But not every woman entrepreneur is pretending her customers can follow the "treat yo'self" mantra into a better world. A truly better world would not be filled with stuffed closets and empty bank accounts; it would feature equal wages and no-bro workplace cultures.

Other businesses are attempting to disrupt the marketplace by making feminist products and using those platforms to have conversations usually absent from empowerment-heavy messaging. Along with her sister Bunny, Taran Ghatrora is the co-founder of Vancouver-based Blume, a chemical-free period-product subscription box that also has an education platform called Blume University. Sure, yes, there's some empowerment branding going on here. But I also don't see other menstrual product companies publishing articles like "Five Tips to Include Anti-Colonial Feminism in Periods," which opens with this framing: "Through my health journey, I notice how much the social structures of capitalism, colonialism, and hetero-patriarchy affect my body as a Sikh-Punjabi woman of colour living in North America." Nor do many of them offer a free book that dishes on your first period, in a frank way, detailing everything from constipation to a step-by-step illustrated guide (featuring a non-white vagina) on how to insert a tampon, with all the information backed by a health committee that includes the executive director of the Women's Health Research Institute.[5]

"Investors would originally ask us, 'Does anybody want to talk about this? Are people going to talk about it on social media?'" said Ghatrora. "It's such a resounding *yes*. When given the space, women want to share these stories.... It's just about time people recognized this happens to 50 percent of the population and it's very normal." She wants her company to be that go-to space for girls and women: the place where their shame dissipates and is replaced by a better experience. There is no parsing of terms here. The word "vagina" is all over the company's branding, and I get the distinct sense nobody would dare call a pad a "napkin." Even more refreshing, both Blume and Bon Temps use a diverse cast of models to represent their brands, in a way that feels more central, less afterthought. I don't know if it's perfect, but it's a worthwhile reminder that feminist endeavours aren't limited to zines and bookstores. There's a multitude of options between Goop and non-profit.

And while it can be difficult to parse the distinctions between ineffectual empowerment and true power-bending politics, a feminist-first enterprise that's built with sincerity can phenomenally change the economic landscape — on both a micro and a macro scale. For what it's worth (millions, actually), women-owned businesses that focus on social good are far more likely to get funding than those that do not.[6] "We find that for female founders, highlighting the social impact of their ventures leads to more positive perceptions," wrote the authors of a 2018 study on female founders and social missions. Indeed, the authors discovered that the more female founders focused on how their business would help others, improve the world, and generally do good things beyond making oodles of money, the less they felt the discriminatory effects of gender bias. That's no inconsequential thing. Thanks to such pervasive gender bias in funding, women in business need all the help they can get. In 2018, for instance, women-led businesses in the United States received a bafflingly low 2.2 percent of that year's total venture-capital funding. For context, offered *Fortune* magazine, that means an entire country's worth of female-led businesses received $10 billion less than one e-cigarette company, Juul.[7] If framing their businesses as do-good ventures can help women get more money, one might argue, then what's the harm?

Female entrepreneurs also face different questions from potential investors than men do. Men are usually asked about their potential gains (what's called promotion orientation), whereas women are asked about their potential losses (prevention orientation), immediately undercutting how a woman might talk about her business.[8] That translates to drastically less money—roughly $3.8 million less, on average—for every question a potential entrepreneur is asked under a prevention orientation mindset. It also means that potential investors describe male investors as "young and promising," "aggressive, but a really good entrepreneur," as well as "extremely capable and very driven," while women are described as "young, but inexperienced," "enthusiastic, but weak," and "lack[ing] ability for venture and growth."[9]

This negative view of women entrepreneurs persists against the reality that female-founded businesses generally perform better. One study that tracked a decade of venture funding in more than 300 firms found that female-founded companies performed 63 percent better than companies with all-male founding teams.[10] What's more, 90 percent of women factor in social impact when choosing which businesses they want to invest in—a marker of how much this different way of doing business resonates, at least with them.[11] Cynically, this can all paint a far less rosy picture: that is, women-led companies can only dodge the gender penalty by conforming to the very gender stereotypes that hound them.[12]

Previous research has shown that for women to be seen as competent, they must also be seen as warm, caring— your typical after-school-special mom on a mission to save starving children and adorable puppies. And, yes, of course women shouldn't have to pay it forward to be taken ser- iously; they should not have to be nice. But after speaking to people like Ogston—founders who are genuinely commit- ted to figuring out entrepreneurial feminism—I wonder if there's another way of looking at it: that women who invest in other women have forced the economy to respond to their priorities.

These priorities not only aim to create a more equitable world, they give women more access to participate in it. And considering that access helps close the power gap in tangible ways, this, really, is something we should all cheer for. Numerous studies have shown that the more women shift the power of the economy, the more wealth it generates for all of us. Research has shown that without new ways of promoting growth and productivity in Canada, for instance, the GDP will continue to stagnate; according to the federal Advisory Council on Economic Growth it could even slow to half the rate of the previous half-century without "bold and immediate" action.[13] What could be more bold than a feminist economy, in which women have equal access and opportunity to both jobs and capital? Imagine more women in male-dominated fields, yes, but also imagine more women creating kinder, non-exploitative social enterprises, products that don't assume male as their default, and essentially disrupting the hell out of the marketplace. Imagine a system that didn't look like capitalism at all.

If Canada were to close the gender gap completely— meaning, if everybody participated equally in the workforce, with the same hours worked and across the same sectors— the country would see an additional $420 billion in GDP in less than a decade, roughly equivalent to a nearly $12,000 boost per person.[14] Additionally, the greatest opportunity for growth is in male-dominated industries, including technology. And although women's representation in the labour force has languished—particularly, again, in male-dominated areas, such as the STEM fields, in management, and among business owners—Canada remains a global leader in equality. In other words, if Canada has so much to gain and it's already, objectively, closer to closing the gap, think about the potential of women worldwide. If we somehow reached the miracle of global parity in the workforce, a staggering $28 trillion would be added to the economy by 2025.[15] Quite literally, investing in women will make us all richer.

But if we ever want more women to enter the workforce, it will mean overhauling the workplace itself and making it into an environment where everyone can thrive, as opposed to what it mostly is now: an endless reflection of funhouse mirrors, with so many repeated hurdles that most of us swallow screams of horror and frustration every day.

Warning: Men at Work

In June 2018, trade magazine *Canadian Lawyer* published an article that enraged women in the legal industry. Not because of anything the magazine did—but because it reignited controversy over the long-standing double standard for lawyers at Osgoode Hall, home to Ontario's highest court. Inside the historic building, there is a robing room for male lawyers to change. The magazine rightly described it as "opulent and spacious with nearly 70 full-length lockers, benches, several mirrors and a spacious bathroom area." Oh, but that's not all! No, men of law deserve nothing but the best. "There is also a comfortable lounge section with a sofa and a large wooden table and chairs for writing any last-minute notes before appearing in court." The atmosphere, noted the magazine, is that of an old-money golf and country club. Walk a few steps down the hall, though, and you'll come to a door with a sign on it reading "Lady Barristers." There are twelve lockers inside, mismatched furniture, and one old desk. One lawyer later joked to me that it was really the "lady barristers' closet." Or, as another lawyer told the magazine, "It is like there is a sign there saying we don't think you are staying long."[16]

Breanna Needham, an associate at Borden Ladner Gervais LLP who focuses on commercial litigation, remembers first witnessing the furor in June. She filed away the information—like, apparently, most everyone else. But then when another lawyer, Fay Faraday, tweeted about the Lady Barristers room again in February 2019, she thought, "How many more times are we going to have this discussion?" She also thought, *This is only* one *representative example of the systemic inequality that exists in our profession.* She knew this inequality wasn't quarantined to the legal profession; it permeated society. People had grown used to overlooking things like the "Lady Barristers" room—to borrow an old cliché, they played along to get along. That strategy was crumbling under the force of women's advancement, yes, but also their re-emerging frustration that things had not advanced enough. "We're at a point," Needham said, "where women are taking a position like, 'Why is there anything but fairness here?'"

As far as symbols of power went, Osgoode made a good target. "To put it in not so eloquent terms," Needham joked, "it's kind of a big deal." So she started a petition to end a divide that endorsed swanky rooms for men and broom closets for women—an especially ridiculous disparity considering nearly half of all practising lawyers in Ontario are women.[17] The solution, she suggested, should not be a fancier room for women, but a larger room accessible to all genders. The men's change room wasn't only a symbol of their lopsided power within the profession; it was also a place where men could, in a very practical sense, get more work done. Their larger, more hospitable room invited mentoring, networking, case discussions, and problem-solving on legal issues. "It goes both ways," Needham argued, imagining the number of missed interactions. "It's not just about the women who are missing out; the men are missing out too. We're all missing out—whether we're men, women, LGBTQ+, or non-binary." The petition drew more than two hundred signatures in twenty-four hours, eventually hitting more than eight hundred, and successfully pushed the Law Society to promise a gender-neutral space.[18] The unfortunate Case of the Lady Barristers Room (Agatha Christie, I'm coming for you!) is an undeniable example of what can happen when a profession remains stubbornly wedded to traditional power structures. That such a visible gender inequality could exist well into 2019 shows how deeply we've come to think of certain professions and places as still belonging to men. Not every see-saw vision of the workplace is so visible. That doesn't mean the more hidden, lopsided treatment isn't as harmful; it's often more so. Workplace dynamics, the expected decorum called "professionalism" in most places, and a commonly implicit (and sometimes explicit) bro-ness all tend to reward a specific type of employee or manager. Put another way, the typical office culture usually benefits straight, white men, but not really anyone else.

The consequences of this exclusion are both measurable and measurably bad. Workplace sexual harassment has particularly deleterious economic effects for women. It is not uncommon for women to leave a job with no safety net simply because their job has become unsafe. I have a friend, who works in the financial industry, who told me about a social gathering with her department at a local bar. Her team leader at the time, an older man, pulled her aside, requesting that she help him figure out what to give their mutual boss for a birthday gift. "Leading me away from the crowd," she told me, "he then attempted to kiss me. I can only describe the experience as being face-raped with his tongue. I left and asked another co-worker to drive me home. I quit the job soon after." At another job, a man who was not her manager, but was a manager on her floor, sat across the table from her at a work gathering, removed his shoe, and attempted to put his socked foot in between her legs. Before that, he would snap his fingers in her face when passing by her in the office hallway, or whistle at her like a dog. Luckily, not long after, he was laid off. "I have only seen him once since then," she told me, "and I almost had a panic attack."

Her experiences are, unfortunately, far from unique. One 2017 study marks the first in-depth attempt to prove, as well as quantify, the economic effects of such toxic work environments. Here's a standard example of what researchers uncovered: a woman, whom they named Candace, reported being the subject of offensive jokes, inappropriate questioning about her private life, and unwanted stares (i.e., gross leering). After raising the issue with her supervisors and receiving no resolution, she later left. Her new job meant a 10 percent reduction in hourly pay. It took her more than five years to meet her pre-harassment hourly wage.

Now is also a good time to mention that men who experience disruptions to their career trajectories are likely to retain relatively high-paying jobs; women are not. I don't think it's inconsequential that women often have far more tumultuous reasons for leaving — ones that, as in the case of another study participant, make them unwilling to enter another male-dominated workplace.

Perhaps even more troubling, the 2017 study also found that misogynistic workplace culture not only interrupted workplace advancement and earnings for those women who were directly targeted, they also harmed women who challenged or refused to participate in such environments.[19] One woman told researchers that, once she spoke out against her workplace culture, she found her job responsibilities significantly reduced and her co-workers' attitudes significantly chilled. "I would *never* become friends with these people," she realized after she spoke out. "My boss would *never* be a mentor, I would *never*, you know, have any relationship with these people. So that was rough and finally I just quit."

Or take the experience of one of my closest friends in one of her first jobs, at a tech start-up. A few women had told her that a manager there made them very uncomfortable, engaging in unwanted touching, sexual comments, and invitations to his home. She spoke with her boss about him; but they didn't have an HR department yet, and nothing was done. Then, one day, a young woman confided in her that this manager had sexually assaulted her during a conference. Shortly after, he pulled my friend aside. "He was extremely amped up, invading my personal space, pleading with me to believe that he was a good guy and the woman was a liar," she said. "I was really scared during that conversation—he seemed unhinged." The rumours spread fast, and many of them framed the woman as a liar. My friend tried to help her, calling both a lawyer and the police to ask about her rights, but, understandably, neither option appealed to the woman. She was transferred to another team and quit soon after. Working with the manager then became a nightmare for my friend. "I was accused of trying to destroy his career, called a narc, excluded from events," she said. "He was still allowed to attend conferences—he was at one just a few months later when he was accused of sexually assaulting one of our clients."

This all means, according to researchers who ran the 2017 study, that "women find themselves in the untenable position of having to choose between participating in misogynistic cultures at work, which does not serve them as women, or resisting these cultures, leaving little chance for growth in their companies."

The potentially damaging outcomes of that resistance have received more attention only since the rise of #MeToo. Many men aren't comfortable mentoring potential protégés if they're women, and instead seek out other men. Some pre-#MeToo research has indicated that upwards of 60 percent of men avoid solo interactions with women in junior positions because they're afraid of what people will say about their motivations.[20] Which, when you think about it, is troubling in so many ways, all of which bring us back to the "men only want one thing" line — and, conversely, that the "one thing" is all women can offer. Because why else might you show an interest in a promising employee? The most damning rumours always have a bit of truth injected into them. On some level, I'd wager, men are so afraid to take junior women under their wing because they know other men who have done the things of which they're afraid to be accused, or they have done those things themselves.

That men's reluctance to mentor women has skyrocketed since #MeToo suggests that instead of solving the problem, many of those in power would simply like to avoid it. One 2019 survey found that almost 30 percent of male managers didn't want to work alone with a woman, more than twice as many as before #MeToo.[21] The number of men who were uncomfortable mentoring women tripled, too, hitting one in six. Men were also far more likely to invite another man to a work dinner or as a colleague on a business trip. There's an insidious message at play here: women can accuse you of harassment at any time, even when you're just a *nice guy* trying to help them. Women are liars. If you're not actually going to harass them, it's probably best to pretend they don't exist.

Needless to say, none of these super-sexist approaches are helping women advance at work, particularly in male-dominated fields where so much is already stacked against them. All of this has perpetuated such a neat cycle of imbalance that the natural, if imperfect, solution to this grossness — find a woman mentor — invites the depressing answer, "Good luck finding her."

Cry If You Want To

Whoever decided there's only one way to run a company and its office culture? (That's a rhetorical question: the answer is "men," a very long time ago.) It took a concussion in her mid-twenties for Amy Saunders to realize that she was sick of it. Stuck in bed for over a week, forced into a sort of quiet contemplation, she began to think that if she wanted to be part of a different work culture, she should build one herself. Call it a *Field of Dreams* moment, for feminists.

"I was honestly fatigued. I was so tired of doing the same fucking thing over and over in all of the places where I worked," she told me. Most of her bosses had been men, slow to adopt change. Most of the women she'd met in upper management enacted the same damage—having, after all, found success by playing the same corporate game. She decided to try something new. "I wanted to break away from that and actually work with a team of women and build the structure of my company by women, for women, from the ground up. Rather than having women's voices running alongside the structure of the company—like something parallel to it—I wanted it to be ingrained at every stage of the company and of our communication and of our processes."

Who knows if it's going to work? she thought. But she did know something: the old model was already broken. How much worse could it get?

First, she thought about her skill set and the work that had always been most meaningful to her. She was a good communicator, with a background in the film industry and a long history of grassroots organizing for women's and LGBTQ+ rights organizations, both communities to which she belonged. She decided that she wanted to work with women, yes, but she also wanted to spend her days elevating their stories and the stories of other marginalized communities. She wanted to see their faces on the front pages of *The Globe and Mail*, *The Hollywood Reporter*.

Second, she decided she'd be able to do none of those things effectively without a different kind of business structure. As a survivor of sexual violence, one question loomed large: What would a trauma-informed business structure look like?

By the time Saunders launched her company, AlphaPR, in 2017, she'd decided that part of the answer had to include a culture that nurtured radical honesty and open vulnerability. On a day-to-day basis, that meant putting her employees' personal health and well-being first. Nobody should be a "boss bitch," working themselves into exhaustion. They should be able to ask for, and receive, any help they needed. Meetings should focus on how an employee was doing, not just the work that had to get done that day. That no women would experience harassment at work was a given, but any woman who had experienced trauma would also be supported, unequivocally. If a woman was having flashbacks to trauma, for example, she should feel comfortable taking a break and going for walk; she should not have to worry about her job if she needed time off. She should not have to worry that nobody would ever respect her again if she cried at work. Saunders still remembers how shocked an intern was when Saunders asked her, as she was clearly struggling that day, what she *needed*, then proceeded to agree that if going to the gym and having a nap would make her happy, that's what she should do.

"How do we facilitate a space where we can do good work, be creative, and be empathetic to ourselves and others?" Saunders asked, adding that #MeToo has only increased the urgency of asking these questions. "If we want to heal collectively, but you can't cry at your desk when you're dealing with the wounds that you picked up in this life from being a woman, how the fuck are you supposed to heal? And how are we, as a society, supposed to heal?"

Sexual violence does cost us, whether or not it happens on the job. One extensive Statistics Canada study has examined the total annual economic cost of sexual violence, looking at everything from court expenses to women's lost income. The impact of resulting mental health issues, such as anxiety, depression, and PTSD, is especially jarring. The report estimated that such mental health challenges collectively cost women more than $180 million in future earnings that year. And that was only the bare beginning of it.[22] Lost wages from resulting physical disabilities and missed school days also significantly gouged women's economic well-being following their assault, pushing them further and further down the economic chain.

Given all this, the goals of #MeToo shouldn't stop with creating better workplace policies against harassment — although that's important. They should extend to creating better, kinder workplaces. Period. A trauma-informed workplace culture isn't only a nice thing to have; it could drastically change a woman's chance of achieving a robust economic future. "I worked in so many different industries," said Saunders. "I've just seen them all fail women. At some point they fail," she added, frustrated. "And maybe they fail women from a mental health standpoint and maybe they fail a woman when she becomes pregnant. Maybe they just don't understand women." Her voice tipped into something hard and incredulous. Because she was *still* sick of it. "It all comes from the fact that workplaces weren't designed by women. It's so simple. We're failing women because we're not designing workplaces for and by women."

A lot of people told Saunders her structure wouldn't work. But she's barely been able to keep up with its growth. They also told her that employees would take advantage of her policies. That hasn't happened either. What's more, as we saw in previous chapters, research shows that while one woman at the top often struggles to enact change in a male-dominated company, a mass of women working together can, as Saunders suggested, build a different sort of work culture. And it's one that is exponentially more profitable. It's far from a secret that Fortune 500 companies with at least three or more corporate directors who are women — the point at which workplace culture actually starts to shift and diversity stops being tokenism[23] — drastically outperform those with zero women directors. That includes an 84 percent higher return on sales, a 60 percent higher return on invested capital, and a 46 percent higher return on equity.[24]

Beyond the board level, if only 20 percent of a firm's workers are women, sales per worker in that firm increase by about 14 percent if the company's male CEO is replaced with a woman. In cases where half of the company's employees are women, sales per worker rise more than 18 percent. Wages for women in senior positions also increase in such scenarios.[25] The reason for all this is that women who take over previously male-led companies can often reverse discrimination, not only by paying women wages that are reflective of their actual value, but also by recognizing that value and by better matching women employees to jobs that suit their skills — something that starts with acknowledging and cultivating that talent to begin with.

Working for healing and against harassment, of course, is only one part of it (albeit a very large part). There are, depressingly, many ways that women become footnotes in a wider, male-centric work culture. Combatting them will take more than talking about the profitability of diversity; people have been making that business case loudly and frequently in recent years. That's a good thing, sure. There are only so many times, though, that women and others can stand to prove their worth. More than that, none of that profit will ever be realized if workplaces remain so toxic that women can't or won't enter them—and are ground down into sand if they do.

So many of the changes workplaces can make are practical, easy fixes, Dr. Lori West told me. West is the director of the Alberta Transplant Institute and the director of the Canadian Donation and Transplantation Research Program (CDTRP). When it comes to keeping more women in the STEM fields and other male-dominated industries, she said, those simple, well-worn solutions—like breastfeeding rooms and child care, for example—are a good place to start. They also have a high payoff that goes beyond mere profit returns. But the next, trickier step is to build workplace cultures that work for everyone.

When West and CDTRP co-director Dr. Marie-Josée Hébert set out to build the organization, they agreed the program's fundamental philosophy must be inclusion. They'd build a sandbox to which everyone was invited, and make it clear that their framework would support various needs, with a strong focus on collaboration. Parents were welcome to bring their children to meetings. They created a training program that assigned a science mentor and a career mentor to every trainee; many of the mentors were women. Trainee curriculum included career development. Within three years, and without specifically targeting women at all, the program had reached gender parity. Women felt called in. So, too, did everyone else. "Women then find their voices more easily, it seems, in this kind of structure," said West.

"And that's what then allows more women to stay in the field and excel in the field—because it's a more welcoming place for them to thrive and flourish."

Not that she and Hébert didn't face a lot of pushback for building the CDTRP the way that they did. Like Saunders, they absolutely faced criticism. People told them they'd run out of funding, that in offering a chance to so many people they'd shortchange themselves. But West believed she was right: they'd develop the best research through the most diverse perspectives. Today, the CDTRP is the first program to ever bring together and integrate solid organ transplant, bone marrow transplant, and donation and critical care research communities—several disparate, but linked, fields. It now connects more than two hundred investigators, students, collaborators, and more. "We had to stand our ground," she added. "That's the other thing that women in leadership need to do. You need to not be shouted down. You need to be able to say, 'No, no, you've missed the point entirely.'"

How to Build a Feminist Economy

Against a backdrop of both grumbling and fanfare, the Canadian federal government introduced its first gender-equality budget in 2018. As Kate Bezanson, a guest columnist for *The Globe and Mail*, put it, the budget was "unlike any of its predecessors, representing a historic and aspirational statement of ambition, with potentially transformative social and economic consequences."[26] Although the budget introduced specific funding and action items focused on gender equity (more on those shortly), what truly made it stand out was the introduction of a new tool for analysis, which the government dubbed Gender-Based Analysis Plus, or GBA+. With it, the government acknowledged that any economic policy, including spending and taxation measures, would affect women differently than men. It also acknowledged that the difference wasn't binary, but on a scale of many intersections, including other genders, race, ability, and so on.[27] Thus, the plus. More than that, the government underscored that those differences *mattered*. The new lens of gender-based analysis declared that no federal budgeting decision should be made without considering who, actually, it helped. No more pretending economic decisions were power-neutral.

However, analysis is not quite the same as action, as many feminist critics noted. That's not to say the budget offered nothing to women. Importantly, the Liberal government introduced pay equity legislation, which requires federally regulated workplaces to examine their compensation practices and ensure that everyone receives "equal pay for work of equal value."[28] The government allotted $1.4 billion in increased financing to women entrepreneurs, and committed an additional $86 million in funding for initiatives against gender-based violence. Yet, for all its lip service to getting more women involved in the economy, it did nothing significant to address affordable child care, a longstanding roadblock for equitable participation in the workforce — an estimated 608,000 women are working part-time either involuntarily or because of caring responsibilities.[29] Likewise, it did not adjust the income-replacement rate for parental leave, keeping it at 55 percent for those who take a twelve-month leave and 33 percent for those who are gone for eighteen months. This does little to mitigate against the "motherhood penalty."[30]

Beyond that, there was also no concrete legislation to

ensure future governments would stick to the GBA+ framework. As journalist Sarah Boesveld wrote in *Chatelaine*,
quipping that the Liberals mentioned the "'g' word no fewer
than 359 times in 367 pages," the analysis tool itself was what
gave the Liberals their feminist cred (or, at least, that seemed
to have been their aim). "And that," wrote Boesveld, "is what
will help the Liberals walk their very loud and frequent talk
about making Canada a more equitable place for women."[31]
If we want to truly build a feminist economy, policies must
go beyond *business-as-usual, but this time with a dash of feminism!* Incorporating analysis of how policies affect women
into decision-making is a good start. A better start would
be to think beyond the usual economic solutions and to
consider more than, say, tax breaks or how to cast a wider
net for the status quo. What if we could instead build the
economy around a desire for equity?

A realignment of fiscal power into other, oft-ignored
areas, for instance, could fix vast, global structural inequalities — ones that currently seem so huge as to be beyond
reach. Imagine if economic policies focused on nutrition
and maternal health. Pregnant women's poor nutrition is
connected to 800,000 newborn deaths every year. But if
economics scaled up nutrition interventions, every dollar
spent would yield $16 in returns. Women around the world
also lack access to safe, modern contraception. Every dollar
spent improving that access would return $120 in economic
benefits. Worldwide violence against women, including
intimate partner violence and sexual violence, costs the
economy about $110 billion globally. Why aren't we doing
more to solve that?

A more equitable economy would also demand that countries invest more in education: every year of schooling for
children increases the average annual GDP by 0.37 percent.

Every year a girl attends school increases her future earn-ings by 10 to 20 percent. Using open-source data in education could create a mind-blowing $1 trillion in economic value every year. And if another 600 million women in developing countries could access the internet, the annual GDP could rise as much as $18 billion across all their 144 countries. The planet would be cared for, too, because resources are not infinite and their endless extraction is only an economic driver for the already privileged. Using solid fuels, like wood and coal, costs everyone $123 billion annually. Poor access to clean water is also an expensive bit of inequality; every dollar invested in water sanitation in developing countries could result in up to $5.50 in returns.[32]

Together, these solutions save lives, build stronger health systems, reduce poverty, facilitate better education, reduce climate change, and help women reach their full potential. All of it ripples out to increase intergenerational prosperity, boost individual and group wealth, eliminate disparity, and, oh, you know, also make sure there's a planet left on which we can all live this better future. So, yes, *that* is what a feminist economy looks like.

Of course, none of those large-scale, global solutions mean discarding everyday solutions that disrupt traditional eco-nomic structures on a smaller, local scale, such as investing in other women or purchasing from their businesses. To truly change (or destroy) economic power structures, we'll need to fight them on all levels, from big to small. The economy is a patriarchal monster. To slay it, many things must happen in parallel, the more boundary-pushing the better. And how else to wound it except to give women more weapons, in the form of increased opportunities to actually use their fiscal power?

Slaying the patriarchal monster that is the economy means busting myths, like the one that says men are innately better with money and better at business. They're not. Studies have repeatedly shown that women investors actually outperform men, on average, by one percent every year. They earn higher returns on their investments and are better savers—in part because men's trading is driven by ego, and wanting to beat the market, whereas women usually have specific end goals, like a sustainable retirement or buying a house.[33] Yet 80 percent of investment advisers are men and, on average, over fifty years old. That can mean an industry that defaults to men's salaries and career paths, which look very different from women's. In recent years, several companies—including, most notably, Ellevest, a firm founded by Sallie Krawcheck, a former CEO of Merrill Lynch, Smith Barney, and Citi Private Bank—have started to target women investors. "Money in a capitalist society is power," Krawcheck has told media. So nobody should be surprised that the most capitalist industry—investing—is also the most manly of the industries. With Ellevest, she has said, she wants to "change the underlying product as opposed to just trying to exhort and cajole women to themselves change."[34]

We need more of this. (We need more of everything.) In many ways, though, even this type of thinking is still inside-the-box—radical only by virtue of many women's vast inability to participate in the economy. But what if feminism itself, and the growing power of the #MeToo movement and women's anger, could be brought to bear on the economy? Remember, women are already far more likely to invest in companies that do social good. Might we shift the weight of how everyone invests, and in so doing force companies to also care about gender equality? Andrew Behar thinks so. Behar is the CEO of As You Sow, a U.S.-based not-for-profit that pushes environmental and social corporate responsibility through shareholder advocacy.

As You Sow hosts several digital "Invest Your Values" tools on its website, allowing investors to screen mutual fund holdings against specific environmental, social, and governance issues. Past screening tools have focused on tobacco-free, fossil fuel–free, and weapon-free funds. And in late 2018, the organization finally debuted one on gender equity. It was something the team had wanted to do for a while, said Behar, and also something many people had asked them to do. But initially they didn't have enough data to truly capture how well a company was performing on gender equity. They didn't just want to look at board representation. To understand how a company thought about gender, they needed to also know its sexual harassment policies, its approach to parental leave, equal pay, reproductive rights, gender ratios in senior management, plus how the company recruited new staff, trained and advanced current employees, and even what its supply chain looked like. It took teaming up with Equileap, an organization that evaluates gender diversity in the corporate sector, to get the right data set. With it, they were finally able to assess and rank thousands of companies on a twelve-point scale, aggregated over an entire mutual fund. Many people never realize what companies are in their fund, a fact that shields the worst of them; now all they needed to do was type the fund's name into a search bar and press enter.

I spoke with Behar days before the new tool launched, and he told me mutual fund managers were already anxious about what they'd discover. No surprise there. Behar had seen earlier As You Sow tools completely shake up investing trends. When the organization first introduced its fossil fuels tool, for instance, only ten mutual funds achieved the highest ranking. Now hundreds do — a change that happened after fund managers called As You Sow in a panic, wanting to get out of the bad books. All of which means that the worst-offending companies either cleaned up their acts or were dropped from those funds, with their profits usually taking a nosedive. Win-win.

"So how does the mutual fund manager pick the companies in the fund, and how do they weight them?" mused Behar. "We believe that gender should be one of the major factors, and right now it's not. It's invisible. This tool is shining a bright light in there and saying, 'Look.'" Once that light exposes which funds are doing poorly, and which companies are within them, capital is going to shift. The economy will stop supporting the misogynists—slowly, perhaps, but inevitably. And maybe not even that slowly. "Women control a lot of capital. And they control a lot of buying power. To have your brand associated with really poor gender practice—you're going to be a marked company. I'm sorry, but your brand is going to be tarnished."

Good.

At the same time, if gender equity goes deeper than tallying the number of women on a company's board, equity itself is more complex than measuring a woman's ability to thrive in any particular environment. For starters: *which* women are we talking about? If I truly wanted to know what it would take to disrupt age-old power imbalances, I'd have to also acknowledge that some people face significantly more hurdles than others. What's more, I'd have to examine how to tear down those hurdles—and how women helped to put (and keep) them there in the first place.

CHAPTER 7

I See You Now

*Representation, inclusivity, and the
end of white, male media*

THE TORONTO INTERNATIONAL FILM Festival did not,
at first glance, seem like the setting for an industry-
shaking feminist rally — or at least not one organized by TIFF
itself. Everywhere I looked, the festival grounds brimmed
with corporate-sponsored booths. At one outdoor feature,
women in matching red berets and blue peacoats ushered
festival-goers in front of an Eiffel Tower replica sponsored
by Air France. At another, people snaked around a Pure Leaf
tea booth, waiting either for samples or for a chance to take
a selfie on a white wooden swing nestled inside an explosion of flowers, or, who knows, probably both. L'Oréal gave
makeovers while also "celebrating iconic women in film."
Most of the barricades marking the TIFF road closures were
7-Up branded. Even as I got closer to the rally site — which
I, amusingly, had RSVP-ed for, in a show of organized dissent — I couldn't shake the sanitized feel. TIFF volunteers

handed out black T-shirts branded #ShareHerJourney and fistfuls of colourful buttons. That the artificial grass didn't move at all as the wind gusted only added to the surreal feeling. It also didn't help that there was only one person in the giant crowd holding a protest sign: "Men of Quality Don't Fear Equality."

Any fear I had about the rally being bland or corporatized, like some of the other features of the festival, however, disappeared when the women started talking. Because they were inspiring and they were furious.

It was 2018, nearly one year after the #MeToo movement went viral, and the rally was meant to push for more women in film. But now that these women finally had a stage, they were ready to talk about so much more—including why the vision for diversity in film could not be limited to a white feminist's utopia. One speaker was Amma Asante, an actor and director whose fourth film was premiering at the festival that year. "Now if there's anybody here who is going to sigh at this point, 'Oh, why does she have to bring race into a conversation about all women?'" she began, acknowledging the tension too often present when a woman of colour speaks about race, and she went on to suggest that anyone sighing should consider how it felt to have society constantly question and dismiss the obstacles of inequality that faced them as women. "Remember how that feels. If we are going to be concerned with equality for women in film, then the very poignant issues for women of colour in film must enter the equation in a hugely significant way."

She was forced to pause, unable to speak over the burst of clapping and cheering, the thunderous *woooo*s rising to meet the air. She would be remiss, she added, if she did not use the platform she had that day to confront the ways in which misogyny and sexism are magnified once race becomes part of the equation—if she did not use her time now to speak for others who were just like her. Or, rather, others who wanted to be like her but were never able to break through in an industry that didn't want to see them. The last time she looked, she said, Black women directors made up not even one percent of their industry. And because those numbers are so minuscule, she added, the motivation to look into their experiences, triumphs, and difficulties has been equally small. Those numbers would never get bigger until advocates and researchers had the courage to dig into Black women's experiences and the problems they face both entering the industry and then navigating it. "We are here," said Asante, "yet we are erased when analysis of the industry absorbs us into pages that look purely at race or purely at gender."

She knew first-hand, she told the rapt crowd, that the unique problems Black women directors face do not evaporate after one film. Asante's fourth film, *Where Hands Touch*, is the film she wanted to make second. Instead, she was told repeatedly that the film was "too big." Its story is set during the Second World War, in 1944 Berlin, and Asante was often implicitly, if not explicitly, reminded that such time periods and genres are usually the domain of white, male directors. So, she said, we must also ask: What kind of movies does a Black woman get to make? How does her access to film's many genres differ from that of other filmmakers? How are those prospects additionally limited, even in the context of the sparse opportunities for all women? What is a Black woman's journey through development, production, and distribution, and how does it differ from that of her white counterparts? We must ask these questions and more, relentlessly, until there are answers, she insisted. Until it isn't so truly, devastatingly rare to see women like Asante leading in the film industry.

She did stay in the industry, she added, because both women and men mentored her and gave her opportunities she might not otherwise have had. As she put it, these people in power "allowed their positions to work for me rather than against." They saw her talent, not their own assumptions. "In short," she said, "they saw *me*." The crowd roared again, cheers and claps domino-ing into each other. They saw her, too. Invisible turned visible. But, she added. *But*. Having used her platform that day to speak for Black women film-makers, having used it to galvanize a crowd of hundreds, she hoped that, ultimately, she'd be able to talk about something else. Something she hardly ever got to speak about: her work. Speaking out about inequality had been a necessity; it wasn't her calling.

"So what I am saying is, oh, to live in a world where any Black woman creative, *any* woman creative and artist, did not have to stand on a platform in 2018 and speak about why power-sharing and equality is essential, unless we choose to do so through and within our storytelling," she thundered. "Oh, to have the privilege that those who do not share my gender or my race have had since time began. Do I want that for my fellow women filmmakers?" She paused, emphatic, as the wind whipped her hair. "*Hell* yes. Because every day I dream of a world in which the necessity to talk about this is absent, and when my fellow women artists can speak about their work, rather than campaign to do it."

I could not hear for all the cheering.

See It, Be It

Stories matter. What are we, really, but the sum of all our stories, spun into human form? They are how we connect with each other, how we learn about each other, how we learn about ourselves, and how we conceive all that is possible. We are constantly inundated with both entertainment and news media, each feeding information and imagination, forming and reforming how we see the world, challenging our conceptions—or, far more often, solidifying our closely held stereotypes into presumed fact. Storytelling is still very much a white man's game, and that matters, too. Because, as easy as it is for the keepers of the status quo to dismiss calls for diversity in media, shouting protective myths like "a good story is a good story," there is so much more truth in "see the change, be the change" thinking. Studies have consistently shown that when media challenges stereotypes, readers, viewers, and listeners do the same. And, in doing so, they acquire the power to reimagine their own stories.

Take, for example, one of the first and most iconic female characters to be featured in a STEM role: Dr. Dana Scully, a medical doctor and forensic pathologist with a degree in physics. Portrayed as a cool-headed and brilliant FBI agent on prime time's *The X-Files*, Scully stood out against the more typical bevy of awkward white men. Over a decade after the show's first run ended, when asked about their opinions on women in the STEM fields, *X-Files* fans exhibited what researchers have called "The Scully Effect."[1] Regular viewers of the show were 43 percent more likely than other women to have considered a career in the STEM fields; many of them also made it a reality. Those who watched the show often were also more likely to have encouraged their daughters or granddaughters to enter the STEM fields, and to believe women in general should have a higher presence there. Two-thirds of women who participated in the study and currently worked in STEM said Dana Scully acted as a role model for them—perhaps because so few real-life ones existed for them growing up.

For those of us who grew up watching female characters save the day in shows like (the way-too-white) *Buffy the Vampire Slayer* or *Veronica Mars*, it probably isn't all too surprising that fictional role models play a major part in women's lives. Nearly all women in a 2016 global survey felt female role models in film and TV were important. The biggest shocker there is that the number isn't 100 percent. But more than 60 percent also said that those role models have been influential in their lives—reinforcing the idea that TV shows and movies are more than a brain-numbing exercise after work or an excuse to eat buckets of buttery popcorn. (Just me?) And almost the same number of respondents said their favourite women characters on TV had inspired them to be more ambitious or assertive in particular. The survey of 4,300 women, across nine countries, spanning from the United States to Saudi Arabia to Russia, also found that, on average, one in nine respondents felt their onscreen female role models had helped give them the courage to leave an abusive relationship. In Brazil, that number was as high as one in four.[2]

What's more, research also shows that this role-modelling starts young. One study from late 2018, by the American-based Women's Media Center in partnership with BBC America, found that boys aged five to nine were far more likely to name a male superhero as their top role model than they were to name their own mom or stepmom. (Dads placed first.) Girls in that same age range were, conversely, more likely to name their mom or stepmom or another family member, in that order, before they named a female superhero. (Dads came in last. Sorry dads.) At the same time, girls—and particularly girls of colour—were more likely than boys to say that watching female superheroes made them feel as if they could achieve anything they wanted. Watching their favourite superhero or sci-fi lead made them feel strong, brave, confident, and motivated.

The problem wasn't that female superheroes were uninspiring to these girls; it was that there weren't enough of them. Girls were, predictably, more likely than boys to say they wanted more superheroes and sci-fi leads who looked like them. After all, little white boys have their pick of superheroes. Girls of colour — who face an even bigger dearth of choices — were also far more likely than their white counterparts to say they wanted more heroes who looked like them. As *A Wrinkle in Time* director Ava DuVernay put it in the introduction to the report, "In *Wrinkle in Time*, literally this girl of color saves the universe — not just the world, multiple planets and galaxies... that's such a radical idea as a woman of colour, as anyone who's outside the industry construct of who's usually put forth as the hero in cinema."[3]

Straight White Men (And Women) Are Everywhere

Perhaps this potential for power-shifting ripples is why there isn't much impetus among media elites to push for change. Depressingly, many women fare worse in leadership and male-dominated fields on TV than they do in real life. Family films are especially likely to influence youth and their visions of a future self, but they offer remarkably grim portrayals of women's ability to succeed. A study of the top-grossing family films released between 2006 and 2011 found that few women characters occupied "clout positions" in any given sector. Only *two* women in the 129 family films released during the study's span were depicted as executive officers of a major corporation. Not one woman was shown as being at the top of the financial sector, legal arena, or media industry. Only one speaking character played a powerful woman in politics across more than 5,800 speaking roles represented in the film sample. *One!* Things are often bleak for women in the workforce, and they are acutely dismal for women in power, but they're not *that* bad. Across all jobs, not just those representative of power, women held only a little over 20 percent of onscreen jobs in family films, and just under 35 percent of those in prime-time programs—a considerably smaller share than those who work in real life.[4] So, great.

And for all that female characters in STEM inspire women, there are too few of them onscreen. Across film, television, and streaming content from 2007 to 2017, male characters that worked in the STEM fields—at nearly 63 percent— notably outnumbered the female characters. Of those STEM characters who were women, most were white, accounting for just over 60 percent. Black women made up 23.5 percent of female STEM characters, whereas only just over 8 percent were Asian, 6 percent were Latinx, and less than one percent were Middle Eastern.

Across all roles, women are overwhelmingly less likely to even speak onscreen, and overwhelmingly more likely to be sexualized. Things are far, far worse for LGBTQ+ and racialized characters. One comprehensive 2016 study showed that at least half of film, TV, and streaming stories did not include a single speaking or named Asian character. More than 20 percent of stories included no Black characters. And, only 2 percent of all speaking characters were LGBTQ+. (Of that tiny number, most were white men.) "The complete absence of individuals from these backgrounds," concluded the report, "is a symptom of a diversity strategy that relies on tokenistic inclusion rather than integration."[5]

Not that everything is bad. Truly. Analysis of the top
100 films of 2018 showed an uptick in both female leads
and co-leads, as well as the number of women of colour in
such roles. Thank you, *Crazy Rich Asians*. More than forty
of those films featured women in those top roles (in 2017
that number was thirty-two), and eleven films put women
from under-represented racial groups to the front (versus
just four in 2017).[6] Still, the fact that it's taking so long for
power balances to shift—and the fact that eleven films is
still just *eleven* films—is inarguably connected to who has
the power to tell stories and who does not. Asante alluded in
her TIFF rally speech to the fact that those behind the camera
control who's put in front of it, how they're portrayed, and
what words they say. Women accounted for just forty-two
directors of the 1,200 top films released from 2007 to 2018.
Of those forty-two, four were Black, two were Asian, one
was Latinx, and none were Indigenous. White women made
up 16 percent of producers; women of colour made up just
under 2 percent. Across all production roles in film, women
of colour did not make up more than 2 percent.[7]

On second thought, maybe everything is still bad.

This lopsided balance of power for women of colour is
echoed throughout many spheres of life: music,[8] business,[9]
politics,[10] to name barely a few. Most film reviewers are also
white men.[11] Put together, this presents a very clear, not-so-
hidden message: white men matter the most, white women
matter a little less, and everybody else hardly matters at all.
If you listen to those in power, this is a happy accident, not
a controlled effort to endlessly reflect systems of power, like
two facing mirrors. Because if stories help us dream what's
possible, they also tell us what isn't possible. And the stories
we tell right now remain in the purview of men who protect
the status quo, who *are* the status quo. It's like a grand echo

chamber, where one group of white men is on one side of a cliff shouting *You're Awesome!* and another group is on the other shouting *It's All About You!* into infinity. Except that men face neither cliffs nor gaps, so that isn't quite right. Okay. Picture these two groups of men standing really close together and shouting *I Matter Most!* into each other's faces. Yes, that's about it.

Who Cares About the Grammys, Anyway?

In 2017, shortly after *Lemonade* should have won Album of the Year at the Grammys, Solange Knowles posted, and then quickly deleted, a call to action on Twitter: "Create your own committees, build your own institutions, give your friends awards, award yourself, and be the gold you wanna hold, my Gs." Media big and small covered the criticism, with most journalists entirely missing the point. Local Ontario paper the *Waterloo Region Record* said Knowles "vented her anger" over her sister's loss and went on a "rant." It also corrected her initial tweet, which lamented that only two Black artists had won Album of the Year in the past two decades: "Solange's statement was factually inaccurate as Lauryn Hill, OutKast, the late Ray Charles, and Herbie Hancock have all won the gong over the last 20 years." Oh, have they *all*?[12] *Billboard* magazine characterized her tweet as a "rather radical suggestion on how to make sure the Knowles family doesn't sit through another disappointing night."[13] Which, I mean, *come on.*

Such subtly racist coverage worked hard to protect the status quo. It said, *Look, here is just another angry Black woman*, and it said, *Look at* them *always wanting more.* What it really said was, *Don't listen.* It said: *Yes, fine, the Grammys — and by* extension the Oscars and the Emmys—can do better, but they're still what matters. Sure, they may be broken, but they're the best we have. Just keep trying to succeed and stay stuck in this system and one day if you try really hard you might be the fifth Black artist to win Album of the Year, and wouldn't that be nice? But don't leave these systems that never planned for your success to build more of your own, that (status quo–enforcing) voice might as well say. Don't stop caring about what the white, male majority thinks. Don't stop striving to win this rigged game. That would be radical! Yet, that is exactly what the next generation of creators is doing. And if that's radical, they're saying, well, good, because radical self-love is also what's going to bring the old exclusionary systems crumbling down into irrelevance.

"Among this generation of filmmakers and my peers," said Tamil-Canadian filmmaker V. T. Nayani, "it's like, 'Yeah it would be nice to get an Oscar or an Emmy, but that's not the point.' If people are seeing our films, that's what we care about. Those awards shows are not really reflective of us. We're all putting less stock in them." In addition to filmmaking, Nayani has also worked as a producer, focusing on authentic storytelling. For her, that means supporting women and non-binary creators from Black, Indigenous, and other racialized communities to do the work they wanted to do, too. It wasn't enough to make her own films, she stressed. She also had to hold the door open. More than that, really. She referenced a constant reminder pinned to her wall, quoting Ava DuVernay: We're not waiting for other people to open the door. We're building our own houses with our own keys and our own doors and then creating opportunities for others.

The Highlander-esque idea that "there can be only one" does not serve creators of colour. That's called the scarcity mentality, said Nayani, and at its core, it does nothing more than inhibit solidarity and work to reinforce white systems of power. The cool thing about the current moment in film, she added, is that technology has worked to democratize creation and to allow for many diverse perspectives. People can circumvent regular pathways to filmmaking (i.e., securing funding and resources from old white dudes) and make the story they want to tell with an iPhone and a minimal budget. That means a huge shift from old approaches to diversity, wherein people of colour were predominantly used as subjects, not granted agency as creators. Now, she said, people are being seen through their own lens. White creators (specifically, white, straight, cis men) have long had the privilege of telling a multitude of different stories about themselves, from infinite viewpoints, reimagining themselves and what's possible over and over again; now people of colour are wresting access to that same privilege of multiplicity.

For Nayani, inclusive and authentic storytelling doesn't mean making space within existing institutions; it means helping people to create their own spaces and to create them everywhere. "I will make a very different film from another Tamil girl from Vancouver or Montreal or even the other side of Scarborough," she said, adding that all those voices together will help to reimagine different futures — to reimagine stories about Black, Indigenous, and other people of colour not necessarily as singular narratives of oppression, prejudice, and racism, but also as stories about people who thrive, love, and have joy. Let's instead feed into the idea of abundance, she stressed. Let's work toward a future in which everybody recognizes that these stories deserve space to be told. Let's dream up new worlds, she said, that allow us to be seen how we'd like to be seen and invent how we'd like our lives to look. Blockbusters like *Black Panther* are not the end goal but rather the very beginning of what's possible.

"The people who have been telling the stories," echoed transgender filmmaker Luis De Filippis, "aren't the people who are living the stories." In the case of transgender characters, they added, that often means directors are not concerned about who their characters are as people. They're concerned about anatomy. They're concerned about the mechanics of transitioning. Transgender characters seem to be either vilified, eroticized, or sensationalized. Even when the story is presumably a positive one, the formula becomes: this transgender character needs to come out; in doing so they learn to accept themselves; and their family, in turn, also learns to accept them (or not). But a transgender person's life does not, obviously, begin and end with their transition, said De Filippis. So where are all the stories about their actual *lives*?

In response to this question, De Filippis created the short film *For Nonna Anna*, which went on to win a Special Jury Award at Sundance[14] and also the Best Short Narrative Award at the Atlanta International Film Festival. The tender, beautiful film shows a shared moment of vulnerability that unfolds between a granddaughter—who, yes, has already transitioned—and her elderly grandmother. The film, De Filippis said, started with frustration. Frustration with not seeing themselves onscreen, not seeing their story onscreen, not seeing their family onscreen. But they almost didn't make it at all. Not because there was no support for transgender stories outside the expected tropes—although that is a challenge—but because they also didn't see any directors who worked outside the stereotypical, aggressive, masculine style. Those were the methods they saw endlessly replicated in film school; they had tried to make films by copying those methods and it had never seemed to work. De Filippis did not have an abrasive personality at all. *Maybe*, they thought, *I'm just not cut out for this business.*

Then they saw a behind-the-scenes documentary with director Sofia Coppola (a person who, they add, does not come without her own problematic perspectives). Coppola had such a laid-back, soft-spoken manner. She spoke with her hand over her mouth. Something clicked. *Oh, that's me!* De Filippis thought. *That's how I direct. If she can do it, I can do it.* So when they filmed *For Nonna Anna*, they decided to run their set differently—exactly how they had always wanted to. For them, it was a new way to approach an old medium. Every morning on set, DeFilippis started with a check-in, going around the circle to genuinely inquire how everybody was doing, how they were feeling, what they wanted to share about themselves. After lunch, everybody—everybody, not just the actors—participated in a dance break. The result was a film set that worked in collaboration, without anger or ego. That is something that takes effort, stressed De Filippis. If you want it, you have to plan for it. It worked, though, they added. Despite doing away with the tried-and-true regimen of a film set, *For Nonna Anna* finished filming an entire day ahead of schedule.

"I was able to be myself on set. And because I knew who I was, I knew how I wanted to run things and that's how they were run," they said. "It wasn't a decision, so much as I was forced into it. Obviously the other way wasn't working." The ability to be wholly, absolutely who you want to be is what power is really about, added De Filippis. "It really has a lot to do with how much society allows you to be yourself and the things you can get away with while being yourself." Take every horrible thing we've heard about men since the rise of the #MeToo movement, for example, they added. "It's just because they've been being themselves and they've been allowed to be such precise iterations of themselves." Men had felt the complete ability to be themselves on any given day, in any given space. They had never felt the need to hide themselves. Well, now neither does De Filippis.

The New Hallmark Moment

If entertainment media has done a poor job of representing those who buy movie tickets and albums, so too has every other form of storytelling. News media, in particular, is a stronghold of the Old Boys' Club, demarcating the issues, voices, and perspectives of those it deems most important under the guise of objectivity. Historically, that has meant a whitewashing of both the news itself and the newsrooms that produce it. It's essential to note that men of colour lose in these systems, too. Former *Globe and Mail* journalist Sunny Dhillon sent much-needed shockwaves through the Canadian publishing industry in October 2018 when he wrote an essay on Medium explaining why he quit. "That final conversation inside the bureau chief's office crystallized what I had felt: What I brought to the newsroom did not matter. And it was at that moment that being a person of colour at a paper and in an industry that does not have enough of us—particularly at the top—felt more futile than ever before."[15]

In his essay, Dhillon pointed to another article published on Poynter, introducing a new tool, "A Survival Kit for Journalists of Color."[16] In the piece, Dr. Seema Yasmin, a John S. Knight Journalism Fellow, explains why she and her colleague Michael Grant, also a Fellow, launched the project. She addressed some common experiences that journalists of colour face in newsrooms in North America. "You left because the editors shut down your pitches," she wrote. "Or because they said yes but never ran those columns, the ones you felt most passionate about, the stories of the El Salvadorian women who folded dough into triangles to send their daughters to private school, the young African American lawyer fighting police brutality cases. You left because a woman at work kept running her fingers through your braids and when your co-workers said: 'Go to HR,' you said, 'But she is the head of HR.'" The toolkit, she added, is meant to help journalists of colour find "quickfire, in-the-moment responses for everyday racist microaggressions," and also to guide them through "deliberative exercises that help you build community and recruit allies in the newsroom."

Such tools can be especially vital for Indigenous women and women of colour in the newsroom. Edmonton-based multimedia journalist Anya Zoledziowski wrote about the layered challenges such journalists face, in a March 2019 *Tyee* article that shared the findings of her recent academic thesis, which she wrote while a student at the University of British Columbia's School of Journalism.[17] "Although many racialized experiences traverse gender lines," she wrote, "women of colour *simultaneously* battle stereotypes about their womanhood (crazy, too ambitious, ditzy) and their racial identities (incompetent, ethnic, only interested in 'diverse' storytelling)." She was not immune to such racism on the job. "In a previous journalism job, I showed up on day one eager to learn and contribute," she explained. "Within just a few months, my boss at the time told me I was hired 'to be the diversity.' The same superior called me 'fiery' after I questioned ethics around our Indigenous coverage. In various other positions, colleagues have asked me how to cover 'people of colour' issues in a way that made it seem they assumed I have a third eye with an omniscient, racialized lens. Situations like these created a lot of pressure."

A 2018 study of newsrooms across the United States showed just how direly white these spaces can be. Media, in general, skews male, with men writing about 60 percent of online and print stories, and being featured as prime-time anchors slightly more than that.[18] On the whole, men write most of the news we read, getting 90 percent of sports bylines, 67 percent of technology and media coverage, and 66 percent of international, news, and political coverage. Women are present, but outnumbered, in management. Of all newsroom managers, just over 40 percent were found to be women. At least one woman was among the top-three editors at more than three-quarters of newsrooms. Among that female minority, women of colour were even less repre-sented in newsrooms.[19] Just over 83 percent of all journalists, including leaders, were white. Of all employees, 31 percent were white women. Meanwhile, slightly under 3 percent were Black women, a tiny bit less were Latinx women, and just under 2.5 percent were Asian women. And, most dis-mally of all, just 0.16 percent were Indigenous women. The percentage of newsroom leaders was roughly the same — still depressing.

These disparities are reflected in the types of stories that are told, and they're also reflected in whose voices appear in media stories. When it comes to "expert" sources, women's voices, and diverse women's voices in particular, are rarely heard. This absolutely feeds into public perceptions of women as leaders, reinforcing the idea that women have nothing to contribute to the conversation and nor do they have the credentials to guide it. They are, in all ways, not part of it. This dynamic is something that high-achieving, groundbreaking women are clearly not keen about. As one woman put it in a 2018 study looking at the exclusion of women's voices in media: "You get tired of hearing just men all the time about everything. I just don't care what men have to say about pretty much anything anymore, not because they are not experts, but it's just—I've heard it, I've heard it, I don't care anymore. I'd rather hear what women or people of colour and Indigenous people have to say."[20]

To help chart just how wide these inequalities are, Canadian organization Informed Opinions teamed up with researchers at Simon Fraser University to create the Gender Gap Tracker. Using big data analytics and text data mining, the tracker provides real-time numbers on the breakdown of men and women quoted in Canadian news media, including the CBC, the *Toronto Star*, *The Globe and Mail*, HuffPost, and more.[21] I spoke with Maite Taboada, the SFU linguistics professor who headed the school's research team, about what the tracker had revealed in its first month of data-pulling. Not once, she told me, had the percentage of women quoted tipped over 30 percent. (The day I checked it last, in April 2019, it sat at 26 percent.) Taboada said that she wasn't surprised the numbers were so low—previous research had consistently pegged representation around that same percentage—but she was surprised that the numbers stayed so consistent, day in and day out, across all media outlets. It was habit. A *bad* habit. Her hope was that by measuring representation every day and by making those numbers public, media would no longer be able to feign ignorance. Consistently, they failed. Consistently, they told the public in so many (lack of) words that some people were experts and some were not, some were smart and some weren't, some were important and some were not, some could be anything and some were too invisible to ever have the chance.

This messaging extends far past entertainment and news media into advertising and brand mascot-ing, into art galleries and onto bookshelves, and into even the smallest and most seemingly innocuous of places. Take, for instance, the Canadian indie greeting-card company To:Her. A group of women got the idea for the company after two of them could not find a card, no matter how much they hunted, that represented anybody but white people. Dorcas Siwoku was looking for a congratulatory card to give a young Black woman in her life. Oana Romaniuc was attending the wedding of two friends, an interracial couple. Where were the cards showing anyone resembling these special people in their lives? Both women shared their dilemma with Monica Romaniuc, who is Oana's sister and also Siwoku's co-worker. She brought them together for coffee and, after chatting, all three decided it was inconceivable that even greeting cards were so white. And not only white: so hell-bent on reinforcing gender roles and stereotypes. They remained baffled even as they worked on getting To:Her off the ground. "At one point, we were like, 'How has this not been done yet?'" said Siwoku. "It's 2017."

I sat down with the trio about one year after they launched, heading into the 2018 winter holiday season. In addition to having their regular line of cards depicting Black women, Black couples, and Black families (not all nuclear, of course), they had also recently debuted a line of holiday cards. One showed a group of women in winter wear, no words. Another cheekily remarked, "Happy Holidays. Yes, I'm still single." One read, "Congratulations on surviving that [awkward holiday gathering] on your own." Their favourite, they said, in between bursts of laughter, was one of a woman in a bubble bath with the caption, "Wishing you a pleasurable holiday." *Because what do we do when we're taking a bath? Wink, wink.* The cards, they told me, were not only meant to redefine who got to experience a so-called Hallmark moment, but what life milestones were worthy of the name. Other cards the company sells include tributes to single motherhood, ending unhealthy relationships ("Congratulations on leaving that asshole"), and excellent intercourse ("Thanks for the great sex").

The women come up with the concepts themselves, with input from their customers and friends, who are also craving a break from all the homogeneity, and Oana Romaniuc designs and illustrates all the cards. Many cards later, the first one the team designed, in response to her initial empty-handed search, is still Siwoku's favourite. It's called "Black Girl Magic," contains no text, and shows a Black woman in a swirling yellow gown. Description copy for the card tells a potential purchaser that she is "confident in her skin" and "unapologetically takes up the space she deserves." Siwoku stressed that what To:Her does is not "heavy." "When I think about what we do," she said, "it's a seemingly small thing. It's a greeting card." But it's also a powerful way for them to influence a larger conversation about who matters, who deserves to be celebrated, who gets to be happy. She knew what it would have meant to her to have that kind of card when she was the same age as the young woman she was shopping for that fateful day, years ago now. It would have meant everything.

Why Diversity Initiatives Fail

Back at TIFF's Share Her Journey rally, actor and director Nandita Das took the stage. "Good morning, everybody. I have no paper, no notes, no thoughts," she told the crowd, laughter punctuating her last admission. "I'm here just to share my feelings. They asked me to speak and I was like, 'Mmm, am I being called because I'm Brown?' Brown representation. You know we're all into diversity in a big way. Is it because I'm Indian? I represent South Asia." In seconds, Das had exposed the inherent tension between diversity and tokenism, and the difficulties in parsing which is which—particularly when you are the person upon which they are being enacted. "I just want to be treated as a person," she said, emphasizing the last word. "But sadly there is no escaping our identity. I think we all have multiple identities. Some given. Some acquired. We move from one to another, depending on the context. I'm a big champion of multiple identities. But I realize the identity of a woman just doesn't leave me. For better or for worse, I'm constantly reminded I'm a woman."

I often wonder if the reason why diversity initiatives fail is because those who create them, fundamentally, do not want to help shift power at all. For those of us who benefit from the status quo, it is both daunting and uncomfortable to acknowledge our stake in maintaining systems of misogyny and white supremacy. It is even harder to truly release our investment in those systems, even if we think we want to (and I'm certainly not convinced we want to). Diversity policies try to solve these inequities with numbers but do little of the hard work needed to probe work cultures, internalized discrimination, and access to power. They say: *You're here, what more do you want?* But we know by now that simply having a presence is not enough; it's the bare minimum. The problem is that white people—white women included—keep thinking we have all the answers. We don't. *I* don't.

Here's the thing: I know that even as I try to shine light on these issues, in a sincere effort to spotlight an integral piece of the wider conversation on gender and power, I am also acting as a gatekeeper. I am deciding who to interview and how to tell their stories. Yes, I am doing my best to listen and to share this platform that I know I am privileged to have. But if I want things to truly change, as I do, I also know I must routinely interrogate what it means to extricate myself from these systems of power in which I am both a loser and a *winner*. Confronting the myriad ways in which we — in which I — benefit from racism, colonialism, and sexism is not a one-time thing. To work, it has to be, well, work. It must become part of a daily practice, something I do over and over, and even then I know I won't get it right. That's only more of a reason to keep trying. Good intentions do not erase racism. That's true for individuals — and it's also true for companies, organizations, and other groups that claim they want to do better. Unless they're truly ready to reckon with what it means to reallocate power, their diversity initiatives are nothing more than feel-good optics, invested not in inclusion, but in ultimately maintaining the status quo.

Which is probably part of the reason why diversity initiatives don't, in fact, work. Equal-employment-opportunity language, one of the most standard diversity-friendly flags that companies use, for example, is actually more likely to deter the people it is intended to attract. You know the phrase, often found at the end of job postings: "Company X is an equal opportunity employer. All candidates will receive equal consideration without regard to . . ." or "We welcome applications from . . ." followed by a list of people the company almost certainly does still discriminate against.

One 2018 study confirmed previous research that showed, yes, such statements do signal to people of colour, as well as people with disabilities and those who are LGBTQ+, that they are less likely to face discrimination and restrictive stereo-typing in the hiring process.[22] (That, unfortunately, is not always a safe assumption.) At the same time, such language also greatly increases the perception of tokenism, a factor that dissuades those outside the status quo from applying and outweighs the benefits of such "we promise we're not racist" disclaimers. This effect was shown to be pronounced in cities with majority white populations, such as Houston, Denver, and San Francisco. There, more than two-thirds of job-seekers who were people of colour believed the statements signalled that they'd be token hires, and their consequent fear of tokenism often made people less likely to apply — 50 percent less likely, in fact, when it came to San Francisco.

People are right to be wary. In general, diversity training often backfires, and in some cases it actually increases animosity toward women and people of colour.[23] Participants fail to grasp the complex and often controversial aspects of dismantling racism and sexism in the workplace, and those same workplaces rarely make those complex discussions part of their regular workplace culture. All of which means that employees who are predisposed to fear challenges to the status quo leave their training rejecting the idea that they are "villains" and bemoaning the fact that they now have to "walk on eggshells" around people who "cannot take a joke." Even when positive effects are detected, they rarely last beyond a few days.[24] Individual bias and workplace culture are just too strong — and the workplace is often not truly diverse enough to reach change organically. Plus, as much as diversity training often triggers backlash, it also reinforces tokenism, sometimes putting women and people of colour into the "spokesperson" position whereby they either have to defend their experiences of discrimination or pretend they don't exist. As a result, they often, understandably, don't speak at all.

"Just once I want to speak to a room of white people who know they are there because they *are* the problem," wrote author Ijeoma Oluo in a March 2019 *Guardian* article that reminded readers anti-racism work is not about making white people feel better.[25] "Myself and many of the attendees of color often leave these talks feeling tired and disheartened, but I still show up and speak. I show up in the hopes that maybe, possibly, this talk will be the one that finally breaks through, or will bring me a step closer to the one that will. I show up and speak for people of color who can't speak freely, so that they might feel seen and heard. I speak because there are people of color in the room who need to hear that they shouldn't have to carry the burden of racial oppression, while those who benefit from that same oppression expect anti-racism efforts to meet their needs first."

That white fragility keeps power structures in check by turning the focus back on white people, painting their racism as misunderstood or unfair or both. Robin DiAngelo is the author of *White Fragility: Why It's So Hard for White People to Talk About Racism*. In a piece published on Medium, in June 2018, DiAngelo explained white people's tendency to shut down dialogue or frame themselves as victims as soon as dialogue in anti-racism workshops departs from abstract concepts. "The moment I name some racially problematic dynamic or action happening in the room *in the moment*— for example, 'Sharon, may I give you some feedback? While I understand it wasn't intentional, your response to Jason's story invalidates his experience as a black man' — white fragility erupts," she wrote. "Sharon defensively explains that she was misunderstood and then angrily withdraws, while others run in to defend her by re-explaining 'what she really meant.' The point of the feedback is now lost, and hours must be spent repairing this perceived breach. And, of course, no one appears concerned about Jason. Shaking my head, I think to myself, 'You asked me here to help you see your racism, but by god, I'd better not actually help you see your racism.'"[26]

Which loops us right back to the reality that diversity initiatives often don't work because white people simply cannot get over themselves. They write half-hearted policies that don't extend past tokenism. The appearance of diversity is valued over true inclusion. People hire people who look like them or share the same interests as them—preferential bias disguised as a spark of connection.[27] Managers give less or no weight to the poor performance of those who look like them, but significant weight to those who do not.[28] People who exemplify the status quo too often want a pat on the back for doing the right thing and yet they want to change nothing about themselves, maintaining the exact power they have, which is all of it.

In confronting this, though, some organizations may find a silver lining. For those that truly want to change, behavioural science has an answer: ditch the diversity initiatives and the long, difficult (if not futile) fight to eradicate organizational bias through individual improvement. Take the decisions out of the hands of individuals and infuse equality into the design of the company itself. In other words, redesign organizations so they cannot make biased choices in the first place.

In her book *What Works: Gender Equality by Design*, Iris Bohnet, a Harvard University professor and director of the school's Women and Public Policy Program, argues for companies to adopt increased transparency (so they can honestly assess how they're doing) and policies that require a critical mass of women and people of colour (something this book has examined in depth). Get rid of tests and evaluation tools that can invite individual bias. Don't go with your gut; it cannot be trusted. Embark on studies that evaluate how current practices work. Basically, realize that every current system invites bias and has to go; build new, better ones based on data, not on what you *think* will work. "Big data improves our understanding of what is broken and needs fixing, blind or comparative evaluation procedures help us hire the best instead of those who look the part, and role models shape what people think is possible," she wrote, adding that, under behaviour design, there is a clear definition of success, determined by a clear definition of engagement. Fair enough, but who gets to decide what those definitions are?

In answer to some of these inequity challenges, certain companies have started to rely on artificial intelligence to delete bias from their hiring and promotion practices. Which highlights another lesson: who gets to decide what's unbiased also matters. Amazon, for example, infamously scrapped its supposedly unbiased recruitment tool after the company discovered the AI had taught itself to discriminate against women. The computer models were taught to vet applicants using job applications from across a ten-year period—most of which came from men. Thus, it learned that male candidates were preferable and started to penalize applications that used the word "women's," as in "women's club."[29] Microsoft's chatbot, Tay, learned racism from interacting with users on Twitter to "get smarter."[30] In March 2019, the American government sued Facebook, claiming it employed discriminatory algorithms that excluded whole swaths of people from seeing housing ads.[31] These are only three examples of many that show humans have, essentially, created AI to be as racist and sexist as they are. Considering who has the power to create technology, however, maybe this shouldn't come as too much of a surprise.

CHAPTER 8

Slay All the Trolls

*A reimagining of women and technology
doesn't end with addressing harassment or
better representation in STEM*

IMAGINE IF, INSTEAD OF responding to every horrible thing on the internet, a piece of code could go into battle for you. In 2015, Sarah Ciston ventured onto Reddit. The more she dug into the platform, the more she saw the deep-rooted threads of misogyny and racism there.

The accepted slang and chat-room short forms alone were appalling.

SMV: Sexual Market Value.

Plate: Woman with whom you are in a non-exclusive sexual relationship.

LMR: Last Minute Resistance.

AWALT: All Women Are Like That.[1]

The Wall: The point in a woman's life where her ego and self-assessed view of her sexual market value exceed her actual sexual market value.

Hypergamy: The instinctual urge for women to seek out the best alpha available.[2]

Oh, and let's not forget this definition from the manosphere:

Feminism: A doctrine built on the pre-supposition of victimhood of women by men as a foundation of female identity. In its goals is always the utilization of the state to forcibly redress this claimed victim-ization....Feminism is therefore, a doctrine of class hatred, and violence.[3]

A notion had struck Ciston: why wasn't there a bot that could explain actual feminism to trolls on the internet? At the time, she was learning the programming language Python. A bot was something she could make. It was the best kind of light bulb moment—a fully formed idea had popped right into her head. She would build that bot.

It was the first time, in all her time learning coding, that she'd felt empowered by technology in a way that made her truly want to engage with it and to learn it. With a background in creative writing, she'd been drawn to digital technology in the first place because she was curious about how much the form of something shaped what could be said within it. How does the actual structure of something like technology and the digital worlds it embodies enable or disable what can happen within those structures? Would a woman operate and move through those worlds in a different way? "I had had a lot of stumbling blocks with feeling like I couldn't access or learn the technology. That it wasn't for me. That I actually wasn't a very good coder," she told me. "This was the first space where I felt like I had a project."

She had big questions about artificial intelligence: How does the fact that it's designed by looking through certain lenses, power structures, and biases shape what it is? Especially, she thought, when everybody assumes such technology to be neutral and rational? Truly, at the base of it, she wanted to know whether technology could intercede in a problem that was created by the technology itself. Could technology speak for her in a digital space where, as a "human, fleshy body," she wanted to retaliate against misogyny but didn't feel she had the power to do so? She had never felt as though she could speak *through* code as she'd seen others do. But this chatbot would let her.

She began beta-testing her new project in early 2016, programming it to scroll through Reddit and search for a compiled list of misogynistic terms. When it found one, like "cunt," the most-used slur, the bot would post a corresponding quote from a feminist author or thinker. To wit: "'A feminist is anyone who recognizes the equality and full humanity of women and men.' — Gloria Steinem."

Ciston called her bot Ladymouth.

During the initial beta tests, Ladymouth operated for twelve hours and three days on two forums, respectively, before it was banned from each. During that time, the bot posted sixty comments and received forty-four responses. A typical back-and-forth went something like this:

Ladymouth: "Women of today are still being called upon to stretch across the gap of male ignorance and to educate men as to our existence and our needs. This is an old and primary tool of all oppressors to keep the oppressed occupied with the master's concerns." — Audre Lorde

Misogynist Reddit user: Women are being called upon for anything? Oh please bitch. It's men who are being called upon. To grow the fuck up and stop falling for the shit tests from feminism. . . . Idiot men freed you. But you only have power when you're young and dumb. And you completely fail to realize that with power comes responsibility. And you'll never understand what that means. Best if we just put you back under control. Everyone, you included, would be happier.

Ciston told me that she had expected her bot to get yelled at. She had expected that some of the exchanges would be absurd. So, on both those fronts, she quipped, "it was completely successful." She was surprised, though, at exactly how successful the bot was. It took so little for Ladymouth to be yelled at. Even the suggestion that women deserve basic human rights provoked violent vitriol. It eventually got to the point where the bot no longer felt like an anonymous piece of code. Ciston had thought she'd be able to let it run and she'd go about her day, letting Ladymouth do the feminist work. But before she knew it, she'd be in the other room, cooking dinner, feeling anxious about how men were responding to the bot online. She started identifying with it. Weren't real women getting the same targeted messages? The comments began to feel personal, especially when some men started direct-messaging the bot. Going through the messages en masse, Ciston felt the cumulative weight of all that hatred.

There was one response to Ladymouth that made her laugh, though. A Reddit user on a men's rights group had written: "It's probably a bot. And very likely coded by a man, because you know ... coding."

When Diversity Becomes Diversion

Conversations about diversity in technology often start and stop with representation. *We need more women in tech. Tech is too white.* True and true. The numbers, by now, are well-known. In 2018 only 21.4 percent of Google's tech employees and roughly a quarter of the company's leaders worldwide were women; only 1.5 percent of tech employees were Black and 2.8 percent were Latinx.[4] At Apple, women made up 23 percent of tech employees and held 29 percent of leadership roles in 2018; 7 percent of Apple's tech staff were Black and 8 percent were Latinx.[5] Over at Facebook that same year, 21.6 percent of tech staff were women, and women occupied 30 percent of senior roles within the company; just under 5 percent of employees were Latinx and 3.5 percent were Black.[6] And so it goes. Each company has promised to do better, and each has seen a glacial growth in its diversity numbers.

Previous chapters have shown that gender equality, however, is more than counting the number of women in any given company; nor can inequality be solved by hiring practices that encourage tokenism but do little to address underlying company and industry culture. In short, discrimination and misogyny run deeper than numbers, which means the corresponding problems run deeper, too. Still, I don't highlight the slow growth in diversity to suggest we shouldn't care about such underwhelming representation; we should. The culture, the priorities, and the products of the tech industry are created by the people who participate in it and, right now, those people are, overwhelmingly, young white men. That means that until these numbers shift, *and* until we stop playing by the rules of the game, technology will remain a stronghold of a certain brand of masculinity—one that literally has the power to define our future. Or, as the epiphany of one *New Yorker* journalist, thousands of words in the making, proclaimed: "It suddenly occurred to me that the hottest tech start-ups are solving all the problems of being twenty years old, with cash on hand, because that's who thinks them up."[7]

That, ultimately, is the problem with letting the conversation get stuck on diversity in the tech field: we never get around to imagining how technology itself might change. How it *needs* to change. Consider the long rehabilitation of Uber, one of tech's most notoriously toxic companies. For context, its diversity numbers mirror those of other big tech companies. In 2018, women at Uber held 21 percent of leadership roles; just 2.8 percent of those in leadership roles were Black, and 1.4 percent were Latinx. Only 18 percent of the company's tech staff were women, 2.6 percent were Black, and 3 percent were Latinx.[8] As is well-known by now, cofounder and CEO Travis Kalanick resigned from the company in June 2017 amidst a growing list of scandals that included a public accusation from a former employee, Susan Fowler, that the company fostered a culture of sexual harassment. In a much-circulated blog post Fowler shared her experience with the company:

On my first official day rotating on the team, my new manager sent me a string of messages over company chat. He was in an open relationship, he said, and his girlfriend was having an easy time finding new partners but he wasn't. He was trying to stay out of trouble at work, he said, but he couldn't help getting in trouble, because he was looking for women to have sex with. It was clear that he was trying to get me to have sex with him, and it was so clearly out of line that I immediately took screenshots of these chat messages and reported him to HR.

Both her HR department and members of upper management agreed that she was being harassed, but added that it was this man's first offence and they didn't want to punish him too severely. Fowler was told he was a "high performer" and that it was "probably just an innocent mistake on his part." She was given the choice to either leave his team, the one that best suited her expertise, or stay, she wrote, with the acknowledged expectation that she would likely receive a poor performance review, but there was nothing HR could do about it because she had been given *choice*. She left the team, and after a year left the company.[9]

Given this environment, perhaps it's no great shock, then, that it took until May 2018 for Uber to revamp policies that previously locked drivers and riders into a mandatory arbitration hearing in cases of sexual misconduct or assault. From no angle could the company be conceived of as one designed for women.[10] With the same announcement, it also scrapped a confidentiality agreement that had prohibited anyone from sharing their experience and speaking out. The policy change wasn't a coincidence; not only did Uber want to clean up its image, it was facing a lawsuit claiming it had created a service conducive to sexual assault.[11] A few months later, its "Chief People Officer" — i.e., its head of HR — left the company after accusations surfaced that she'd repeatedly ignored internal allegations of racial discrimination and had made derogatory remarks about the company's global head of diversity.[12]

The tension between diversity and actual equity — by which people have an equitable share of power, status, and influence[13] — permeates all areas of STEM, right down to the educational level. Take, for example, the infuriating experience one seventeen-year-old girl shared with me. She was the only female on a team of fifteen students who were tasked with building an electric vehicle for a major engineering competition. As part of the project, students presented to various teams of potential investors, with hopes of earning more funding to build their car. Keen, she had already sketched a prototype design for the car. But, rather than look at it, her team insisted that, instead of working on the car, she focus on the investor presentations. At first, she assumed they were simply acknowledging that she was a good presenter. She knew she was. Then, one of her fellow students let slip that they thought they had a better chance of getting money if she were the face of the group. Wasn't everybody keen on including girls in STEM fields now? "It felt as if they were taking advantage of a system that was used to overturn the oppression that women in STEM had to face," she said. "I agreed to do the presentation because I knew they were right, but I refused to exclude myself from the engineering part of the project."

It's not a big stretch to draw a line from that teen's experience to that of the thirtysomething woman who told me about her experience working at a major tech company. After the woman who had hired her left, a man became her boss. He had little understanding of the role she had been brought on to perform, and soon combined her job with that of another woman. "We'd each been hired for our expertise, but that had been erased without even talking to us," she said. "After that, they immediately began to exclude us from meetings, reports, and even conversations with the very clients we were tasked to take care of. I saw my role diminish in stature and purpose and impact. I went from leading strategy discussions with stakeholders to silently taking notes, in a very short amount of time." Tasked as the new note-taker, she found it difficult to participate in meetings or lead an agenda. As a direct result, she found it more difficult to build relationships with stakeholders and get the information she needed. When she raised the issue with her boss, she was told to take better notes.

"When bonus time came around, I was told that because none of my bosses had set any goals for me...I was ineligible for the payout that every other person on the team got," she said. "Of course, no one ever got a bonus for being good at taking notes."

Incidents like these underscore how little we've thought about diversity beyond simple optics and the shrug of *because...ladies.* Technology companies may say they want women and people of colour, and schools may encourage these demographics to sign up for tech clubs, but they haven't thought much about how to support them once they're in the room. Numbers rise through a lens of gaining tokens, not talent. As a consequence, some women and people of colour arrive and then crumble under the culture. They grow so tired from earning, and then keeping, their place. They're downright exhausted from trying to fit into a field that is still not fundamentally for them. So, of course, once they're there, they do not have the opportunity to spend much time thinking about what they might create. How do you ponder innovation, invention, and new ways to imagine the world when you're simply trying to survive? Even when women are in the room, and that room is not overrun with IRL trolls, it can feel like we're intruders, carefully navigating spaces men trample through with ease. But we stay because we want to love it. Or we leave because it breaks our hearts. That's the trap we're in.

Whenever I now think of the complexities of challenging STEM's narrowness, I find myself reflecting on the question-and-answer portion of a tech event I went to, in late February 2019, called "deBrogramming App Studies." If any place should have been a vision of a feminist tech space, it was this one. The room of fifty was about half women, two of the three presenters were women, and the entire theme of the night was, after all, focused on expunging the "bro"-ness from one of tech's new(ish) fields of study. One presenter, a researcher from Ireland, made a point of repeatedly asking "Do you ever feel like you don't fit?" and "Do you ever feel like the technology you use doesn't work for you?" The answer to each of these questions, it was suggested, took the form of the classic breakup salve: *It's not you, it's them.* She also spoke openly about the difficulties in getting anybody who's not a white man — the default tech-industry employee — to show up to things like open learning sessions. "Just because they're advertised as being open to everybody," she said, "it doesn't mean everybody will show up" — because women and people of colour can read the fine print of who belongs in a space, even if it's in invisible ink. Another presenter talked about the overwhelming "bro"-ness on apps like Tinder (hello, eggplant; hello, unsolicited dick pic). At the end of the night, the "bro" could not be escaped, even there.

After some others had asked questions, a young man raised his hand in response to the presenter's detailed explanation of her research on the rampant sexual violence and harassment on platforms like Tinder — and Tinder's tone-deaf response to it, which was to debut what the company called its "menprovement" initiative in 2017. (This allowed users to throw a virtual drink or send an eye-roll gif;[14] many women felt it trivialized the problem, and some men felt it engaged in misandry.[15]) The young man with a question wanted to know if the presenter had heard of Lego's massively multiplayer online (MMO) game that got cancelled several years ago because people kept building "dicks." Moderators couldn't keep up with scrubbing all the non-family-friendly content and had to scrap the game.[16] He was laughing. Was, like, that harassment too? Did the presenter know about it? What did she think?

Nobody asked another question after that. A male presenter, who was also acting as a de facto moderator, urged the audience to continue. "Is this really the question we're going to end on?" he asked, shaking his head. "Okay, then, we're going to end on dick detection."

In the same way, Sarah Ciston is rarely able to present her Ladymouth research — which she has turned into both live poetry and video art installation — without a man admonishing her for trolling the trolls. It's as if she was breaking some gender code by, first, using the technology, and second, using it to *not* be the bigger person. It's the burden, Ciston tells me: women are expected to be nice, to educate people, to always invite them into the conversation. Her chatbot is a prime example of what women might build if they weren't being kept busy advocating for their right to be there and speaking out about equality. What they might build if they had access to the funding, research, and teams. What women might build if they were building for themselves. Sure, men might also be invested in ridding digital spaces of violent, hateful rhetoric against women, but this particular piece of technology was not built with them *first* in mind. With Ladymouth, Ciston has stepped far out of bounds, in multiple ways, earning a degree of power in the process. Many people would like to stuff her back into her expected place. They'd also like to dismiss the severity of the violence online. "When people say, 'Aren't you just adding fuel to the fire?' they're kind of missing the scale to the issue," she said. "As if my tiny match would do anything to this fucking forest fire that is misogyny and toxic masculinity."

Oh, the Things We Would Build

Around 2016, it became popular to debate whether techno-logical innovation was, in fact, slowing down. Numerous media articles and research studies pointed out that while it had become conventional wisdom to believe in the accelera-tion of invention, technology had not drastically evolved. People were not making new things. "We can expect a significant slow down in the years to come," warned one article.[17] "In a three-month period at the end of 1879, Thomas Edison tested the first practical electric lightbulb, Karl Benz invented a workable internal-combustion engine, and a British-American inventor named David Edward Hughes transmitted a wireless signal over a few hundred meters," lamented another in the MIT *Technology Review* (naming all men, naturally), adding that even modern-era technology wasn't so impressive. "Think the PC and the Internet are important? Compare them with the dramatic decline in infant mortality, or the effect that indoor plumbing had on living conditions."[18] Past innovation, added a *Washington Post* article, meant "finding ways to increase Americans' material well-being by reducing the cost and improving the quality of goods," whereas today's innovation focuses on small technological shifts that do little to improve everyone's base quality of life.[19]

I wonder how different the technology forecasters' visions might look if it weren't the same demographic endlessly inventing our future. So, too, does Sarah Sharma, director of the McLuhan Centre for Culture and Technology, whom I first spoke with about the #MeToo movement. Looking at the most ubiquitous technology today — the kind that has changed the texture of everyday life — she pointed out, as others have, that a lot of the latest innovation is really just duplicating the "Mom" role in robot form.

"We're inventing the post-Mom economy, which — not to insult mothers or anything — should make us all happier and richer and finally bring us the leisurely future we were promised 50 years ago," argued one *Newsweek* article, dubbed "Silicon Valley Needs Moms!"[20] An instalment of the web comic *Joy of Tech* that circulated around this same time joked that developers were merely replicating technology to replace mom's loving reminders: "It's a beautiful day. Go outside and play!" (Fitbit); "Don't use that tone with me, young man" (Siri asking, "Could you please rephrase the question?"); "I'm not your maid" (Roomba).[21] Since then, Mommy apps have only become more entrenched: TaskRabbit for chores, Uber and Lyft to drive you to the mall, LiveBetter to alleviate your boredom, Rinse to clean your clothes, Skip the Dishes to feed you, and on and on.

The singular focus on Mommy apps, warned Sharma, is not as innocuous — or as universally beneficial — as people want it to seem. "The classed and heteronormative obsession with work–life balance, efficiency, and time management displayed by Mommy's-basement apps suggest that one can escape patriarchy or gendered labor in an instant—one just needs the right app! But this propaganda obscures the inescapable realities of care work that so many women, people of color, and precarious workers undertake out of survival," she wrote in the *Boston Review* a few months before we met in fall 2018.[22] As she later told me, the endless reimagining of technology as mere replications of women's traditional roles, without doing anything to change those roles, keeps us from creating a future that looks any different. It says, over and over, *this is what innovation looks like*, while simultaneously excluding women from the reconstruction of their supposed roles. What might a feminist vision of care technology look like? We've hardly had a chance to find out. Or, as Sharma put it at the close of her article: "The technology that comes out of Mommy's basement will never liberate Mommy *from* the basement. It is about control and the maintenance of power."

At the same time, before many women and people of colour can imagine building their own jetpacks and flying cars, they want to imagine what it would be like to be safe. Such a goal is, in its own way, revolutionary—a direct response to the types of things we might make if we weren't driven by the needs and wants of a particular subset of the population. Because if STEM has failed to account for women in its design, so too has the engineering and design of most things, including the cities we live in. Perhaps this isn't wholly surprising. Over the course of history, "respectable" women in cities all over the world were expected not to leave the house, or at least not without the protective presence of a chaperone. Nobody really guessed that one day women or people of colour would be traversing the city, with the presumed power to engage with it as the men who built it might. I say "presumed" because it hasn't really worked out that way.

How to Engineer a Feminist City

Today, the design of both urban and suburban landscapes often means that many people still don't have the freedom of mobility that most white men have. In fall 2018, the Rudin Center surveyed New Yorkers about their travel habits and learned that women spend a median extra $25 to $50 each month on taxis, Uber, or Lyft for safety reasons — for example, when travelling alone at night — because they perceive such methods to be safer than public transit. The median extra cost for men was $0.22. "The financial discrepancy raises red flags in late-night service safety," wrote the study's lead author, Sarah Kaufman. And there are implications for women's capacity to safely take part in the economy of night work, like nursing, janitorial work, and bartending.[23] Other, similar studies have found that women also take more onerous, expensive, time-sucking routes than men, owing to household and child-care duties, and this can influence their decision to take or stay in a job.[24] This isn't even taking disabilities into account, and how vastly inaccessible (and thus expensive) our cities can be for those who have mobility issues. Nor does it take into account how a person's various identity intersections may contribute to their safety concerns, further curtailing movement.

"With most companies, institutions, and corporations, the culture was not necessarily designed to put women forward or to have women in mind," says Aisha Addo, founder of the company DriveHER, based in the Greater Toronto

Area. The rising gig economy (or what Sharma might call the "Mommy app" economy) did not, she added, give serious consideration to the safety or mobility of women, even though much of it focused on transportation, whether that's a gig worker zipping around the city or a passenger in a car. Whenever something new was designed, she said, nobody really thought about how it would "work for us." As a ride-sharing service for women only, both at the driver and passenger level, DriveHER, on the other hand, was designed entirely around the "work for us" mission. "When we talk about safe space, for instance, at DriveHER, we're not just talking about putting a woman behind the wheel, we're not just talking about having a woman as the passenger," Addo said, "we're talking about the entire experience." A safe space, she added, is not just about making an *existing* space comfortable or free from violence. "A safe space is thinking from the very beginning, *What is my encounter with you? What is my experience with you? And how does that translate into action?*"

Addo founded the company after her own uncomfortable late-night cab ride home to Mississauga from Toronto. The driver's conversation quickly turned sexual, and he asked Addo personal questions, and also whether she lived alone. I've had similar rides, and so have many women I've known, including a man who remarked on my "exotic" looks and insisted on dropping me off at my street address, even though I'd only entered the intersection; another man who demanded to know why I wasn't married, while insisting he needed to find a good woman to date (*hint, hint*); and another man who, upon learning I was heading to the nutritionist, asked if I needed to lose weight and speculated on whether or not it was working. The only time I've ever felt safe in an Uber, Lyft, or cab was on the rare occasion when my driver was a woman—but more than three-quarters of Uber's drivers are men.[25] And still, for many women I know, these options feel *safer* than public transit at night. Many of us, including me, brush off these incidents as a creepy but necessary gamble—a still-awful experience, but a less awful one than we might find on public transit. It's worth asking, though, as Addo did, why we think it *has* to be that way.

For Addo, DriveHER is not just an app. It's a way to address the uncertainty of safe transportation and how it curtails a woman's ability to move through the city, thus diminishing her opportunities. Similar questions of safety, mobility, and design were on AnnaLise Trudell's mind when she successfully pitched the idea of London, Ontario, becoming a United Nations Safe City to councillors in 2017. As the UN puts it, the Safe Cities initiative (not to be confused with sanctuary cities) is "the first-ever global programme that develops, implements, and evaluates tools, policies and comprehensive approaches on the prevention of and response to sexual harassment and other forms of sexual violence against women and girls across different settings."[26] Trudell, who is a manager at London's Anova, a shelter plus counselling and resource centre for abused women and their children, wanted to see how a city's very geography influenced the safety of those who lived in it. While London isn't the only Safe City project in Canada—others include Montreal, Vancouver, Edmonton, and Winnipeg—it is one of the few in the world that has undertaken the initiative using geo-mapping.

While most other cities have used more conventional methods, such as focus groups, Trudell wanted to gather quantitative data using crowd-mapping and -sourcing technology. Why not use technology to make a city more humane, livable, safe? She wanted to be able to see where people felt most unsafe — where the hotspots were, and what the "geography of harm" looked like in London. "It's broader than the moment of 'someone hurt me here,'" she told me. "It's 'I feel unsafe here for all kinds of reasons.'" One of those reasons might be a physical attack, yes, but feeling unsafe could include a multitude of cross-sections between spatial use, belonging, and a perceived threat to safety: say, cat-calling and leering, but also unlit parking garages and isolated transit stops. The map itself can be seen by members of the public, who are all able to drop pins, but only project members can view the reasons someone might give for feeling unsafe. When I met with Trudell in late October 2018, a few months before she and her team had finished collecting the data, they'd already discovered that about 70 percent of the pins were related to sexual violence, by its broadest definition, which includes things like street harassment.

"We don't want women to navigate the world based on that map," Trudell told me. Meaning, she didn't want a Band-Aid solution that focused merely on alerting women to the "hot spots" and doing little else — just another solution that limited them. Trudell stressed that the project was not an "academic" one, either. Stakeholders included the city council, its urban planning department, the London Transit Commission, and the city's police force — all groups that had the power to transform how the city operated. To create their new Safe City, these groups would examine the gathered data and use it to plan real, concrete change. Physically, the city would not even *look* the same after they were done. That could mean adding street lamps to public parks, or it could mean changing bus stop locations. It could even mean rerouting roads or creating pedestrian-only streets. They'd let the data — and, by extension, women's own stories, feelings, and experiences—determine how their future city would work.

Certainly, that would include changes to the city's downtown core. I met Trudell there at a bright and trendy-looking coffee shop with pastel Eames-style chairs, polished concrete floors, and white-painted brick walls. Outside, a sign announced: "Coffee is always a good idea." It seemed quaint and quiet, but Trudell told me that, just a block away, at the city's core intersection, was the place that had so far received the most pin drops: more than six hundred. I walked by the spot later, looking at the jostling line of commuters waiting for the bus in front of a church courtyard. Yes, I could see feeling vulnerable there stuck in line, sandwiched between strangers, especially at night.

Women like Addo and Trudell might not be creating new technology—in fact, Addo quipped to me, "I'm in the business of women, not necessarily in the business of technology"—but they are devising applications that are tailored for new audiences and users. For *us*. At their core, what they are really doing is changing power balances. So, naturally, both initiatives have been attacked.

Trudell was hacked one day, she told me, by someone dropping over 200,000 pins in a matter of twelve hours, all full of useless data. That wasn't the worst, she added—although, she grimly joked, "It does show that people are invested in fucking with us." The worst was reading the online comments section after three women shared their stories of navigating the city with local media. People were debating who was more "rapeable," said Trudell, with much of the discussion focused on a young Muslim woman who wore a hijab. Meanwhile, DriveHER was back in testing mode after a man hacked the platform and proudly went public, boasting to media about his data breach. Addo was forced to put the company on hiatus while she made sure it wouldn't happen again. She knew she wasn't targeted randomly; they wanted to focus on a company that catered to women and their safety. The man wanted to make them feel *unsafe*. "There are a lot of giants that we have to slay on a daily basis," she said, "but you have to keep going."

Break the Internet

As a digital editor, I'm someone who spends most of my days (and nights) online. I was lucky enough to start my digital career working largely with women. Unlike others whose working lives intersect with technology, I did not have to witness a "bro"-saturated workplace, live with daily mansplaining, or have my skills and knowledge constantly undermined because of my gender. Offline, I have never been made to feel like I don't belong. Online, though, it can be a different story. Every time I've published a story in a digital space, the trolls have arrived to slay me. From the comments I've read, it's clear that I am the villain — poisoning a place of presumed pristine maleness with my lady-mouth — and they are the heroes. I've been called a race-traitor, an idiot, a bitch, and various other iterations of things horrible people call other people they don't like. I've been told to get raped and killed, sometimes in that order, sometimes reversed. Think about that for a second.

I don't use social media because I do not find this discourse to be beneficial to my life. Admittedly, I often wonder if I've made the right decision in opting out. It isn't only that I cannot help others turn the tide against such online violence if I'm not on social media, although there is that. It's that I often feel I'm missing out: on good conversations, on marketing opportunities for my writing, on connection. Our online lives have become part of our everyday lives, offering many people a sense of richness and community that they might not otherwise have. I know that the ability to transcend geographic boundaries has saved many people from loneliness, from shame, from disconnection. Like anything else, social media has positive aspects that present a foil to all its negativity. Still, those fleeting feelings of isolation are never enough to make me wade through the inevitable messages about how I must be the stupidest person on the planet, the threats of bodily mutilation, and worse. (If you don't know how it can get worse, then—bless you!—you have never had to spend large amounts of time online. Rejoice!)

Even so, there's no question that I move more easily through technology spaces than many others. Takara Small is a Toronto-based technology journalist, web developer, and founder of the non-profit Venture Kids, which aims to help under-served and low-income communities learn how to code. Despite its myriad challenges, Small was drawn to tech because of what she sees as the even greater multitude of opportunities within it—something she believes has the potential to outweigh its lack of diversity. When it takes diverse voices into account, technology can help people create some truly amazing things. It can change the lives of users *and* creators. It can uplift entire communities. After all, technology is, by its nature, a field that makes an infinite number of once-impossible things possible.

None of this means that Small is naive when it comes to the incredible challenges that form a fortress-like wall around diverse participation in technology. As a Black woman, she knows first-hand how rare it is to find a face like hers in a sea of white—and, consequently, what that means when she walks into tech-centred spaces.

"It's very apparent," she told me, "and I say this all the time, that whenever I enter a conference or enter a room I might not necessarily be welcomed with open arms. I can tell you so many stories." Small attended one major U.S.-based conference while working as a journalist for a major publication — and here she carefully clarifies that this type of incident is not specific to this conference, but something she encounters often in tech spaces. It was the first year she'd gone to the event. At some point, she went to walk into the dedicated press room, as any journalist would. A white woman stopped her, telling her the room was for journalists only. Small assured her she was media. The woman assumed Small was confused. Perhaps she was looking for the booth area? The not-so-subtle assumption underlying that question: Small must be a "booth girl," helping to showcase products. She has been mistaken for a booth girl, or for hotel staff. In this case, Small pulled out her press pass. The woman asked her how she got it, suggesting it wasn't hers. So, Small pulled out her wallet and produced her ID.

"I saw her immediately blush a very deep crimson red, and then welcome me with open arms," said Small. "And every time I walked into the press room after that, she would go out of her way to offer me coffee, offer me food, ask me if I needed a phone charger." It wasn't the first time something like that had happened, she added, and she knew it wouldn't be the last.

Constantly encountering such biased, and outright racist, behaviour hasn't pushed her out of the industry, however. It has only made her more ambitious. Every time she gets admonished for not knowing where a bathroom is at a conference (something she told me happens often) it only makes her that much more focused on creating a more diverse space within technology. Venture Kids came out of that determination. "Under-served" does not have to mean "racialized," she stressed. Such considerations should also encompass those who are LGBTQ, disabled, newcomers to Canada, and more. As someone who grew up in a small farming town, she also wants to ensure that rural children are given greater opportunities to learn coding skills. For her, the future of technology must incorporate diversity in all of its forms. If we want to get anywhere *different*, she believes, we can't afford to keep thinking in the same binaries: men and women, white people and people of colour, rich and poor, ability and disability. We have to embrace intersectionality. We have to think creatively.

For many people who inhabit the technology sphere, a different way of thinking extends past the things we make with technology to the internet itself. They ask: What if the mistake came at the very beginning? What if, to fix the toxic inequality that permeates the internet, we have to break it first? To do so would mean pushing for deeper solutions, ones that question the very purpose of the internet and its model of, as T. L. Cowan and Jasmine Rault put it to me, a maximum network, maximum exposure, sharing economy. In other words, it would mean questioning what we've previously been sold as the internet's greatest strength: its ability to connect everything and everyone, give us all the most massive platforms and soapboxes we could ever desire, and allow us to access and publish every piece of information invented, to live online, seemingly forever. Prizing those things isn't necessarily wrong, but even critiques of our hyper-connected lives rarely consider how, practically, the internet could look any different.

Cowan and Rault are both faculty at the University of Toronto, where they study digital cultures through a trans-feminist and queer lens. They first came up against these questions when they set out to create a digital archive of the Montreal-based queer cabaret Meow Mix.[27] With grant money in hand to gather photos and stories from the event, held monthly for several years, they wanted to create an online networked space where people in Canada could be in conversation with people in, say, Buenos Ares, all learning from each other. They could discuss cabaret as a political act, engage in each other's social lives, talk about survival strategies. Everybody would discuss the methods they used to address their specific, local issues, and they'd all learn from each other. In this way, Cowan and Rault could be part of a growing movement that's questioning how women and others are erased from digital spaces—and, more than that, how they're often exploited.

It's this final point—the idea of complicity and exploitation—that gave the two academics pause. Yes, the project sounded great. But would it have unintentional consequences for those people who would join the archive, were it to go online and be connected to the entire digital world? "As soon as it was going to go online," said Rault, "we were like, 'Oh damn, this does not feel right.' And it didn't feel right for a lot of different reasons."

For starters, they didn't have everybody's names. Even if they did, though, Rault added, they began to wonder if it would be enough. They realized they wanted to ask people if it was okay if they used video of their work in the online archive. That would mean tracking down dozens of people who performed in the 1990s. What if their names had changed? What if some of them had transitioned? What if, in trying to find performers, said Rault, they set off an "algorithmic detonation system across Google" that put people at risk? Every conventional research method encouraged in the Online Age, they realized, came with huge ethical pitfalls, particularly for those who wanted to do research in a way that valued the people and practices they were studying. Together, they began to ask new questions: What are we putting online? How? What are we keeping *offline*? What are better ways to engage with the extreme latitudes digital research can provide? And, ultimately: Just because we can put all this material—this content—online, *should we*? They'd started to make a mistake, but in stopping themselves they decided to fuse the internet and their research in ways few others were doing.

"You can never assume you know what somebody wants. And that's just basic feminist consent," said Cowan. Seeing your work (and yourself) used online in a way you never intended can feel like a "violence of scale," they added. In terms of a cabaret performance, it could be that the original person only said yes to participating in the show because they knew it would be seen by a small audience of mostly friends. To see the scale of that change without consent, added Cowan—an audience reaching into the thousands, with exposure to misogynistic and transphobic trolls—is a massive potential violation of that initial performance. The silver lining in all this, said Rault, is that both the lived experience of harm—losing control over online content; experiencing digital violence; feeling the mass influence of toxic social media—and the fatigue of constantly navigating your life through today's digital expectations and parameters is fuelling change. People know something feels off. It's just a matter of figuring out what, exactly, isn't working, and why. Cowan believes that urgent sense of "not working" is hurtling toward a Take Back the Internet moment: finding a way to recreate an online space that prioritizes safety, vulnerability, and connection, while also protesting against violence.

Practically, that could mean online spaces that don't stay online forever—not necessarily because they've done harm and need to be taken offline, but because they were envisioned on a different scale. It also means a willingness to take content offline that *is* doing harm. Or it could mean gathering information in ways that are participatory, collaborative, and transparent, not extractive. In many ways, it's as simple and as difficult as asking for permission to include something or somebody—as simple and as difficult as believing the internet, for some people, is not an easy, free, and infinitely large playground where we all share information and content. Beyond that, it could mean restricting access to some people, or closing access for some parts of the year.

Take, for example, one content management system (CMS) that's gaining ground, called Mukurtu.[28] As an Indigenous-created, grassroots project, Mukurtu is designed to help communities manage, share, and digitally compile their heritage in ways that are both ethical and culturally relevant. At the core of this CMS are cultural protocols that allow those using it to determine "fine-grained levels of access" based on what a community needs: from completely open to strictly controlled. Everything is there, but not everybody—especially those outside the community—needs to see it.

For many people, the idea of *not* seeing something is antithetical to the internet itself. After all, we've been told that's where we derive our power online: as sort of Great and All-Seeing Wizards of Oz, with the apparent freedom to say and take and do whatever we want. But Oz was an illusion, his power smoke and mirrors. Breaking the internet doesn't have to mean making it smaller, more restrictive. It doesn't have to mean increasing regulations (although both those things may be *part* of it—hello, Facebook, I see you). What it does mean is letting the humanity back in. It means asking what equitable digital spaces would look like. It means, as Rault put it, designing these spaces according to anti-colonial, trans-feminist, and queer cultural protocols. "Honestly," they said, "it's not an easy thing to see. People are cobbling it together all over." The point is that they've started. "It's fun and frustrating and slow," added Cowan. "That's what we all know now: most things that are ethical move quite slowly."

And if that breaks the ultra-fast, too-big internet — good. We're already building something better, something for *us*.

CHAPTER 9

Unconventional Women

*From motherhood to politics, women are
redefining old narratives for the better*

IN MANY PLACES AROUND the world, there is perhaps no
unconventional endeavour that thrusts women into the
spotlight as much as a career in politics. And because there
are also few other pursuits that present such opportunity
for power, little else can match the extreme resulting pressure for women in politics to be ultra, well, *conventional*.
When media, campaign managers, and voters aren't busy
telling a woman in politics to *get out*, they're busy demanding she become the ultimate Mom-in-Chief. It's as if they
want to mitigate the potential for power with assurance
that, underneath it all, women are still members of the supporting, second class. Women candidates are often framed
as benignly, conservatively attractive (or else benignly, conservatively unattractive), their pantsuits rendering them
softer imitations of powerful men — ready to take on a
PTA meeting, not a country. Nonetheless, during election

cycles, certain members of the media still over-analyze their appearance, whether they'll have the emotional chops for the job, and, most of all, how it will affect their home life. That is, how it will affect their role as mother. No matter her experience, it seems, or her childbearing status, the ability of a woman in politics is often measured by her (perceived) ability to mother.

We're simply obsessed with the idea of politics and motherhood. Take, for example, Hillary Clinton, who is the mother of an adult daughter. Her election team worked hard to frame her as, in the words of her husband Bill, "the best mother in the whole world."[1] Or consider the top Google search for German chancellor Angela Merkel, which is about how many children she has. (The answer is: she has no biological children.)[2] We might even point to New Zealand's prime minister Jacinda Ardern, who was celebrated for being the second world leader to give birth while in office. Ardern is an interesting example. Pessimistically, one could argue that her pop-progressive fame got a boost from her blatantly visible motherhood—which put her nurturing femininity on full, constant display. Given everything we know about women in politics, it's an easy conclusion to draw. And yet, there was something subversive about seeing Ardern walk the literal halls of power with her rotund, pregnant belly. Just by doing her job well, while pregnant, she interrupted the constant pendulum swing of the contradictory, can't-win expectations for women, power, and motherhood. Because while society likes to remind women their *real* job is to be a good mother, rewarding or punishing them accordingly, it likes it far less when women set their own terms for motherhood and their careers. Ardern not only defied every assumption we have about women, politics, and motherhood by breaking convention, she doubly defied assumptions when she announced that her partner, to whom she was not married, would be raising their child as a stay-at-home father.

Months later, Ardern was celebrated yet again for showing the world how to do power differently. The day after deadly attacks on two mosques in Christchurch shook the world, Ardern was photographed wearing a black hijab, her sorrow plain on her face, visiting Muslim and refugee families. The soon-to-be viral picture showed Ardern embracing a Muslim woman who wore a lavender head scarf. Many people around the world interpreted the gesture exactly as Ardern meant it: *you are us, we are you, the country is united in grief.*

This photo didn't lodge in my heart and mind because Ardern was there showing the expected womanly compassion; keep in mind that she also acted swiftly to introduce new gun-control measures. It struck me, and others, so deeply because she was there acting *human*. She presented through her actions another, alternative approach to power—not because of any innate biological qualities, and not because she was expected to fulfill the side role of being nice or motherly. But because, to her, that's what power looked like in that moment: a shared connection across communities, a common elevation. Such expressions of power and leadership have the potential to benefit all of us, which is of course what makes them so scary to the dominant ranks.

To give more women a chance to do power, and politics, differently, we also have to give them a chance to break convention. We have to help them, and, as we've seen in other chapters, we have to show them that such convention-breaking is possible. People have to see that, yes, it's possible to be both a mother and a politician. It's possible to *not* be a mother and be a politician. They have to know what it looks like.

Nagwan Al-Guneid is the president of the Calgary-based organization Ask Her, which was founded to help reach gender parity within Calgary's city council. As such, Al-Guneid thinks about representation and power in politics. She thinks about parity and diversity. Challenging who we see as Canada's political leaders. There are specific barriers for under-represented populations in government, too, she told me, and we can't successfully describe the problem and craft the solutions by referring to those who are excluded simply as "women."

"We can't just say 'women,'" she pointed out, and assume we are including all women in the discussion. Many women face different barriers. Many women experience different levels of access to power. Many women have different networks, connections, and levels of financial wealth. And, yes, said Al-Guneid, a new mother herself, many women are also worried about how they'll juggle being a parent with running for office. Will it make them a bad mother?

Women are all-too-aware of the numerous barriers they face, said Al-Guneid, and it often leads to them self-selecting out of politics. When I spoke to her, Ask Her was focused on the 2021 municipal election. On average, she told me, women need to be asked seven times before they agree to run for office.[3] Certainly, many women politicians have spoken about needing to be asked, repeatedly, before they stepped up — and they've spoken about the fact that they needed to be asked at all, as opposed to coming forward on their own initiative.[4] Research has shown that the gap begins early, when a woman is university-aged. One American study revealed that men were twice as likely to say they planned to run for office; women were 50 percent more likely to say they'd never run. Even when asked which upper-echelon jobs they found most appealing, imagining all received equal salaries, men were twice as likely to desire a future position in Congress. A young woman would rather be a salesperson than a mayor. In fact, 90 percent of the young women surveyed in the study chose a non-political position as their dream job. That's despite being as politically engaged as young men when it came to things like voting, participating in a rally, or discussing political issues on social media.[5]

Researchers named it the "ambition gap" in women. And, they argued, that gap was instilled in women from a young age. Growing up, girls were far less likely than boys to be presented with politics as a valid career ambition. While both fathers and mothers were less likely to talk about politics with their daughters over dinner, on the whole most kids were equally exposed to political discussion in their homes. Daughters were even *more* likely to talk about certain political issues with their parents, particularly same-sex marriage. Still, more than 40 percent of the men surveyed said their parents encouraged them to enter politics at a young age, compared to 29 percent of women — who were, in turn, more likely to receive clear discouragement. Whether it's grandparents and friends or coaches and teachers, most influential figures in a young woman's life were significantly less likely to tell her to one day run for office.

If we want to boost the presence of women in politics, says Al-Guneid, we have to start by realizing that we first need to help women and girls see themselves in decision-making roles. They have to see themselves in office. Instead, they're told from the beginning that it is not for them, through both explicit and implicit messaging, which deters their ambition from even flickering. Maybe it's no wonder, then, that while women are more likely to vote, they are also less likely to speak up for their political views or try to persuade someone to their side.[6] How do we overcome that?

One thing is certain. If we ever want to make it to a point where women can explore and seek out these alternate visions of themselves, we need to get over our aversion toward women who want power. Because if women face an apparent ambition gap, that's not solely on them. It's on us—all of us who, collectively, want to contain their ambition. Stifle it. Make it go away. Demand they be something else—something *conventional*—instead.

Women Can Win

Given today's tumultuous political climate, the utter lack of women in office, and the general disparagement of women in leadership roles, you might reasonably assume that we don't generally like the idea of women in politics. The reality, as usual, is more complicated. Dating back to the 1980s, studies have repeatedly shown that, when they run, women are just as likely as men to win. *And* they are just as likely to raise as much money as men, and sometimes more.[7] In the United States, Gallup has been asking the public since 1937 if they would vote for a woman as president, providing she was qualified for the job. In that first year, about a third of Americans said yes. By 2011, that number was up to 95 percent.[8] While this suggests a gender-neutral political system—a baffling claim to swallow for anybody who's paid even cursory attention to American politics in the past five years—those affirmations do come with some caveats. Less than one-third of Americans who would vote for a woman said they would do so with enthusiasm; one in seven still expressed reservations. Meaning, sure, they'd vote for a woman in theory, but perhaps not *that* (nasty) woman. Beyond that, research shows that women candidates are usually far more qualified than male ones, and that this exceptionality can help mitigate the gender penalty on election day.[9]

Still, when women run in elections in general, they win at roughly the same rates as men and accrue roughly the same number of votes, if not more.[10] Remember that Clinton famously beat Trump by nearly 3 million in 2016's popular vote.[11] All of which makes the overwhelming scarcity of women in politics even more frustrating — women are exceedingly unlikely to reach the supposed gender-neutral end stage. This boomerangs back to the idea of an ambition gap. In addition to receiving less encouragement to pursue politics, young girls are socialized out of the professions that most commonly feed into politics: business and law. They are also, traditionally, fiercely socialized to not be competitive, and to disavow those traits viewed as compatible with the political sphere, particularly our newest, high-octane modern version: anger, assertiveness, aggression. These gender expectations run deep, forming persistent ideas about who belongs in politics and which archetypical qualities succeed. And if coaches, teachers, and parents are more likely to encourage boys to enter politics, then party leaders, elected officials, and political activists are likewise more inclined to ask men.

Taken all together, women say "no" long before they even know they can say "yes."[12]

To some very, *very* small extent, that is changing, thanks, in part, to Trump.[13] "It is hard to overstate Democratic women's dismay with the president," wrote researchers Jennifer Lawless and Richard Fox, who studied the "Trump Effect" on the U.S. 2018 mid-term elections. The mid-terms saw Democrats elect ninety women to the house, thirty-five of them new female members — marking the largest number of new women ever elected by one party to Congress in a single election cycle. "When asked whether they'd rather have a colonoscopy or a private lunch with Trump, more than half of female Democrats chose the colonoscopy." Lawless and Fox have been studying women's low representation in politics for more than a decade, focusing largely on why women choose to run at such diminished rates, and they wondered how this disdain of Trump — and his brand of power — affected women's political motivations. For a number of Democrat women it certainly did. Before Trump imploded the world, the 2012 election cycle had the highest record of female primary candidates, at 298, including both parties. But in the 2018 mid-terms, 476 women stepped up. Three-quarters of those women were Democratic Party candidates. What's more, those Democrat women outperformed the men in their party during the primaries, and continued to perform well in the election. Republican women, on the other hand, plummeted to their lowest numbers in the House since 1994.

Trump himself may be repugnant to many women, but he's also emblematic of a certain ultra-masculine expression of political power. Both his style and his policies embody many of the characteristics women are taught to distance themselves from. He is uncompromising, unkind, volatile, self-centred, egotistical, loud, performative, *confident*. And while society has not always prized the Trump-esque expression of these qualities in its world leaders, it has never condemned such qualities in powerful positions, either — provided those positions are occupied by men. Boys are taught to exemplify many of these traits, and both their masculinity and their agency — itself an expression of gender constructs — is tied tightly to expectations that they will seek power.[14] If you don't want to be powerful, then you're not a man. Women's socialization, on the other hand, often centres around avoiding attempts to exercise power, especially over men.[15] And so, people make allowances for the darker edge of these qualities in men; they are, especially now, the qualities people commend and cheer. *In men*. A woman would be loathed if she behaved the way Trump, Ford, or any of the other political strongmen acted.

But Only If They Don't Want Power

When women do gain influence — or some semblance of it — many of them bring a different flavour to power. Not necessarily stereotypically feminine, but different. Beneficial. Women are shown to deliver more spending to their jurisdictions and to sponsor more legislation. Women politicians bring a more co-operative leadership style, with an emphasis placed on coalition-building and communication. They are less likely than men to focus on hierarchy. They're more likely to support rehabilitation. At the municipal level, they are more likely to approach fiscal challenges with transparency and a will to fix them.[16] And, yes, they are more likely to speak about women and to consider how policies and legislation will affect them.[17] Research has also shown that when women are represented by women in their jurisdictions, they are more likely to be engaged in politics — to know the issues and to talk about them.

While a lot of the proven strengths of female politicians can be dangerously skewed as "women are good at *feeeeeelings*," my hope is not to separate out women's power from men's. It will do little good to reinforce what research has repeatedly confirmed: that voters see male politicians as lacking compassion and political effectiveness in child and family issues, whereas women politicians are expected to perform poorly on economic and military policy.[18] No, my hope is to embrace a new vision of power that values qualities such as collaboration and consensus-building, no matter a person's gender.

But that's not what's happened, at least not yet. If research offers surprising optimism about women's chances at the polls, it offers expected bleakness about perceptions of women in power, and how they're able to use it. Studies indicate that men are likely to run for election because they have a "raw desire" to hold office; women choose to run because they care about a specific policy issue.[19] As it turns out, voters respond keenly to this mirroring of expected gender roles: the agentic man and the caretaking woman. But what about women—like Clinton, for example—who do not successfully mould themselves into the Mom-in-Chief role, whether it be because they don't want to, or because the public won't accept them as such? We know that while people respond favourably to long-established, successful leadership traits in men, they assign lower status to the same traits in women: anger, self-promotion, competitiveness, task-oriented speaking styles, an authoritative manner, swift discipline, criticism. But how do they treat women who make clear their desire for advancement, who merely intend to seek power, and do not yet hold it?

Alas, by now, we know how this goes. Published in 2010, one of the first studies to tackle the interplay between gender and power-seeking found that would-be women politicians were, predictably, penalized for showing stark ambition.[20] Men's blatant ambition, on the other hand, actually *improved* reactions to the candidate. Consistent with previous studies that looked at power-seeking intention in other contexts (such as within a company), researchers found that ambition was seen to negatively counteract perceptions of communality and care — deficits that only affect women. Meaning, just seeing a woman in a stereotypically male role is not enough to spark backlash, said researchers. That happens when people view women as violating expected gender roles. That's bad news. So long as care and community are seen as a salve against power-seeking women — a way to assure the public that they're not straying too far from their prescribed function — leadership styles that model those values will be limited from entering male-dominated spheres in any meaningful way. And women politicians cannot be expected to shoulder the emotional burden of an entire country (or company). Especially when there are so few of them.

These expectations also work against women once they're in office. It's generally assumed that the more power a person has, regardless of gender, the more time they'll spend talking in a group setting, commanding the attention of others. Not so. Powerful women who talk disproportionately longer than others in a room are seen as significantly less competent and less suitable for leadership, by all genders in the room. Conversely, men in power who talk *less* than others in the room are also seen as less competent and less deserving of leadership.[21] Powerful women are best able to maintain their power when they are *silent*. (Case in point: Jody Wilson-Raybould.) These dynamics can translate into so-called career ceilings for female politicians — those who have served in office for a long time, but have not yet attained a powerful position within their government. Women generally spend less time in politics, as they do in other male-dominated professions, and they are over 40 percent more likely than men to retire when their ability to influence the legislative process stalls (perhaps a culmination of all that frustration).[22]

Essentially, the pattern of power working against women exists in politics, as it does everywhere, sprouting roadblocks like weeds. If we want to truly change the nature of power, and women's access to it, then we need to loosen the restraints on our expected (celebrated, coveted) gender traits. In particular, we need to stop slotting women into the "Mom" role, whatever that might be in any given context — whether it's making women responsible for an organization's caretaking competency or simply expecting them to be mothers first, period. To be sure, the impossibility of smoothly balancing a high-demand work life with the expectations of motherhood hangs over women's ambition like an axe. It's something we haven't yet figured out because it's not something those in power believe they have a stake in helping us to figure out. The presumed duties of motherhood — and the overwhelming, guilt-ridden implications of failing at them — are used to hem us in. And so long as they have power, we will not.

Mommy Dearest

Sharon is a thirty-eight-year-old mother who has applied for advancement within her company twelve times. She's been turned down every single time. Some of the un-won opportunities have been direct promotions from her current job, and others have been similar roles within the organization. One application turndown, she told me, was for a leadership role in another department. She had seven years of previous experience in that same role with another company, and her current role "only added a very valuable wealth of experience." She believed she would have been able to greatly help the struggling department. She was told she wasn't "a good fit," with no further explanation. The kicker, she told me, was that in addition to being turned down for a role she'd already held at one point, she'd likely still hold that role if she hadn't become pregnant and taken maternity leave.

"It made me really doubt my abilities," she said, "even though I have never had a bad appraisal rating in my entire career. I am always seen as a superstar and my ratings show that I outperform everyone else, and not by a little. I have tried applying two further times to this [particular] role but didn't even get an interview. I don't think I am able to overcome this one. Now, having been passed over so many times, I don't even want to apply to any more jobs. If I can't advance after many years of experience and twelve attempts, it really makes me feel like I am not good enough, despite all the evidence against it."

Without realizing it, Sharon had described a classic example of the "motherhood penalty." That is, the direct link between a woman's mom status in the workplace and perceptions of lower competence and commitment, a lower likelihood of hiring and promotion, lower recommended salaries, and higher professional expectations.[23] The penalty can cost women in real dollar figures: up to $16,000 a year in lost wages.[24] Combined with our fear of overachieving women, it can be deadly to a woman's career, her ability to control her future—and her perception of herself.

It can also come into play before a woman even has children.[25] Consider what one twenty-six-year-old woman told me about her experience with a job interview in the insurance industry. When she let the male interviewer know she would be getting married that year, she saw his facial expression change. He had a copy of her resumé printed out and he wrote down the information across the front. She didn't know why he did that: getting married wouldn't change her work ethic or her career goals. No, she didn't *understand* why, but she knew why: interviewers assume that once a woman gets married she will have children, and once that happens she will either quit or become less productive, less professional, desire less responsibility, *blah, blah, blah.* "I couldn't respond or react to his action because I was in the middle of the job interview. I was worried that if I reacted negatively, it would affect my interview result. So I had to appeal that I wouldn't stop studying for my exams nor pursuing my goals in this industry," she said. "But I'm 90 percent sure that he wouldn't have bothered to write a memo...if I were a guy."

She's likely right. There is no equivalent fatherhood penalty for men. If anything, men are more likely to garner a premium when they become dads at work.[26] Married men who become fathers see wage gains of about 4 percent— in addition to the 7 percent premium they see for getting married in the first place. That's directly at odds with the wage penalty for women, who see a decrease of 4 percent for each child they have.[27] Fathers who are married to other men, who are single, or who are not white don't receive the premium; women see a penalty regardless of marital status or race or sexuality.

Beyond that, research is emerging that undermines the efficacy of gender-neutral policies put in place to mitigate such penalties. Take, for instance, the practice of tenure clock-stopping policies used in universities. The policy allows all genders to put tenure-track requirements, such as the mandate to publish a minimum number of research papers, on hold when they become new parents. One study that examined almost two decades of data found that such policies corresponded to a decrease, by 22 percentage points, in the probability of a woman assistant professor earning tenure at the same university where she took her leave.[28]

Men, meanwhile, saw their probability increase by nearly 20 percentage points. That's because they spent their time off tenure track trying to get papers accepted into more prestigious, riskier journals; women did not.

Complicating all this winning and losing is the pervasive cultural messaging that tells women they won't be happy unless they have children — that it is, above all, their purpose in life. Their ultimate role. The manner by which they can access power and achieve influence (if they have a boy!). As I discussed in a feature for *The Walrus* in 2018, we live in a pro-maternity culture.[29] It's marked by everything from the royals' baby watch to Beyoncé's epic Instagram pregnancy reveal (which broke the record for most "likes" in 2017, earning a total of 11.18 million,[30] only to be eclipsed the next year by Kylie Jenner's baby reveal[31]). It drives women to seek motherhood and to perform it perfectly; it drives others to expect perfect motherhood from them. And it suffocates out anything else.

Academics and activists call this mindset "pronatalism." As Laura Carroll explains in *The Baby Matrix*, pronatalism is "the idea that parenthood and raising children should be the central focus of every person's adult life."[32] More than that, it's the idea that it's the "normal" path to adulthood. Pronatalism teaches women that children are synonymous with success and stability, and, if they do it right, *the* answer to the question of life's meaning. It teaches them that motherhood is not so much a choice as it is a higher calling. To step off that path is not only inconceivable, it's unnatural: a surefire way to an empty life and a sad death.

The term was first introduced to mainstream audiences in the 1970s, most notably with Ellen Peck and Judith Senderowitz's book *Pronatalism: The Myth of Mom & Apple Pie*. The book followed Peck's bestseller from a few years earlier, *The Baby Trap*, in which she argued that motherhood was not innate, but rather something that was marketed and sold to women — to keep them tractable, to preserve strict gender roles during a time of social flux, and, perhaps most significantly, to establish an industry around motherhood and thereby fuel the economy.[33] Peck, who would go on to found the National Organization for Non-Parents, also used her book to make a simple point: that the addition of children often meant a subtraction of something else. In an interview with *People* magazine in 1976, she stressed that the motherhood-and-apple-pie image has long existed: "The beatific mother with golden hair in the shampoo ad may look young, but she is really 10,000 years old."[34]

More than forty years later, Peck's criticism of our baby-obsessed society holds — even as women's equality has exponentially advanced. Consider the ways in which pronatalism has also influenced the past decade's pop-culture products. It has given us mega-family reality shows, such as *19 Kids and Counting* and *Jon and Kate Plus 8*.[35] Pronatalism is the reason why the protagonist of the *Hunger Games* movie series earns motherhood as her reward for saving the world,[36] and it is why, in real life, reporters recently asked one of the world's first "female" AI robots where she stood on motherhood (surprise: she seems to want kids).[37]

There is arguably no public or private realm that pronatalism misses. In the workplace, it is what drives us to bring newborns to the office; what has us ask, by way of introduction, how many children a co-worker has, what lets those with children go home early and causes those without kids to pick up the office slack. In school, it is what makes young students protectively carry around eggs or sacks of flour with scribbly baby faces drawn on them,[38] and why so much of our foundational, outdated sex education curricula focused on the right time to have a baby, not whether there *is* a right time. It's what makes us contribute to the continued rise of global retail sales for products geared toward kids, including clothes, health care, toys, and food, which hit a combined US$350 billion in 2016.[39] And it's how we got everything from child tax benefits to the Nyquil slogan, "Moms don't take sick days."[40]

With such pervasive messaging, it's no wonder that many women find it difficult to convince others, let alone themselves, that any life that doesn't revolve around ideal motherhood is viable. As a consequence, women slip into motherhood without always understanding what it will mean—whether that's how much their life will change or how much they'll regret that it did. Taboo as it is to discuss it, regret does happen; that does not make somebody an ice queen. In 2017, Israeli author Orna Donath published *Regretting Motherhood: A Study*, which drew on a five-year project in which she interviewed twenty-three mothers from a variety of backgrounds, ranging in age from twenty-six to seventy-three. For Donath, the regret many of these women expressed about having children stemmed from the way society pushed them into motherhood as a default path without providing adequate systemic support, or even an honest conversation about the long-term cost to their careers, ambitions, and happiness. We assume that having "it all" for women means children and a career; rarely do we allow for the fact that having kids can greatly, undesirably, *disrupt* a previously carefully crafted life. "Regret is an alarm bell that should not only alert societies that we need to make it easier for mothers to be mothers," writes Donath, "but that invites us to rethink the politics of reproduction and the very obligation to become mothers at all."[41]

Just Plain Selfish

Before Cecilia Lyra got married in April 2011, nobody ever asked her if she would have children.[42] They just assumed that she would. It wasn't until after she wed her husband, Bruno, that the question of *when* started up. She found the incessant curiosity annoying, but not strange. She thought she would have children one day, too. Still, she wasn't in a hurry. Both Cecilia and Bruno were busy, successful lawyers; they had met in Brazil at the law firm where they worked. After their marriage, the young couple bought a house, advanced in their careers, and got a pet. People would look at their English Bulldog, Babaganoush, and ask, "When is the real baby coming?" *Not now*, Cecilia would say, *but eventually.*

At the same time, she was beginning to realize something else: she was content with her non-nuclear family of three. She wasn't afraid to be a mother, but she didn't have a strong desire to become one, either. Today, neither she nor Bruno remember when they finally decided not to have children. There wasn't a tough, hand-wringing conversation. "For me," said Cecilia, "it wasn't an ambivalence. It was me not seeing that *not* having children was a possibility." Many people expect their lives to be either glamorous and extravagant or lonely and immature, she said, but she described their life in Toronto as quiet, comfortable, and happy. It feels *full*. "I'm not worried I won't have a daughter's graduation or a son's wedding to go to, or that I won't have grandkids," she told me. "It doesn't even cross my mind."

As the default structure for women's lives, the motherhood imperative is not just about apparent fulfillment. It is a stand-in for order, an assurance that everyone is exactly who, and what, they are supposed to be — someone who nurtures, sacrifices, populates. Only five years ago, in 2012, the *National Post* ran a column titled "Trend of couples not having children just plain selfish."[43] And in 2013, *Newsweek* ran a story called "Why the choice to be childless is bad for America."[44] It argued that the so-called eroding family unit would create "a culture marked by hyperindividualism and dependence on the state." That same year, *Time* magazine featured a cover story on the child-free life, arguably mainstreaming the conversation, and stirring controversy.[45] Conservative media outlets, like Fox, hosted panels in which participants said things such as, "Have you ever seen anything more selfish, decadent, and stupid?"[46] Two years later, when *The Atlantic* ran a review of an essay collection on the decision not to have children, cheekily titled *Selfish, Shallow, and Self-Absorbed*, the article received nearly 4,000 online comments.[47] That same year, Pope Francis plainly stated, "The choice to not have children is selfish."[48]

There is a sense that women who don't have children, or may be contemplating a decision not to have children, don't know their own minds—that the world knows better, and, if they would just listen, it would save them from a wrong move. I talked to Irena Kramer, a twenty-nine-year-old child-free lawyer based in Southern Ontario, who said that people still cannot picture what life outside of motherhood looks like for adult women. We are at ease with nuclear families; less so with stable, single, grown women. When it comes down to it, we often still think of women without children as missing something essential.

Mixed into all this is the fundamental idea of who should be a mother and who should not. That is, the model mother is usually white, middle- to upper-class, educated, able-bodied, healthy, and coupled. While many women who match this profile have reported trouble obtaining tubal ligation (read: sterilization) from doctors who stress that the process is irreversible (forgetting, perhaps, that that's the point), others have found it all too easy. One is a Calgary-based woman named Sarah Moon, who describes her no-children status as a choice, but one with layers, some of the onion bitter. As someone who lives with addiction and disability, she says that, at first, she felt pressured to undergo the procedure. She wondered at her own choice: *Am I doing this because I'm too disabled?* Was it because she truly didn't want children, or because she believed the messaging around who makes a good mother? When she spoke with me, she said she felt as though her child-free status gave her freedom, but her feelings remain entangled.

There seems to be no right way to approach children, whether you have them or not, added Kramer. Nothing is ever good enough. "I see people commenting on mothers that stay home, mothers who don't stay home. Mothers who breastfeed, mothers who don't breastfeed," she told me. "There's an endless list of things to criticize women on" — and it all starts with motherhood. We are always asking if women are doing motherhood right, and we're always asking if they can do anything else right if they're doing motherhood. Can women be politicians and mothers? CEOs and mothers? Judges and mothers? Scientists and mothers? To take yourself out of the constant debate over motherhood, said Kramer, is really uncomfortable for people. "I find people don't even know what to say. I've never had someone automatically say, 'I totally respect that choice and it's up to you.'"

As a consequence, many women don't recognize that it is up to them. Growing up, Victoria Carter never realized it could be a *choice* not to be a mother. A thirty-six-year-old Cree woman based in Nanaimo, B.C., she told me that as her friends and family began to talk about having children, she realized she wasn't interested in the conversation. She felt so out of place that she even went online and googled "I don't want kids — what's wrong with me?" In her culture, she added, the importance of family structure and of carrying on the bloodline is particularly ingrained. "As a woman — as an Indigenous woman — you have kids," she said. "Everyone who is a woman in my family has kids, except me."

Carter has other child-free friends who have also felt the added weight of how their wider culture views women's roles and values motherhood. The child-free community, she said, can only gain from hearing more diverse perspectives. That can include different racial, cultural, and religious backgrounds, but also a diversity of socio-economic backgrounds, those in the LGBTQ+ communities, women who experience mental health issues, those with disabilities, and more. "It would be empowering to know there are similar women out there," said Carter. "That you're not alone. And there is nothing wrong with you."

She added that her life without children didn't really solidify until she found a like-minded community. In her googling, she discovered a group in Edmonton, where she was then living, called Babes without Babes, founded in 2003 for women thirty-five and older. Since then, she's travelled to Mexico with the Babes, attended monthly get-togethers, joined book clubs and restaurant clubs. She no longer worries there's something wrong with her, or that people might judge her. This sense of liberation has carried her through other decisions in her life, such as a recent career change, and a decision to go back to school. These days, she said, she no longer wonders about her choice: "I'm not going to keep thinking about it. I want to continue on with what's left of my life. I want to *live* my life."

Who Do You Think You Are?

None of this is to say that the end solution for women's power relies on eschewing children and motherhood. But it is all tied together. Much of what has kept women from power in the past is connected to the limits we put on their perceived roles and "natural" interests. Women's life-narrative leans heavily on who we should be, what roles we should play, how we should find fulfillment. But how one woman defines a successful life, can — and should — be different from how another woman does. We will have power not when we're all motherless world leaders, but when the variety of possible roles, jobs, and life paths reflects our freedom to choose for ourselves. Instead, we have a toxic, divisive, hyper-masculine version of leadership that prefers to subsume women under one monolithic vision. We tell women what they should want, starting from a very young age, and then we punish them whether they achieve it or not. People fear child-free women so much because an absence of motherhood is seen, at its core, as a rebuke of traditional, masculine power. It says: *I want more than what I've been offered, what everyone has told me I should want, since the beginning of all time.* This rethink is an essential part of reimagining motherhood, as well. We'll never figure out the answer to a woman's work–life balance without dismantling the idea that her first responsibility is to be a good mother: to mother well wherever she goes, care-taking everyone she encounters, from colleagues to constituents.

There's an everyday pervasiveness to women's and girl's "role-making" that feels monotonous. It grinds us down. It may shout "dream big" but it whispers constantly that "this is what you *should* want." Our achievements are relentlessly measured against patriarchal standards. We must look and talk the right way. Our bodies must be sculpted to just the right degree, with the right amount of curves and flat planes, so that our clothes are pleasing to the eye. Our voices must be soft but not too high, deep but not tilting toward vocal fry. We must measure out the right amount of ambition, teaspoon by teaspoon, and we must never announce just how badly we want that success, unless we're also willing to grit our teeth and say we want it so that it will benefit everybody but us.

Too often it feels as though we need permission to co-operate and build coalitions, and even then we must pretend it is *not* because we want to advance ourselves and others who seek equity; we are allowed to build these things calmly and to do well only within the confines of a wider, patriarchal society. We must play our roles and we must perform them flawlessly to criteria we never set. If we want to achieve equality, we will do so by measuring ourselves against men's goals, by moving through men's systems, and then we will fail, because these things society has demanded that we do — these contradictions — are impossible. They are a way to maintain and exert control, and it's time to say that we are done with them.

Because if we define power as also having the ability to control our own fates, then many of us do not have it yet. We don't have the power to decide for others and we don't have the power to decide for ourselves. Any solutions we undertake now are corrective: we are unlearning everything we were taught as children, trying to undo and remake systems and socialization methods that have been ingrained in us for generations.

These are urgent, worthy goals. But what if we could interrupt the cycle before it even begins?

CHAPTER 10

Rebel Girl

*Radical new ways to teach girls and
young women how to push back*

GROWING UP, CAROLINE MARFUL was "a very ideal-istic kid." She always saw the best in people and in the world. Then she took Grade 11 American history. "Just cuz," she told me, laughing. The more she learned about slavery and Jim Crow laws, the more that idealism slipped away. As a young Black woman, she had, of course, known those horrible things happened. Yet before that class she had seen them as a by-product of history—examples of outdated thinking, sure, but not really anybody's fault. "It was the first time I sat there and thought, *No, no, no, it's the* people *who write policies. It's the* people *who are voted into office*," she told me. "They choose these things, and they chose things that I think are terrible." They also did what they thought was best for *them* at that time. If she wanted things to change, she realized, she'd have to be in the room when such decisions were made. When it came time to choose her major, she set aside her interest in English and chose to study politics at Queen's.

While she was there, she realized she'd need more than her university education to gain access to those rooms. "These rooms are usually behind closed doors," she knew. "They're usually full of white men." To start, she co-founded a political leadership conference for women at Queen's. She wanted to help other women combine their knowledge and skills, rather than seeing them all facing the same issues and getting pushed down individually, continuously. At the time, it never occurred to her that she *couldn't* pull off the conference, or learn how to open the necessary doors. "I always feel the need to give my parents credit," she said. They both immigrated from Ghana when they were Marful's age, in their early twenties. They didn't have any networks, but they both went on to get their master's degrees. "When they raised my sister and I they never really spoke about the barriers that existed in society. It was a very conscious choice. They were never like, 'Oh, because you're a girl *this*,' or 'Because you're Black *that*.' It was never the narrative, even though it's true. They just didn't continuously vocalize it."

As a result, she added, she just "goes for things." So when she had the opportunity to apply for the Girls on Boards program through the not-for-profit G(irls)20, she did so without hesitation. The organization focuses on fostering leadership and decision-making among girls from eighteen to twenty-five years old. In many ways, says Heather Barnabe, the organization's CEO, they are the forgotten demographic. People love seeing girls look empowered. Companies can see the benefit of bringing on women with experience, someone who might be in their diversity pipeline. But girls in university are politically disruptive, in both their thinking and their actions. To Barnabe, that's when women really begin to comprehend not only their rights, but also what they're owed—by their education, by the wider systems in society, by those around them. They also begin to understand how they can contribute to the change they want to see. Which, Barnabe figured, should make them incredibly valuable to both corporate and non-profit boards.

Of course, it's exactly this potential for change-making that made boards so nervous about signing on to the program and inviting young women—after extensive training and coaching—to serve a one-year term as a "Young Director." An even tougher sell: Barnabe insisted that if the young women were to participate, they'd not only get a seat at the decision-making table, they'd get a voice. It's a two-way street, she told me. The young women should feel as though their lived experience matters, because it does. They will have points of view that many of the boards—which are still largely composed of older white men—have not had access to. That's why, in addition to working on governance training with the young women in their program, G(irls)20 also works with the boards themselves to educate them on how to value and interact with young women in board settings. "What we don't want is that tokenistic piece," said Barnabe. She didn't want to mimic convention that preached training women and letting boards continue on with the status quo. "In reality, it's the boards who have to change their approach."

The organization's approach is innovative, and it's also challenging. For everyone. No matter how much training the women have, said Barnabe, if there's one theme among the women, it's that "none of them feel good enough to be in our program." It frustrates her. "At the same time," she added, "of course they don't. They've been messaged their whole lives that they don't deserve to be in this space."

Even Marful, for all her confidence and conviction that she belongs in such spaces, found herself surprisingly intimidated when she showed up to her first meeting. She suddenly realized how much she had to learn. It wasn't until her third board meeting, she told me, that she began to feel like she belonged — an underestimation of her skills and value, she stressed, that was entirely of her own making. Before that third meeting, the executive director of the organization had called Marful and asked her to sit on the executive committee as secretary. Marful's first response was, "I don't know anything." She thought she wasn't ready. She was still in school, taking the train back from Kingston for every gathering.

Sitting in that first executive meeting, though, she discovered nobody knew everything. They worked together to combine their knowledge. "It's when I realized the best asset of me being on the board was being me," she said. They may have known a lot of things she didn't. "But none of them know what it's like to be Black, and none of them know what it's like to be young in today's day and age." She stopped trying to model herself after everybody else and started channelling her own thoughts and experiences. It clicked.

Now a graduate, Marful has completed the Girls on Boards program. People always ask her, she added, if she wants to see more Black women in the room. *Yes*, she'll answer, *100 percent*. She wants to be in the room, and she wants to bring twenty others with her. But she has also realized something else from her time on the board: "If there's no one in the room, I'd be okay with being the first."

Girl in a Box

The summer that Adrienne McRuvie's daughter turned eight, she decided to read *The Mother-Daughter Project*. Written by psychotherapists SuEllen Hamkins and Renée Schultz, the book posits that, despite the notoriously rocky time, relationships between mothers and daughters can actually thrive during adolescence. If that happens, the book argues, teen girls also stand a better chance at thriving through what is often a tumultuous transition. The authors' solution: a "simple but revolutionary idea" to gather moms and daughters into small social groups that meet regularly. In the book, the authors talk about how they developed activities that focused on self-esteem and other issues of growing up, such as friendship and puberty, and eventually body image, drugs, sexuality, and violence against women.[1]

McRuvie knew immediately that she wanted to try something similar with her daughter. She thought back to a yoga class she'd taught when she and the other students were new mothers. They'd had a sense of collectiveness that she'd missed after everyone finished maternity leave and went back to work. Their children would all be the same age. She contacted four of them, who had daughters. *Yes, yes, yes, yes.* A group of five mothers and daughters, they've been meeting once a month ever since.

Sometimes, they'll gather and just bond—do something fun, like go to a movie. But, more often than not, McRuvie and the other mothers try to find guest speakers to come in and chat with their girls. When their kids were younger, the mothers, like the book's authors, focused on things like friendship. As they've grown older, they've had a naturopath come in to talk about periods. Another woman taught the girls about money, its value, what you can buy with it, how much energy it costs to make it. One filmmaker helped open a discussion about beauty. They held a clothing swap with a stylist who led a conversation on style, personality, and self-expression through clothes. Being different, they tell their daughters, is not a bad thing. They should always be able to express themselves to the world. When I spoke to McRuvie, she'd recently invited a sex therapist to chat with the group. The woman focused on consent and why it's important. She also talked about pleasure and masturbation—teaching the girls that it is totally normal, totally okay.

The mothers have also brought in a sense of ritualized memory. Every time one of the girls in their group gets her period, McRuvie told me, the mothers gift her with a memory box. They ask her grandmothers to write letters about growing up. They've given bracelets and inscribed copies of the bestselling novel *The Red Tent*. She laughed when she admitted that the first girl to receive one of the boxes was "super embarrassed." But, McRuvie added, she still has the box, with all of those things inside. She hoped the girls knew why the mothers had given them the period boxes: *We don't want you to have experiences like we had.* McRuvie said she remembered what happened when she got her first period. "[I was] sitting in a bathroom at a wedding, in my pretty dress, thinking I was dying," she said. Nobody had told her what would happen when she got her period. Nobody had told her much about it at all. "This is showing them and telling them that we're here and we can talk. We're supporting you and telling you. Your period is not a curse. It's not the worst thing that's happening to you. It's part of your power. It's who you are."

McRuvie believed her role as a mother was to create opportunity for her daughter. To give her infinite choices and to help her create the life she wanted. Sure, the world was going to throw up all sorts of roadblocks. But she was doing what she could to ensure her daughter didn't self-select out of opportunity before the world even told her "No."

Many young people begin to experience — and name — gender inequality at a young age, long before many adults assume they do. In fact, on average, children reportedly first notice gender inequality at eleven years old, and more than half of girls first notice it between the ages of ten and thirteen, according to a 2018 Girl Guides of Canada/Ipsos survey. The survey also discovered that one in three girls between the ages of twelve and seventeen believe they've been treated unequally or unfairly because of their gender. (Incidentally, the wage gap has also already started by the time teens are working summer jobs, with girls earning about $3 less than boys.) Such experiences chip away at what girls and boys each believe they can do. For example, one-quarter of young people surveyed believed that boys are more capable than girls at sports, science, math, and leadership roles. Two in ten believed that girls should aspire to mimic traditional gender goals, like marriage and children. The same proportion believed boys are superior to girls, period.[2]

And while half of girls surveyed said they believed in feminism, 30 percent of them said they were scared or hesitant to speak out for their rights. This fits (depressingly) neatly into the extreme drop in confidence girls experience as they head into adolescence. Between the ages of eight and fourteen, girls' confidence levels drop by 30 percent, according to a 2018 YPulse poll commissioned by the authors of *The Confidence Code for Girls*.[3] Between the ages of twelve and thirteen alone, the percentage of girls who say they aren't allowed to fail increases by a staggering 150 percent. During that same, scant year, the percentage of girls who feel pressured to be perfect jumps by 46 percent. "There is virtually no difference in confidence between boys and girls until they hit age twelve," write the authors, Katty Kay and Claire Shipman. "After age twelve, a confidence gap opens between boys and girls that doesn't close through adolescence." It doesn't even close by the time those girls become adults in their thirties.

"Our culture is teaching girls to embrace a version of selfhood that sharply curtails their power and their potential," argues Rachel Simmons in her book *The Curse of the Good Girl*. "In particular the pressure to be 'Good' — unerringly nice, polite, modest, and selfless — diminishes girls' authenticity and their personal authority."[4] It's what drives girls to fear failure, become averse to risk, and to become overly cautious, silent. Once they're in adolescence, girls are also more exposed to stressful interpersonal events, like conflict with peer groups or social isolation, and they also tend to ruminate on those events more than boys, leading to higher risks of depression.[5] Seen against such a dismal backdrop, ventures like mother-daughter groups — which promote self-love, respect, and community while trying to infuse confidence without selling it as a panacea — seem downright radical. And if we could teach girls to be tender and kind to themselves through adolescence, I wondered, could we also teach them to be angry, aggressive? Could we teach them to be "bad"?

Nice Girls Don't Yell

Pan Am Games gold medal winner Gemma Sheehan is standing in front of a group of giggling thirteen-year-old girls. The mixed martial artist founded Girls Who Fight after she retired from cage fighting in her early twenties.

With her whole life before her, Sheehan thought about what she wanted most and became determined to teach young women how to protect themselves. To her, that didn't stop at learning how to break free from somebody's grasp. If anything, she told the girls assembled there that day, the best thing they could do if somebody attacked them was to run away. A drop-kick in real life rarely worked like it did in the movies. No, if they really wanted to *protect* themselves — the core of who they were — they had to learn how to stand their ground, be a leader, speak out. It would mean forgetting how to be quiet and learning how to yell.

"You aren't going to learn this from a lot of people," she told the group. "People are not going to teach you to speak assertively and not be nice all the time." But *she* would.

It was close to the end of a full day of activity. The girls had learned how to break an attacker's grip and they'd learned how to strike someone. They'd talked about the perils of social media and the bullying they faced online. Yelling at someone, though, was proving to be the most difficult thing they'd done the entire day. Imagine, Sheehan said, that the girl standing next to them in the circle was someone who did not take their "Stop!" as a "stop" — whatever it was they wanted them to stop doing. Now, she told them, practise what you'd say next. Don't be shy, she said. Don't worry about looking cool.

They did a few practices as a group. Don't make it a question at the end, Sheehan added after listening for a moment. Keep eye contact. Keep the bounce out of your voice. Don't be inviting. Be loud. "Keep it short," she quipped, "but don't be sweet."

After a few more minutes of coaching, she told the group that they were going to turn it into a competition. If they laughed while they said the phrase "Stop doing that!" to the girl next to them, they had to sit down. They were out.

The first girl spoke: "Can you please stop doing that?"

"No 'please'!" shouted Sheehan.

The next girl laughed when she was done saying the words, and sat down. "I sounded like I was going to kill her," she said, surprised.

Another girl tried, but broke down in laughter. "I'm out. I'm out."

The next girl raised her arm, took a deep breath, and drew her fingers together. "I can't," she said.

The other girls coaxed her. "You're talking to your mom! Pretend you're pissed!"

She almost whispered it.

"Don't rush it," said Sheehan. The girl laughed, trying to get it out. "Eye contact," coaxed Sheehan.

Finally, she said it: "Stop doing that."

"Good," said Sheehan. "But you could be meaner. You could be meaner."

And so it went around the circle. Most girls laughed, and laughed even more uncomfortably when they managed to get the words out. As if they were astounded with themselves for speaking so forcefully, for saying "no," even if it was all pretend.

Sheehan told me that their mothers had signed them up for the class, maybe with #MeToo on their minds, maybe with the general messy state of the world. Earlier in the day the girls had gone around and said why they were there, what they wanted to be when they grew up. Two of them wanted to be engineers. One wanted to be a surgeon. Another a pediatrician. One a scientist. They told the group they were there to "learn how to kick somebody in the gut," to "stop someone with a knife," to "break someone's nose," to know how to defend themselves. One girl said that she just "wanted to learn how to be strong." Another said her mom had forced her to be there.

I wanted to be able to leave that day and see that it had changed the girls. I wanted to witness a clear moment of "before" and "after," in which the "after" became an epiphany of assertiveness and rebellious belief in themselves. I wanted to see them learn not how to kick somebody in the gut (they did not do this), but what it was inside them that made them want to learn these things. The anger and the injustice and the truth of themselves at the centre of it all. What I saw instead was a subtle war.

The martial arts club where they met was a giant room, lined on one side with mirrors so that the club's participants could monitor technique while they practised. The girls repeatedly drifted toward the mirrors, almost subconsciously. There, they posed, sticking out their bottoms, tugging down the fronts of their shirts, pursing their lips, sucking in their tummies. There they examined themselves from all angles, frowning or smiling in turn.

A trio of girls, who spent most of lunch scrolling through their "Insta" feeds, decided to take a group selfie at lunch. They all posed, expertly contorting their thin bodies into camera-friendly shapes. "How cute do I look?" asked one. *Flash. Flash. Flash.* They gathered to look at the results. I heard one girl scream. "Ew! No, no, no," she shouted. "My arm looks disgusting!" Already, she thought she looked too fat; earlier, she'd complained about another girl, dismissively waving one manicured hand, "Bye, bitch." The second girl shrugged, her face unsure; she'd pretended to seductively hump one of the punching bags during a snack break, asking her friends to take a picture. The third in the trio made to post the group picture anyway, but seemed to decide against it when the first girl angrily exclaimed, "What the fuck are you doing?" When Sheehan later asked them to turn away from the mirror, a chorus of panicked *nos* flew into the air.

I felt chilled. These girls seemed to want so much for their lives. And they were up against so much. Wanting them to walk out of there as bad girls who didn't care about looking perfect or speaking too loudly was a lot to ask in one day. But I hoped it was a start.

"It is quite a complicated thing to teach—confidence," Sheehan later told me. "It's not like one can go up to a group of girls and say, 'Be confident. Don't listen to social media.'" They might nod and agree, she added, but they'll still face an avalanche of messaging telling them otherwise as soon as they leave. Unless they begin to train with her consistently, which many girls do (especially those whose parents become dismayed that their daughters have become too timid, too shy), the most she can hope is that they walk away from the day with an open mind. As it is, she always tries to subtly instill assertiveness and even aggression into every activity, whether it be a one-day session or ongoing training. She wants the girls she trains with to become comfortable with telling others what they want and what their boundaries are, whether it will upset someone else our not. She wants them to be able to feel no shame in voicing their competence. They should be able to say, "I'm good at this," without having to fear someone's reaction. She wants them to learn to be a little selfish. To take the lead without caring whether anyone thinks they should be a leader.

"After we do a certain move, I'll ask something like, 'Who thought that technique was hard or easy? Who really liked that technique and who didn't?'" Sheehan told me. "The girls will look at each other before anyone raises their hand. 'Why do you have to look at someone else to decide what you think about what you just learned?' I'll always grill my students about that kind of stuff." Sheehan added that she also teaches co-ed classes in high schools. That's where she notices the starkest difference between boys and girls. Whenever she introduces a technique, or even when she merely asks them to start jumping around and warming up, she said, the boys will dive right in. But the girls won't. Often, she said, they'll play a game of *You go first* and *No, no, you go first*, right on into indecisive infinity. They're afraid of people watching. They're afraid of looking silly. They're afraid of being first. "Just do it!" she'll tell them. "Don't be afraid of being judged for wanting to be a leader." Her hope is that the sport will teach them competitiveness, leadership, assertiveness, discipline—all things "girls aren't finding at a lot of other places."

The uncomfortable truth is that girls *are* judged for being leaders. The even more uncomfortable truth, as we are learning, is that even though the judgement won't easily or even always disappear, they have to find their own way to start leading anyway. If we want adults to embrace new styles of leadership and demolish harmful gender stereotypes, part of the answer, surely, is to start interrupting those limited power structures early so that it won't be such an uphill journey to break conventions later in life. Opening the world of sports to girls and women—and the values and skills that come with it—does, indeed, work. Research has shown that girls and women who play competitive sports are more likely to enter other competitive domains like business and STEM.[6] Others argue that sports help women gain and develop their communication skills and teamwork, as well as, yes, their competitiveness, their assertiveness, and their discipline.[7] One 2015 study found that more than half of women C-suite executives had played sports at the university level, and nearly 95 of them continued to play sports.[8]

It also found that 80 percent of female Fortune 500 executives played competitive sports at one point in their lives.[9] Even more striking: former athletes were paid, on average, 7 percent more than non-athletes.[10]

Not that it's all as simple as grabbing a ball or a puck and passing your way to the C-suite. As Sheehan herself said, certain sports for women are often not seen as an option. It's no coincidence that sports also teach success, failure, and competition within highly masculine constructs. In so many ways, sports are prepping women for the masculinity contests they'll face later in life, teaching them how to be competitive, and to value winning. No wonder women have historically been barred from these literal men's games, and even today such structures often try to wrestle them into wearing a uniform of perfect femininity when they play (see the skirt-based uniforms in the 1940s-era All-American Girls' Professional Baseball League; now see the furor over the black—initially banned—catsuit that Serena Williams wore to the 2018 French Open).[11] This is changing as women's participation increases dramatically, and as girls themselves are beginning to challenge how they're socialized into sports.[12] As girls are beginning to change sport itself.

So, yes, it was a start. A start that couldn't start and stop with one afternoon. A start that needed to transform into a constant interruption—one that blared in over and over again, right into early adulthood and beyond. Then again, preaching the necessity of living a feminist life and actually figuring out how to do it are two very different things.

Welcome to Feminist Camp

In early January 2019, sitting at a conference table in New York City with a group of young women, men, and non-binary feminists, I tried to perform an abortion on a papaya. I held the heavy fruit as another woman, also from Toronto, attempted to firmly grip the narrow edge of the papaya with the blade-tips of a speculum. After a few tries — the fruit was slippery — she got it, under the careful guidance of the doctor on hand, a woman who also works as an abortion provider. "Careful," she told our group. "Remember, all these tools would be sterilized in real life. Don't let them touch anything else." We were practising manual vacuum aspiration. A common method for abortion, it removes the uterine contents through suction, applied through a cannula, which another member of my group began to prepare. (Instead of a hand-held syringe, some aspiration procedures use an electric pump; some women choose to medically induce their abortion via pills.)[13]

Taking turns, my group members used the cannula to draw out some black papaya seeds and deposit them onto the paper covering the table. A papaya was used because it closely resembles a uterus, said a staff member with the Reproductive Health Access Project, which hosted the workshop.

Earlier, the group had spent some time chatting about abortion myths, with group members calling out some of the ones they heard most often: it's immoral; it's murder; it's "everywhere"; if you get one you're "going to hell"; you'll never get pregnant again; the whole process is creepy. They engaged in some role play to show the group what respectful, neutral conversations should look like in clinics. Before we split into groups to try with our own papayas, we watched the doctor expertly, smoothly, quickly extract the seeds from her own papaya. The whole point of the workshop, she added, was to cast the procedure as what it is: part of an everyday medical process. Something completely normal.

Welcome to Feminist Camp: a packed week of workshops, presentations, job-shadowing trips, and a smattering of other events that included an off-Broadway play and a trip to a swanky penthouse cocktail party. Launched over a decade ago, and founded by the *Manifesta* authors Amy Richards and Jennifer Baumgardner, the camp gathers young feminists of all genders in New York City every year so they can learn, essentially, what it means to build a feminist life. Most of the campers were from all over America, but others hailed from Sweden, Italy, Scotland, and Canada. A lot of them were in university or college; others were recently graduated; one was in her fifties with adult children of her own. About half of them had only recently discovered feminism. As many of them introduced themselves on the first day, they were amazed to learn they weren't the only ones who came from conservative backgrounds, from deeply religious families, from entire communities that, as one young woman put it, "literally raised me to be a mother." More than one confessed, with a troubled look, that their entire family had voted for Trump. They had no framework to live a feminist life. *What did that even mean?* they wanted to know. Could they get a job and be a feminist? Would they ever make money? How would they step outside of academia and disrupt power structures in the real world?

The week introduced them to prison abolitionists who told them how little it took for a Black woman to be sent to jail, and discrimination lawyers who told them how much it took for a company to protect its harassed employees. Campers met UNICEF employees who travelled all over the

world, and they met naturopaths who incorporated traditional Chinese medicine into their practices. They learned
about emotional labour, the toll it took, and practical steps to
address it. Together, we all travelled to a trendy meditation
studio, where we sat on oatmeal-coloured pillows, closed
our eyes, and took a moment to be calm. We watched a live
taping of *Democracy Now!*, and the campers all shook their
heads over the government shutdown. They bought books at
the Feminist Press, and buttons, hoop earrings, and women-
made clothes from the feminist retail store Bulletin, which
offers a bricks-and-mortar space to online brands — it also
gives creators back 70 percent of sales and donates 10 percent
of its own profits to Planned Parenthood. One of the staff
members called the store a "total girl-powered safe space"
and remarked that the ethos of the store was, "Yes, I'm shopping for cool shit, but I'm also helping sisters in need." Inside,
the store was an explosion of pink and lemon; outside, a
sandwich board read "Impeach Trump but make it fashion."

On the last day, we all travelled out to Queens to sit
inside Judge Toko Serita's courtroom, where she presides
over the innovative Human Trafficking Intervention Court.
Run from a harm-reduction perspective, with a stated mission of keeping women *out* of jail, the court works with
community leaders to find solutions for trans and cis women
who have been charged with prostitution. As a journalist,
I have been in a lot of courtrooms, but I have never been
inside one where the judge smiles at the people brought
before her and starts with asking, "How are you?" Not only
did the inquiry seem genuine, Serita also asked the people
before her if they were happy. Were they getting the services they needed? How were their children? Once she was
satisfied that the survivors before her were doing well, she'd
dismiss their cases.

At a morning break, Serita and the court's various social workers, victim-services support workers, and community liaisons met to chat with the campers in an empty court-room, portraits of esteemed white men lining the walls. "I want our visitors to see who is involved in this court," she said, gesturing to the line of people, mostly women, beside her. "Even though I'm the one wearing the robe on the bench, this court could not be successful without collaboration."

In so many ways, the week presented the campers with the various iterations and contradictions within femin-ism. That was deliberate, Richards told them at the week's close. We start the journey thinking feminism is one thing, she said, and then we learn there is no wrong or right way to practise feminism or to be a feminist. She hoped, she added, that they had also learned from the week's tensions — "because that's how we find our own voices." Surely, the week did have some tensions. When I spoke to some of the campers in the following weeks, all of them pointed to one session, with an artist, as one that stood out most for them.

It had started out benignly enough, in another board-room, this one borrowed from one of the city's top law firms. The presenter was an artist who was speaking about her work. The first crack came when she mused about choos-ing a symbol to represent feminism. Many of the campers were (rightly) uncomfortable with anything that referenced gender binaries. The pink pussy hat received some heated criticism, as campers (rightly) stated that "not all pussies are pink and not all women have pussies." The fist was also considered and then dismissed, after some campers carefully criticized that it was too close to the Black Power symbol. The conversation darted to flags, and then on to other things. But then, the artist mentioned the word "ally." Many of the campers shifted in their seats. A few bounced with barely contained emotion, seemingly frustration, anger. None of them particularly liked the word "ally." One didn't want allies, but comrades, accomplices, people who were invested in the same goals. Another wondered if the best path was to change the meaning of "ally," not the word itself. A different camper felt allies were performative activists. A fourth said allies were too concerned with equality and not concerned enough with equity, with the differences between the two. Soon the whole table was talking about language and access to language. "You can't punish people for doing their best," ended one camper. "You can't punish baby feminists." The campers had completely, unexpectedly, usurped the presentation.

I was interested in speaking with some of the campers a few weeks later to see what they thought, now that there had been time to let it all sink in. One of them, Leslie Lopez, a self-described first-generation college student at the University of North Texas, told me that the week had, in fact, changed her life. She had been scared that she would be in a room of middle-class white women. She had also been worried that she'd be given a seat at the table, but not a *voice*, something that had happened a lot in the past. Thankfully — intentionally — that was far from the case. Lopez had come to the camp with deep questions about her path after university. She wanted to become an art therapist, but had thought the job would mean abandoning her feminism. Being seen and heard throughout the week, and seeing and hearing other diverse perspectives, had helped her to see that her future as an art therapist *was* feminist. It had helped her to see other things, too. There was a lot of power in access to language. She thought of one reading she'd completed at school, heavy with academic jargon, only to eventually realize the piece was talking about people with the same lived experience as *her*. It was her life, shrouded in language many people outside academia wouldn't understand. She wanted to see more lived experience in her feminism.

One of the other campers, Roman Staebler, a Florida-based artist and former academic who identifies as non-binary, seemed to want to see more radical thinking, more discussion. At twenty-eight, when they attended, part of their reason for coming to the camp, they said, was to figure out what kind of meaningful work they might find outside of academia — a deeply restrictive, patriarchal profession that had ground them down. In that, they said, they got a partial answer: they'd likely have to move outside of their town in Florida if they wanted something else. Yet they were surprised and also disappointed that the itinerary was so jam-packed with sessions and job workshops. What about making space for political discussions, for talk about climate change, for sharing strategies on organizing? They had expected more earnest discussion, more plain urgency. Things, after all, they remarked, were *kind of on fire around us*. "Whether you want to talk about it locally, nationally, globally, we have got maybe ten years to pull the emergency brake on this thing," they said. "And so some of the questions that I've been grappling with, both big-picture and small-picture, they didn't come up."

But they needed to.

Fix the System, Not the Girl

With my mind on Staebler's remarks, I thought back to the last day of Feminist Camp. We'd made our closing remarks at the Elizabeth A. Sackler Center For Feminist Art, housed inside the Brooklyn Museum. Outside, over the entrance of the building, in all capitals, red letters announced "DO NOT DISAPPEAR INTO SILENCE." Inside, Judy Chicago's iconic 1970s installation *The Dinner Party* stood on permanent exhibit. I snapped a few photos of the massive triangular table, its large goblets and utensils, the ornately embroidered fabric, all of which appeared to be set for giants. Which, in a way, it was. Huge plates adorned with or shaped into ornately stylized vulvas marked reserved spots for notable women throughout history: the Primordial Goddess, Mary Wollstonecraft, Virginia Woolf, Georgia O'Keeffe. Widely hailed as celebratory, subversive, and revolutionary at the time, it's also much criticized today, and for good reason. There is only one place set for a woman of colour at the table, and her plate, unlike the rest, is *not* a vulva, but three faces. As Alice Walker observed in her critical response to the piece: "It occurred to me that perhaps white women feminists, no less than white women generally, cannot imagine that black women have vaginas."[14]

In 2018, Chicago responded to the latest round of criticism, saying, essentially, that times had changed. "We need to *build* upon each other's achievements if we are ever to break the cycle of erasure that I tried to overcome through *The Dinner Party*," she wrote.[15] Perhaps everybody was right. Surely, feminism had to change, *was* changing. If feminists built a table today, it would not be so white, it would not be so focused on a binary view of anatomy. Already, we were disrupting old narratives and building new ones, new tables, in their place. In the same way, we could not rely on old methods to disrupt (very old) power structures.

I thought about the many people I'd spoken to about re-envisioning power and leadership. The methods that seemed to work the best — that inspired me most — were less about fixing the girl, fixing the woman. They were not the ones that demanded she change to fit the workplace, the organization, the family, the world, the system. They were the ones that demanded the systems change. More like: they were the ones that demanded the too-broken systems be demolished and completely rebuilt.

So far, I'd focused on individuals, organizations, movements contained to North America. But were we capable of uniting for one huge reckoning on power? And what would it even be? To answer those questions, and to see what that might look like, I needed to join the entire world in Vancouver.

CHAPTER 11

Because It's 2020

*Inside the new global reckoning
on women and power*

BC CHIEF INTERNATIONAL CORRESPONDENT Lyse
Doucet has just welcomed eighteen-year-old activist
Natasha Mwansa to Canada from Zambia. The two are on
stage together in Vancouver, seated in front of nearly 2,000
people. I can barely see either woman from the media section in the back of the cavernous ballroom, but I'm not about
to complain. I've been waiting months for this massive,
three-day conference. Dubbed Women Deliver, and held
triennially in a different place around the world, this year's
gathering is centred around one equally massive theme:
Power. The still-huge crowd I'm in is only a fraction of the
conference's 8,000 attendees, who have travelled to British
Columbia from over 160 countries. Doucet is the moderator
for the opening panel, "The Power of Us," and Mwansa is
one of seven speakers. To her left is Prime Minister Justin
Trudeau, and seated next to him is the president of Kenya,

Uhuru Kenyatta. Also on stage are the president of Ghana, Nana Addo Dankwa Akufo-Addo, and the president of Ethiopia, the only woman world leader here, Sahle-Work Zewde.

Luckily, there are giant screens on both sides of the stage that project the panellists' faces to the crowd, rendering them into giants every time the camera lands on them. It's a good thing. I doubt anybody would have wanted to miss what happened next.

Doucet turned to Mwansa, asking her first question after their brief hello. "You're a young female activist, in a world full of men, who are" — she paused, smiling — "a little bit older than you," she settled on, drawing out the "i" in little. "Let's be polite." A little laugh and another pause, this time, I think, for emphasis. "Do you really feel you have power?"

It felt like an odd question. I'm not sure what Doucet expected Mwansa to say. Perhaps that, no, she did not feel powerful. Perhaps that she'd like to, one day. Perhaps we all expected Mwansa to answer with humbleness, with a plea, with her own politeness. Surely, few in the room were prepared for Mwansa to exuberantly shame three presidents and one prime minister.

"I do demand for that power," Mwansa responded, seemingly incredulous, swooping her arm. "I mean, look. I'm on the stage with president[s]." At this, the crowd began to cheer. "I think one thing that really has to be emphasized is that there is no way anything is going to be done for us without us. Because that's just doing it against us." By "us" Mwansa meant youth and women. She was tired, she added, of other people deciding what was best for her and then expecting her to go along with it. She told the crowd she had a "key message" — one she was going to share. It was clear she meant to go on, whether it had anything to do with what Doucet wanted to ask her or not. But first, there was something else. "Can I stand?" Mwansa said, not waiting for an answer as she rose to her feet and walked toward the centre of the stage. "I feel more powerful when I stand."

From there, she continued on. She no longer wanted to see politicians making decisions about young people's health, education, and more, without also letting them make the decisions, too. The way she saw it, world leaders expected people to benefit, but they gave them no power at all to decide *how* they might benefit. They were expected to say "thank you" and nothing more. Mwansa did not say this, but to me there was another implication in her message: if women and youth are expected to only wait for better policies and systems, then we'll never close the power gap. They might receive better education and health care, but they'll never decide for themselves what that looks like. They'll always be second (or third, or fourth, or dead last). "We're not [just] going to be beneficiaries," Mwansa said. "That's not happening anymore. It's 2019. So give us power. We need positions of power." She turned to the leaders. "We need gender equality, and we need this reflected in national priorities." And with that, Trudeau rose to his feet, clapping. Then Kenyatta. Then the whole room.

The glorious moment didn't last. Demands for power are a tricky thing among world leaders, even when they are self-professed feminist allies. It's one thing for women and others to say we need seats at the table. It's another, it turns out, to ask that they be given. For an eighteen-year-old to tell several world leaders, to their faces, to step up — well, that's a thing that hadn't been invented until right then.

At the end of Mwansa's speech, Doucet turned to Ghana's president, Akufo-Addo, who hadn't yet had a chance to speak. First, she remarked positively on Mwansa, then on how closely Akufo-Addo had been listening. She asked him for his response. She might as well have said, *Look, buddy, that's a tough act to follow.* The president made a broad gesture, moving his hands from a prayer steeple to either side of his body. He began to speak, pointing a finger at Mwansa. "She's a politician," he quipped. *She is,* he insisted. He named the two other men on the stage—apparently forgetting the president of Ethiopia—remarking that his fellow politicians would agree. And then he dug himself a hole.

"At the end of the day," he opened, "communities or groups talking for themselves and being representative does not translate into power." Power, he continued, is when you sit at the table where decisions are enforced; it's the table where those decisions become the norms and regulations of a society. He seemed oblivious to his dismissal of the power of community leaders and social movements, many members of which were in the room. I remember dropping my pen and holding my breath. This was not in the male-wokeness script. For a few moments, we stayed in small-hole territory: it's not wrong, I thought, watching thousands of Mwansa-inspired, fired-up feminists begin to murmur, to advocate for more women at the decision-making table. It's not wrong to suggest that's where we can make the most change. But, of course, that wasn't his point. His point was this: women weren't doing enough. The murmur became an outcry. He did not stop.

"What I've seen in the two and a half years that I've been in office," he continued, "is that not enough movement is being made by the 52 percent of the Ghanaian population that are women to be able to be in the positions to make these decisions." At this point, the panellist next to him, Dr. Alaa Murabit, a UN High-Level Commissioner on Health Employment and Economic Growth, made a face that was unmistakably amused, scornful. The giant screen captured her expression perfectly. I took out my phone to snap a picture, focusing on her face, which was smiling a smile that was not really happy, a face that I knew exactly mirrored my own. People have remarked on this smile of mine; I make it when I'm recounting something particularly awful, like I'm shielding myself from how bad things really are, how angry I really am.

As Akufo-Addo continued, Murabit's face worked into one exasperated look after another. I heard other women around me laughing softly. *Look at her.* It wasn't funny. We knew it wasn't funny. But we could only laugh with her as he went on and on. "We're not seeing enough dynamism and activism on the part of those who are seeking this new [power]," he said. "We're not. We're not. We're not. I'm—"

And at this point Murabit shot straight up in her chair, words bursting forth. "I have to respond to that." Her hand went up, finger raised.

"We're not," Akufo-Addo plodded on. "I'm talking about dynamism where it matters." Murabit tried to interrupt again, but he spoke on. "Dynamic is not sitting around here talking and talking about electing people to parliament." Dynamism is control. It's being in office. In *power.* "We're talking about decisions, not wishes and hopes."

Murabit raised her arm again, but this time it was Doucet who interrupted the Ghanaian president. "Let's not put all the problems, all the responsibility, at the door of women." Men, after all, she added, hold the cup.

After the clapping subsided, Murabit tried again to speak. Her face looked open, friendly. Maybe she knew the crowd was on her side. "You know," she started, "I just—you and I need to have dinner." Then she reminded everybody that Akufo-Addo was not the only man who believed women were to blame for their own lack of power. A lot of people thought that way, she said. "It's fundamental," she continued, "that we begin to understand and we begin to explain in a way that people can actually understand how much systems have been shaped to ensure that women do not get to be in positions of power."

Yes, the crowd thundered. *Yes, yes, yes.*

"It's incredibly, incredibly important to recognize that there are dynamic, incredible women that the door remains closed to—"

"So how is it going to open?" interrupted Akufo-Addo. "How is it going to open?"

"I'm telling you. I'm *telling* you."

"You're not telling me. I'm telling you"—mansplaining at its best—"what you're saying will not open doors."

Exasperation. "Stop interrupting me and I'll tell you."

"What you're telling me—"

Perhaps sensing a blowout, Doucet stood up. Akufo-Addo went suddenly silent.

"It's incredibly important for male allies in positions of power, like yourself, to look around and recognize the incredible, impactful, dynamic women in their communities and amplify them," Murabit said, her voice rising, at last no longer contained. "Not empower them—because they have agency—but amplify them and put them in positions of power. That's how it changes." She stopped, readying her voice for emphasis, loudness. "It's on *you*, too."

As the crowd stood once more, and as Akufo-Addo gawped, still saying nothing, Murabit, at last, smiled what looked like a real smile.

Equality Is Not a DIY Endeavour

The preceding chapters in this book have argued that equality is not a DIY endeavour. Yes, there are amazing individuals who are leading themselves and their communities in a re-envisioning of power. They are pushing forward, against our systems, when the systems (inevitably) refuse to budge. They are saying, *It doesn't matter what we have always done, let's do it this new way. Let's try option B and C, all the way down to Z, and then let's create a new alphabet, because the old one isn't always working for us.* We need more options. We need infinite ways of being. These new leaders are charting changes in technology, in politics, in business, in the arts, at work, in their cities, and at home. What they're not doing—what we should all be sick of doing—is deciding that they need to fix themselves to gain equality. They are not saying, *If only I were more of a girl boss. If only I just leaned in. If only I did it better, then I would get ahead.* Sure, there's always room for self-improvement. But we cannot improve ourselves to equality.

This is not a self-help book. It is not a book of easy answers and 10 Steps To a Better, More Powerful You. (Although, where along the line did we start believing this endless fixing of ourselves was the best solution for *more?*) It is a book that demands we open our feminist appetite for solutions to addressing the systems around us. To breaking and rebuilding them. It is a book that rejects what those like Akufo-Addo would have us all believe: that the reason we don't have power, and the power to enforce equality, is because we simply are not trying hard enough. Or, put another, more insidious way: if women and other groups truly wanted power and equality so badly, they would have it. As Murabit said in her closing statement, after their exchange, "If a young girl does not feel like she has power over her own body...to go up to her and say, 'You should run for parliament' is ridiculous." Which is really to say: you cannot spend the whole of history building a society designed to keep women and others away from power, and then expect them to one day rise to the top simply because they want to.

If anything, Women Deliver only proved how complex, and interconnected, the push for power is across the globe. The Vancouver Convention Centre became home to a microcosm of the world's brightest, most tireless feminists. And I quickly learned that we had a lot to say. There were so many sessions, workshops, discussions, and big stage events to choose from that one person could have a completely different experience from another. I agonized over the schedule, often wishing I could clone myself and be in several places at once. I'd come to Women Deliver so that I could see what people from around the world were doing to challenge power structures and to upend traditional systems. I'd wanted to see what models they were using and developing, but also to hear what challenges they faced—where they were fighting hardest and how. Naively, I'd thought three days would be enough. It should not have come as a surprise that the most consistent comment I heard was that there simply wasn't enough time.

Here's some of what I did experience: I saw women and men from around the world discussing what's next for the #MeToo movement; I listened as activists from Europe, Brazil, the United States, and more warned how the pushback against women's progress was shaping their countries; I heard Procter and Gamble's global director of diversity and inclusion, Deanna Bass, explain how her mega-corporation was trying to undo the "perfect housewife" image it had created; and I heard Melinda Gates push some of technology's most innovative people to share how they planned to close the gender gap in their industry. That was just on the first day. I'd go on to hear Hina Jilani, an advocate of the Supreme Court of Pakistan, describe how an abused woman seeking aid was once shot in her office. She was at a lunch session talking about how women leaders worldwide could rise to parity. I heard actors from the MTV show *Shuga* describe how the hit program helps raise sexual health awareness across all of Africa. And I heard wise advice from Lopa Banerjee, the director of the civil society division at UN Women: "Clearly what's next on the trajectory [to power] is impatience."

By far the most crowded session I attended was called "Building the pleasure movement: because she decides to seek pleasure." The panellists spoke about the racialized stereotypes of who seeks pleasure—i.e., the idea that only white women care about it—and of tackling the patriarchy with pleasure. They reminded everybody in the room that pleasure-seeking is not wrong or dirty, and that all the shame and guilt and silence that's wrapped up in it is really only another form of control. A scientist on the panel discussed why we still know so little about female pleasure, and how misconceptions are used to damage us. After all, if we don't know what's supposed to feel good, and we're not encouraged to seek it out, how do we know when something feels bad? Near the end, we split up into four gigantic groups and wrote fictional advertisements for things like consent and contraceptives. The prizes for the winning group: vibrators, dildos, handcuffs, lube. It was fun and wonderful, but it was the question session that came after the laughter that stuck with me.

First, people asked about lube and vibrators and how

to know what was best. Then, with a trembling voice, one woman asked for advice on pleasure for those who'd been forced to undergo female genital mutilation. What then? As the panellists fumbled for an answer, another woman in the crowd answered her: the advocacy centre she worked with had resources; she could supply them. They'd connect afterward. Another woman raised her hand: she'd had personal experience and she could help, too. Then came the next question. What do you do if you have PTSD from sexual trauma and you're not at the point where sex toys look like fun? Heads nodded in agreement. Women called out suggestions and support. Some offered hugs. The woman beside me spoke up. She'd experienced childhood sexual abuse. She rarely spoke about it, but she felt safe in that room. A woman next to her rubbed her shoulder. Then another woman spoke. She'd recently enjoyed sex for the first time after her rape. The room cheered.

It reminded me of all our differences and also all our similarities. In this search for power, we could honour both. It wasn't the only time I was reminded of how quickly distinctions could snap into commonalities, like a rubber band. One morning, I was leaving my hotel, my press badge on, when I ran into another woman with a press badge. With a small town's worth of attendees, this was not uncommon. We started chatting. She was from Guyana, and excited to meet other women there from her country; there were some attending that she knew but had never spoken to, face to face. I asked her what she'd seen and if she felt the conference had provided enough on the biggest issues she felt women in her country faced. She said yes. What were those top issues? I asked. By way of an answer, she told me a story. In her newsroom, she said, she was one of the best editors. She was also one of the only women. She knew she made less than the other editors. "I'm sure they make twice as much as me," she said. "And I work twice as hard." Borders and distance do not change some things.

There is a simple revolution in women acknowledging that, all around the world, we need power. We need to redefine it, reimagine it, and decide, for ourselves, what that looks like. We need to help each other do it. From the outside, from the place where you've never had to work twice as hard for half as much, such a conference can look like inaction. It can look like idleness. From the outside, it's hard to see how special it is that 8,000 women from nearly every single country in the world are meeting, unfettered, to discuss and inspire change. From the inside, it recalls the power of #MeToo: women from around the world talking together, sharing their experiences, finding anger and healing, and doing so all without the involvement of the systems that too often harm us.

Once, in between sessions, I wandered down to the exhibit hall. There, I saw a wall that asked: "How do you feel powerful?" People had written so many things: When I shine a light on injustice. When I speak up. When we work together. When I help young people achieve. When I know I've made a difference. When I empower others. When I let myself be seen. When I choose to lead. When I speak for change. And, with simple underline: All day every day.

Behind Every Man

Women Deliver was the second time in less than a year that I had seen Trudeau open a feminist conference. At both, he talked about Canada's commitment to gender equality and the importance of embedding women's rights into legislation and government funding. At both, he was charming and measured, as close to the perfect male ally that anybody could ask for — especially if that ally was currently running your country. This was, after all, the man whose face adorned the cover of a hot-pink book I'd seen earlier that year, on sale for $22.95: *My Canadian Boyfriend, Justin Trudeau*. On the cover, he's making a heart shape with his hands over his own heart. Years after 2015, Trudeau was still a feminist meme brought to life. I was not surprised when the crowd at both events responded to him with wild applause and standing ovations. They seemed to love him. Most women I met seemed to want me to love him, too.

On the second day of the Women Deliver conference, Trudeau met with us journalists, in a small room, to announce that he would raise funding to reach $1.4 billion annually, starting in 2023, to help support women's and girls' health worldwide.[1] Also as of 2023, he said, $700 million of that would go toward reproductive health rights. The goal, he stressed, was to "build on Canada's leadership on global gender equality." It was a good line, and he delivered it well. I sat in the front row and have dozens of pictures of his face, moving through the motions of what looks like sincerity, close listening, empathy — kind of like, yes, a person might imagine their ideal boyfriend looks at them when they're doing something important. Many of the women beside me gushed over it, nodding along and smiling back. I couldn't decide if I was a proud Canadian in that moment or if I thought he was a robot.

When he walked off the small podium, the reporters around me broke their silence. One woman from Finland remarked, "I just love him." She continued, a little embarrassed, "I know I shouldn't say this. I should be objective." A woman from Costa Rica asked me, "How old is he?" When I said I didn't remember offhand, she went on as if she hadn't heard me. "He talks good." They both agreed: he answered all the questions, not like their own leaders. Later, when I went to get coffee in the press room, people saw the word "Canada" on my name badge and congratulated me — as if I had single-handedly birthed Trudeau into office. One said, "I'm still so star-struck by your prime minister." Another joined in, "He's so charismatic." The first continued, "To me, he is the definition of sexy." Several more women nodded along. I was lucky, they told me. *So* lucky.

I wanted to be skeptical. I wanted to burst the Trudeau Perfect Feminist Bubble. This was only scant weeks after the SNC-Lavalin controversy first broke, and his treatment of Jody Wilson-Raybould, as well as the other female MPs who spoke out against him, was still on my mind. It wasn't too long ago that his feminist star had been ready to hurtle from the sky; now he was back on top. Like many allies and superstars, Trudeau is adept at showing people — and particularly mainstream feminists — what he wants them to see: a man who cares. Of all the possibilities, this is not the worst thing. As Canadians, we only have to look to our closest geographical leader, Trump, to see that, comparatively, glossy feminism is much better than no feminism at all. In the coming weeks, Trump would respond to another rape allegation, this one made by well-respected advice columnist and author E. Jean Carroll, with the gut-churning comment: "Number one, she's not my type. Number two, it never happened."[2] Within the same week, he tweeted about Team USA soccer star Megan Rapinoe, who, earlier, had told a reporter that if her team won the World Cup, she wasn't "fucking going to the White House." He wrote that "Megan should WIN first before she TALKS! Finish the job!" adding that she should "never disrespect our Country, the White House, or the Flag."[3] (The team won; Rapinoe did not go to Chez Trump.) Knowing the inevitability of these things (Trump has a pattern, after all), and knowing what other leaders had done in other places around the world, kept me smiling that day at Women Deliver. It kept me laughing with these women and sipping coffee. It kept me from telling them what I believed I knew: that a good man couldn't save us.

I knew why they loved him. On the whole, Trudeau was at least doing something, consistently, for women and girls. Sure, maybe he just wanted political points. Maybe it was all part of a persona. Most likely, it was a mixture of sincere and surface, real and phony, all at once. But, at the end of the day, how much did that matter? Here I was, with a powerful male ally, and I wanted to throw him back. How ungrateful could I get? That was one way to look at it. And, yet...I thought back to Mwansa and her ground-quaking speech: we're done with simply being beneficiaries. Yes, we wanted to see policies change, to see new legislation, to see governments budget for women and girls. We wanted action. The real question was, *whose*? I was done handing out feminist cookies to nice guys. I was exhausted from waiting for them to make change. And I didn't want them to speak for what we needed anymore. You see, here's the thing about spending half a week with thousands of powerful people who are not white men: you begin to see there are so many other options.

This is what I'd think of as the 2019 federal election approached in Canada: why is an ally the best we can hope for? Sometimes, I was glad Trudeau could proclaim his feminism, even if it often felt flawed. (To be fair, whose feminism isn't?) The NDP's federal leader, Jagmeet Singh, has also preached feminist values.[4] Even then Conservative Party leader Andrew Scheer once said he was a feminist.[5] But in more than two years of looking deeply at power structures, and in speaking to dozens of people about how they were changing them, I knew that allies wouldn't be enough. *Better than nothing* had trained us into believing that we couldn't do it better. It had, however unintentionally, made us stand *behind* our allies—putting us second, even as it masqueraded as putting us first. This is what happened when decisions were made for us, without us. We settled for what little power we could get.

"The danger in cavalierly claiming feminism and feminist victories," wrote two political science professors in March 2019 in the *Ottawa Citizen*, at the height of SNC-Lavalin, "is that it can mask the reality of little substantive change and can leave unchallenged Ottawa's deeper, masculinized power structures." The problem with that, they continued, is that "it can make it much harder to get important feminist issues on the agenda as change appears to have already been made."[6] Exactly how much Trudeau has benefitted from — and relied on — those deeper, masculinized power structures became evident as Canada headed into its 2019 federal election.

In September, two photos and a video dating from the 1980s to 2001 emerged of Trudeau in blackface and brownface. When media confronted him about the extent of his racist dress-up, he responded that he was "wary of being definitive" about how many times he'd done so — a fairly transparent effort to guard against the emergence of other possible evidence.[7] He also apologized. Twice. "I have always acknowledged that I come from a place of privilege," he said at a Winnipeg media conference, "but I now need to acknowledge that that comes with a massive blind spot." Sure, but this is not like forgetting to check your mirror when you park. Blackface is one hell of a blind spot. By repeatedly engaging in such a profoundly racist practice, Trudeau exposed what can too often happen when someone believes in their own inherent power, their own innate privilege: they perpetuate some real bad shit. It's not for me to know whether Trudeau has truly changed, whether he's learned to confront his so-called blind spots, or whether he is, at his core, another over-woke bro who is just a little bit racist. What I do know is that it's an arguably short journey from tokenizing people of colour for laughs at an event to tokenizing people of colour for votes in an election. In both cases, the targeted people and communities are reduced to a tool used to elevate somebody else's brand, their vision — whether the goal is to charm other privileged people at a party or to charm them into giving you even more power.

Later research from McGill University's Digital Democracy Project indicated that social-media discussion around Trudeau's blackface surged when the news broke, but dropped dramatically after three days.[8] A substantial amount of the Twitter activity came from Conservative partisans. But even they soon stopped tweeting about it. As we all know by now, Trudeau won the election. His victory speech was, unsurprisingly, textbook Trudeau. He talked about common goals, about hearing his critics, about doing better and bringing the country together, and about rejecting division and negativity.[9] He will have to work harder now to make those sentiments appear authentic, but they are, on the surface, good sentiments. Still, I'd rather turn to Jody Wilson-Raybould for inspiration. In running as an independent candidate, she refused to give up her own power and chose, instead, to play by different rules. She won, too. In her own victory speech, Wilson-Raybould stressed the importance of tossing the Old Boys' Playbook.[10] "We accomplished showing Ottawa, showing our political process, that independent, strong voices matter and that we can do politics differently," she told the crowd in her Vancouver-Granville riding, adding that business-as-usual politics won't solve the country's most urgent issues, including reconciliation and the climate crisis. "We need to collaborate, we need to come together, we need to, again, work across party lines to address these big issues and I know that we can do it."

Because It's 2020

At the very end of Women Deliver, we danced. Angélique Kidjo, a Grammy award–winning Beninese-American singer-songwriter, took the stage, and it felt like pure joy. Her voice, transcendent, was everywhere, and people just *rose*. And then they swayed. And then they stomped their feet and raised their hands, singing and making noise even if they didn't precisely know the words. They pressed to the front, and when Kidjo jumped from the stage to the convention centre floor, they followed her. She strode through the crowd, and it undulated around her. I saw people locked at the hips, their arms around each other, smiling wide. Some women passed out little flags. When Kidjo returned to the stage, preparing her exit, people kept on dancing. Even after the music stopped, they danced. It felt like a small moment of letting go, after days — or a lifetime — of hard, draining, worthwhile work. But even that's not quite right. We weren't letting go. Really, it was a moment of lifting up. Of looking around, seeing we weren't alone, and feeling like, Okay, we've got this. *We've got it*. Let's dance.

Throughout the conference, every moderator asked the same question at the close of the main stage panels: How will you use your power? At first, I thought it was heavy-handed, the kind of question privileged white women ask one another because they have the luxury of doing so. It seemed cheesy and perfunctory, too close to #GirlBoss creed for my initial liking. But as I heard more and more people answer, I began to change my mind. Viewed another way, this question was a way of reminding everyone there that they did have power, now, even if it didn't always feel like it—even if their power didn't look anything like traditional power. It was a way of telling everybody that what they did mattered. Community work mattered. Reproductive health care mattered. Politics mattered. Sports mattered. Technology mattered. Work mattered. Self-care mattered. All of it put a drop more power into this new bucket. It evened things out. It remade the world.

Those were the last words anyone spoke on stage that day: How will you use your power? I wonder if that question was on people's minds as they slowly, slowly filtered out of the room, by the hundreds. Everyone seemed reluctant to stop celebrating. They lingered and swayed their hips, singing and humming. I heard people talking about what they'd tell their friends, colleagues, and fellow activists back home. I heard them saying they wished they could have seen so much more. I saw people hugging and exchanging contact information and rushing to catch flights. And, like I saw throughout the time I was there, I saw a long line of people gather at a sun-yellow rendering of the word "POWER." Each letter stood as tall and as thick as me, a simple sculpture meant for selfies. Woman after woman stood in front of it, taking their pictures and their friends' pictures. After each one, they looked down at their phones and smiled. Here, for a moment, was everything they needed.

Notes

INTRODUCTION

1. Beard, Mary. *Women & Power: A Manifesto*. New York: Liveright, 2017.

2. Eagly, Alice H., and Linda L. Carli. *Through the Labyrinth: The Truth About How Women Become Leaders*. Boston: Harvard Business Review Press, 2007.

3. Macdonald, David. *The Double-Pane Glass Ceiling: The Gender Pay Gap at the Top of Corporate Canada*. Vancouver: Canadian Centre for Policy Alternatives, 2019.

4. Erlichman, Jon. "One in 100: Canada's 'embarrassing' lack of female CEOs among top TSX companies." BNN Bloomberg. July 6, 2018. https://www.bnnbloomberg.ca/female-ceos-noticeably-absent-from-canada-s-c-suite-1.1103584.

5. McCarten, James. "How Trump's attack on Chrystia Freeland may have been the catalyst that clinched a new trade deal." *Financial Post*. October 1, 2018. https://business.financialpost.com/news/economy/u-s-president-cheers-new-usmca-trade-deal-heralds-end-of-nafta-era.

6. Lilley, Brian. "White House not amused with Freeland's 'Tyrant' antics." *Toronto Sun*. September 20, 2018. https://torontosun.com/opinion/columnists/lilley-white-house-not-amused-with-freelands-tyrant-antics; Ivison, John. "Liberals eye potential electoral gains from 'taking on the tyrant' Trump." *National Post*. September 12, 2018. https://nationalpost.com/opinion/john-ivison-liberals-eye-potential-electoral-gains-from-taking-on-the-tyrant-trump; MacDougall, Andrew. "What if Donald Trump has a point with Chrystia Freeland?" *Maclean's*. September 27, 2018. https://www.macleans.ca/politics/what-if-donald-trump-has-a-point-with-chrystia-freeland/.

7. Catalyst. *Quick Take: Women in Science, Technology, Engineering, and Mathematics (STEM)*. June 14, 2019. https://www.catalyst.org/research/women-in-science-technology-engineering-and-mathematics-stem/.

8. Stop Street Harassment, Raliance, UC San Diego Center on Gender Equity and Health. *The Facts Behind the #MeToo Movement: A National Study on Sexual Harassment and Assault*. January 2018. http://www.stopstreetharassment.org/wp-content/uploads/2018/01/Executive-Summary-2018-National-Study-on-Sexual-Harassment-and-Assault.pdf.

9. CTV *News*. "Alberta student creates database of missing, murdered Indigenous women and girls." September 8, 2018. https://www.ctvnews.ca/canada/alberta-student-creates-database-of-missing-murdered-indigenous-women-and-girls-1.4085895; Sovereign Bodies Institute. MMIW Database. https://www.sovereign-bodies.org/mmiw-database.

10. Women and Hollywood. *2018 Celluloid Ceiling Report: Number of Women Directors on Top 250 Films Falls to 8%*. January 2019. https://womenandhollywood.com/2018-celluloid-ceiling-report-number-of-women-directors-on-top-250-films-falls-to-8/.

11. Women's Media Center. *The Status of Women of Color in the U.S. News Media 2018*. http://www.womensmediacenter.com/assets/site/reports/the-status-of-women-of-color-in-the-u-s-media-2018-full-report/Women-of-Color-Report-FINAL-WEB.pdf.

CHAPTER I: POWER HUNGRY

1. Rothkopf, Joanna. "The Sexiest Thing About Justin Trudeau Is His Cabinet's Gender Parity." Jezebel. November 4, 2015. https://theslot.jezebel.com/the-sexiest-thing-about-justin-trudeau-is-his-cabinets-1740585053.

2. Chartrand, Fred. "Trudeau's 'Because it's 2015' retort draws international attention." *Globe and Mail*. November 5, 2015. https://www.theglobeandmail.com/news/politics/trudeaus-because-its-2015-retort-draws-international-cheers/article27119856/.

3. Wilson-Raybould, Jody. "Statement from the Honourable Jody Wilson-Raybould." https://web.archive.org/web/20190114231051/https://jwilson-raybould.liberal.ca/news-nouvelles/statement-from-the-honourable-jody-wilson-raybould-minister-of-veterans-affairs-and-associate-minister-of-national-defence-and-member-of-parliament-for-vancouver-granville/.

4. Rabson, Mia. "Jody Wilson-Raybould became thorn in Liberals' side before SNC-Lavalin case." *Global News*. February 9, 2019. https://web.archive.org/web/20190209181837/https://globalnews.ca/news/4943451/jody-wilson-raybould-place-in-liberals/.

5. Rempel, Michelle. Twitter post. February 9, 2019. https://twitter.com/MichelleRempel/status/1094260757582118912; Syed, Fatima. "Politicians denounce Trudeau government for sexist treatment of Jody Wilson-Raybould." *Canada's National Observer*. February 11, 2019. https://www.nationalobserver.com/2019/02/11/news/politicians-denounce-trudeau-government-sexist-treatment-jody-wilson-raybould.

6. Union of B.C. Indian Chiefs. "Open Letter: The discriminatory, sexist comments about Minister Jody Wilson-Raybould being spread by government officials and staff are appalling and condemnable." February 2019. https://www.ubcic.bc.ca/discriminatory_sexist_comments_about_minister_jody_wilson.

7. Brake, Justin. "PMO calls comments about Jody Wilson-Raybould 'unacceptable.'" APTN *National News*. February 14, 2019. https://

aptnnews.ca/2019/02/14/pmo-calls-comments-about-jody-wilson-raybould-unacceptable/.

8. Olsen, Tyler. "Abbotsford-area MP apologizes for 'inappropriate' comments." *Abbotsford News*. February 28, 2019. https://www.abbynews.com/news/wilson-raybould-testimony-sour-grapes-abbotsford-area-mp-says/.

9. *Global News*. "Jody Wilson-Raybould's testimony—read the full transcript of her opening remarks." February 27, 2019. https://globalnews.ca/news/5006450/jody-wilson-raybould-testimony-transcript/.

10. Tunney, Catharine, and Peter Zimonjic. "Trudeau pushes back on SNC-Lavalin, says he was 'surprised and disappointed' by Wilson-Raybould's resignation." *CBC News*. February 12, 2019. https://www.cbc.ca/news/politics/wilson-raybould-snc-lavalin-1.5015755.

11. Stone, Laura. "Liberal MP Celina Caesar-Chavannes says she was met with 'hostility, anger' in private Trudeau talks." *Globe and Mail*. March 8, 2019. https://www.theglobeandmail.com/canada/article-liberal-mp-celina-caesar-chavannes-says-she-was-met-with-hostility/.

12. Kalvapalle, Rahul, and Amanda Connolly. "Jody Wilson-Raybould and Jane Philpott kicked out of Liberal Party caucus." *Global News*. April 2, 2019. https://globalnews.ca/news/5123526/liberal-caucus-wilson-raybould-jane-philpott/; Aiello, Rachel. "Wilson-Raybould, Philpott 'disappointed' by ouster from Liberal caucus, PM on defensive." *CTV News*. April 3, 2019. https://www.ctvnews.ca/politics/wilson-raybould-philpott-disappointed-by-ouster-from-liberal-caucus-pm-on-defensive-1.4363910.

13. Harris, Kathleen. "Trudeau ejects Wilson-Raybould, Philpott from Liberal caucus." *CBC News*. April 2, 2019. https://www.cbc.ca/news/politics/liberals-wilson-raybould-philpott-caucus-1.5080880.

14. FiveThirtyEight. "2016 General Election Forecast." November 8, 2016. https://projects.fivethirtyeight.com/2016-election-forecast/.

15. Wang, Sam. "All estimates point toward HRC>50% probability. What determines the exact number?" Princeton Election Consortium.

November 2016. http://election.princeton.edu/2016/11/06/is-99-a-reasonable_probability/.

16. Reuters. "Moody's Analytics election model predicts Clinton win." November 1, 2016. https://www.reuters.com/article/us-usa-election-research-moody-s-idUSKBN12W56J.

17. *Orlando Sentinel*. "Female leader of Canada is the most popular in 30 years." August 17, 1993. https://www.orlandosentinel.com/news/os-xpm-1993-08-17-9308170734-story.html.

18. Farnsworth, Clyde H. "Campbell, Though Liked, May Not Win in Canada." *New York Times*. October 15, 1993. https://www.nytimes.com/1993/10/15/world/campbell-though-liked-may-not-win-in-canada.html.

19. *The Canadian Encyclopedia*. "Kim Campbell." February 2008. https://www.thecanadianencyclopedia.ca/en/article/kim-campbell.

20. Green Party of Canada. "Liberals set up new debate commission with fair rules: Elizabeth May will be in the 2019 leaders' debates." October 30, 2018. https://www.greenparty.ca/en/media-release/2018-10-30/liberals-set-new-debate-commission-fair-rules-elizabeth-may-will-be-2019; CBC Player. "May pleased that Greens allowed in federal leaders debates." October 30, 2018. https://www.cbc.ca/player/play/1356818499651.

21. Coletto, David. "Only 1 in 5 Canadian millennials believe they will see global gender equality in their lifetimes." Abacus Data. September 2018. https://abacusdata.ca/only-1-in-5-canadian-millennials-believe-they-will-see-global-gender-equality-in-their-lifetimes/.

22. Maloney, Ryan, and Zi-Ann Lum. "Trudeau's Speech To Daughters Of The Vote Spurs Roughly 50 Delegates To Turn Their Backs." HuffPost. April 3, 2019. https://www.huffingtonpost.ca/2019/04/03/trudeau-daughters-of-the-vote_a_23705757/.

23. Harris, Kathleen. "MP Celina Caesar-Chavannes quits Liberal caucus." *CBC News*. March 20, 2019. https://www.cbc.ca/news/politics/liberal-mp-caesar-chavannes-caucus-1.5064544.

24. Kappler, Maija. "Sheila Copps Stands By Controversial Twitter Statements About Jody Wilson-Raybould." HuffPost. March 10, 2019. https://www.huffingtonpost.ca/2019/03/10/sheila-copps-jody-wilson-raybould-snc-lavalin_a_23689089/.

25. Desilver, Drew. "A record number of women will be serving in the new Congress." Pew Research Center. December 2018. http://www.pewresearch.org/fact-tank/2018/12/18/record-number-women-in-congress/.

26. Interview with Alice Eagly, February 20, 2019.

27. Government of Canada. "Full history of 'O Canada.'" https://www.canada.ca/en/canadian-heritage/services/anthems-canada/history-o-canada.html; Vomiero, Jessica. "'O Canada' lyric change sparks debate, but the anthem was originally gender neutral." *Global News*. February 2, 2018. https://globalnews.ca/news/4002268/oh-canada-originally-gender-neutral/.

28. World Economic Forum. *The Global Gender Gap Report 2018*. http://www3.weforum.org/docs/WEF_GGGR_2018.pdf.

29. Rotenberg, Cristine, and Adam Cotter. "Police-reported sexual assaults in Canada before and after #MeToo, 2016 and 2017." Statistics Canada. November 8, 2018. https://www150.statcan.gc.ca/n1/pub/85-002-x/2018001/article/54979-eng.htm.

30. RAINN. "The Criminal Justice System: Statistics." https://www.rainn.org/statistics/criminal-justice-system.

31. Canadian Women's Foundation. "The Facts about Gender-Based Violence." April 2016. https://www.canadianwomen.org/the-facts/gender-based-violence/.

32. MacDougall, Andrew. "Jody Wilson-Raybould has Trudeau in checkmate." *Maclean's*. February 24, 2019. https://www.macleans.ca/opinion/jody-wilson-raybould-has-trudeau-in-checkmate/.

CHAPTER 2: THIS TIME IT'S DIFFERENT

1. Burke, Tarana. "Address to Change-Makers: An Evening with Tarana Burke." Toronto, February 16, 2019; Ohlheiser, Abby. "The woman behind 'Me Too' knew the power of the phrase when she created it—10 years ago." *Washington Post*. October 19, 2017. https://www.washingtonpost.com/news/the-intersect/wp/2017/10/19/the-woman-behind-me-too-knew-the-power-of-the-phrase-when-she-created-it-10-years-ago/; Burke, Tarana. "The Inception." Just Be, Inc. https://justbeinc.wixsite.com/justbeinc/the-me-too-movement-cmml.

2. Anderson, Monica, and Skye Toor. "How social media users have discussed sexual harassment since #MeToo went viral." Pew Research Center. October 2018. http://www.pewresearch.org/fact-tank/2018/10/11/how-social-media-users-have-discussed-sexual-harassment-since-metoo-went-viral/.

3. Li, Kenneth. "cbs ceo Moonves resigns amid new allegations of sexual misconduct." Reuters. September 9, 2018. https://www.reuters.com/article/us-cbs-moonves-settlement/cbs-ceo-moonves-resigns-amid-new-allegations-of-sexual-misconduct-idUSKCN1LP0W8.

4. Higgins, Tucker. "Ex-cbc ceo Les Moonves will not receive $120 million in severance pay after sexual misconduct probe." cnbc. December 17, 2018. https://www.cnbc.com/2018/12/17/cbs-says-former-ceo-les-moonves-will-not-receive-severance-pay-after-sexual-misconduct-probe.html.

5. Cachero, Paulina. "19 Million #MeToo Tweets Later: Alyssa Milano and Tarana Burke Reflect on the Year After #MeToo." Makers. October 15, 2018. https://www.makers.com/blog/alyssa-milano-and-tarana-burke-reflect-on-year-after-me-too.

6. Roscigno, Vincent J. "Power, Revisited." *Social Forces* 90, no. 2 (2011).

7. Safronova, Valeryia. "Catherine Deneuve and Others Denounce the #MeToo Movement." *New York Times*. January 9, 2018. https://www.nytimes.com/2018/01/09/movies/catherine-deneuve-and-others-denounce-the-metoo-movement.html.

8. *The Economist.* "After a year of #MeToo, American opinion has shifted against victims." October 15, 2018. https://www.economist.com/graphic-detail/2018/10/15/after-a-year-of-metoo-american-opinion-has-shifted-against-victims.

9. Edwards-Levy, Ariel. "Here's What America Thinks About The Me Too Movement Now." HuffPost. August 22, 2018. https://www.huffingtonpost.ca/entry/poll-me-too-sexual-harassment_us_5b7dcbdde4b07295150f7e5e.

10. Canadian Women's Foundation. "Survey finds drop in Canadians' understanding of consent." May 16, 2018. https://www.canadianwomen.org/survey-finds-drop-in-canadians-understanding-of-consent/.

11. McCann, Carly, and Donald T. Tomaskovic-Devey. "Nearly all sexual harassment at work goes unreported – and those who do report often see zero benefit." The Conversation. December 14, 2018. https://theconversation.com/nearly-all-sexual-harassment-at-work-goes-unreported-and-those-who-do-report-often-see-zero-benefit-108378.

12. Garber, Megan. "Christine Blasey Ford Didn't Come Forward in Vain." *The Atlantic.* October 6, 2018. https://www.theatlantic.com/entertainment/archive/2018/10/did-christine-blasey-ford-come-forward-nothing/572380/.

13. Arnold, Amanda. "Christine Blasey Ford Speaks Out About the Threats She's Faced." *New York Magazine.* November 26, 2018. https://www.thecut.com/2018/11/christine-blasey-ford-threats-gofundme.html; Baker, Peter, Sheryl Gay Stolberg, and Nicholas Fandos. "Christine Blasey Ford Wants FBI to Investigate Kavanaugh Before She Testifies." *New York Times.* September 18, 2018. https://www.nytimes.com/2018/09/18/us/politics/christine-blasey-ford-kavanaugh-senate-hearing.html.

14. Sweetland Edwards, Haley. "How Christine Blasey Ford's Testimony Changed America." *Time.* October 4, 2018. http://time.com/5415027/christine-blasey-ford-testimony/.

15. Levenson, Eric. "Larry Nassar sentenced to up to 175 years in prison for decades of sexual abuse." CNN. January 24, 2018. https://www.cnn.com/2018/01/24/us/larry-nassar-sentencing/index.html.

16. Sullivan, Kate. "Christine Blasey Ford makes first public statement since testimony: 'We all have the power to create real change.'" CNN. December 13, 2018. https://www.cnn.com/2018/12/12/politics/christine-blasey-ford-gymnast-larry-nassar-sexual-abuse/index.html.

17. Carlsen, Audrey, Maya Salam, Claire Cain Miller, et al. "#MeToo brought down 201 powerful men. Nearly half of their replacements are women." New York Times. October 29, 2018. https://www.nytimes.com/interactive/2018/10/23/us/metoo-replacements.html.

18. Duffy, Andrew. "Bekah D'Aoust reveals herself as victim in high-profile sexsomnia case." Ottawa Citizen. March 7, 2019. https://ottawacitizen.com/news/local-news/bekah-daoust-reveals-herself-as-victim-in-high-profile-sexsomnia-case.

19. Roumeliotis, Ionna. "'And then he was raping me': Victim goes public about shocking attack to reveal justice system flaws." CBC News. March 2, 2019. https://www.cbc.ca/news/canada/national-sam-fazio-metoo-assault-justice-system-1.5037881.

20. Cherry, Paul. "#MeToo: More women get OK to go public in Bertrand Charest sex-assault case." Montreal Gazette. June 5, 2018. https://montrealgazette.com/news/local-news/bertrand-charest-case-more-sexual-assault-victims-want-to-speak-out.

21. "Bekah D'Aoust has publication ban removed in sexsomnia case." CBC News. March 5, 2019. https://www.cbc.ca/news/canada/ottawa/sexsomnia-publication-ban-survivor-1.5042964.

22. Chang, Clio. "Alexandria Ocasio-Cortez's State of the Union Guest Is a Message to Survivors." Jezebel. April 2, 2019. https://theslot.jezebel.com/alexandria-ocasio-cortezs-state-of-the-union-guest-is-a-1832327419.

23. Pengelly, Martin. "'Go back home': Trump aims racist attack at Ocasio-Cortez and other congresswomen." The Guardian. July 15, 2019. https://www.theguardian.com/us-news/2019/jul/14/trump-

squad-tlaib-omar-pressley-ocasio-cortez; Swaine, Jon. "Trump renews racist attack on Squad: 'They're not capable of loving the U.S.'" *The Guardian.* July 21, 2019. https://www.theguardian.com/us-news/2019/jul/21/trump-racist-squad-democrats-omar-ocasio-cortez-tlaib-pressley.

24. Nora MacIntosh, Avalon Sexual Assault Centre, in presentation to Law Needs Feminism Because forum, Halifax, Nova Scotia, February 23, 2019.

25. Craig, Elaine. *Putting Trials on Trial: Sexual Assault and the Failure of the Legal Profession.* Montreal and Kingston: McGill-Queen's University Press, 2018, 36–7.

26. Government of Canada, Department of Justice. "Restorative Justice." March 2018. https://www.justice.gc.ca/eng/rp-pr/jr/rg-rco/2018/mar08.html.

27. Evans, Jane, Susan McDonald, and Richard Gill. "Restorative Justice: The Experiences of Victims and Survivors." *Victims of Crime Research Digest* no. 11. Accessed at Government of Canada, Department of Justice: https://www.justice.gc.ca/eng/rp-pr/cj-jp/victim/rd11-rr11/p5.html.

28. Wemmers, Jo-Anne. "Judging Victims: Restorative choices for victims of sexual violence." *Victims of Crime Research Digest* no. 10. Accessed at Government of Canada, Department of Justice: https://www.justice.gc.ca/eng/rp-pr/cj-jp/victim/rd10-rr10/p3.html.

29. Moore, Oliver. "All-female cab-company proposal spurs debate in Halifax." *Globe and Mail.* November 23, 2018. https://www.theglobeandmail.com/canada/article-all-female-cab-company-proposal-spurs-debate-in-halifax/.

CHAPTER 3: WOULD IT KILL YOU TO SMILE?

1. University of British Columbia, Sauder School of Business. "A mandate to promote diverse leadership: Professor Jennifer Berdahl." April 10, 2014. https://web.archive.org/web/20180730212017/http://

www.sauder.ubc.ca/News/2014/A_mandate_to_promote_diverse_
leadership_Professor_Jennifer_Berdahl.

2. Berdahl, Jennifer. "Work as a Masculinity Contest." *Journal of Social Issues* 74, no. 3 (2018), 422–8.

3. Berdahl, Jennifer. "Did President Arvind Gupta Lose the Masculinity Contest?" (blog post). August 8, 2015. http://jberdahl. blogspot.com/2015/08/did-president-arvind-gupta-lose.html.

4. Berdahl, Jennifer. "Academic Freedom and UBC." (blog post) August 17, 2015. http://jberdahl.blogspot.com/2015/08/academic-freedom-and-ubc.html; interview with Jennifer Berdahl, December 12, 2018.

5. Smith, Charlie. "Documents show ex-UBC chair John Montalbano and ex-president Arvind Gupta had a sometimes rocky relationship." *Georgia Straight.* January 27, 2016. https://www.straight.com/ news/626851/documents-show-ex-ubc-chair-john-montalbano-and-ex-president-arvind-gupta-had-sometimes; Sherlock, Tracy. "UBC releases documents on former president's departure but reason he left remains unclear." *Vancouver Sun.* January 27, 2016. https:// vancouversun.com/news/local-news/ubc-releases-documents-on-former-presidents-departure-but-reason-he-left-remains-unclear.

6. Berdahl, Jennifer. "Academic Freedom and UBC"; interview with Jennifer Berdahl, December 12, 2018.

7. Smith, Lynn. "Summary of the fact-finding process and conclusions regarding alleged breaches of academic freedom and other university policies at University of British Columbia." https://president.ubc. ca/files/2015/10/Summary-of-Process-and-Conclusions-Final.pdf.

8. Tansey, James. "Academic freedom at UBC: The case of Arvind Gupta and Jennifer Berdahl." *Globe and Mail.* May 15, 2018. https:// www.theglobeandmail.com/opinion/academic-freedom-at-ubc-the-case-of-arvind-gupta-and-jennifer-berdahl/article26055674/.

9. Gerszak, Rafal. "Not every professor's remark is 'academic.'" *Globe and Mail.* May 15, 2015. https://www.theglobeandmail.com/opinion/ editorials/not-every-professors-remark-is-academic/article26931880/.

10. *Globe and Mail.* "Globe editorial: Why did McGill fail to defend Andrew Potter's academic freedom?" March 23, 2017. https://www.theglobeandmail.com/opinion/editorials/globe-editorial-why-did-mcgill-fail-to-defend-andrew-potters-academic-freedom/article34411662/.

11. Freedom House. "Democracy in Retreat." Freedom in the World 2019. https://freedomhouse.org/report/freedom-world/freedom-world-2019/democracy-in-retreat; also full report, *Freedom in the World 2019.* https://freedomhouse.org/sites/default/files/Feb2019_FH_FITW_2019_Report_ForWeb-compressed.pdf.

12. Walkom, Thomas. "How Doug Ford is different than Donald Trump." *Toronto Star.* May 8, 2018. https://www.thestar.com/opinion/star-columnists/2018/05/08/how-doug-ford-is-different-than-donald-trump.html; Brown, Drew. "Doug Ford Is Not Donald Trump North." *Vice.* June 8, 2018. https://www.vice.com/en_ca/article/7xmdzd/doug-ford-is-not-donald-trump-north; Loewen, Peter. "Did Canada just elect a 'Trump light'? Not exactly." *Washington Post.* June 8, 2018. https://www.washingtonpost.com/news/global-opinions/wp/2018/06/08/did-canada-just-elect-a-trump-light-not-exactly/?noredirect=on&utm_term=.8e4aacb18e5d.

13. Amnesty International. "Toxic Twitter—Women's Experiences of Violence and Abuse on Twitter." March 2018. https://www.amnesty.org/en/latest/research/2018/03/online-violence-against-women-chapter-3/.

14. McKeon, Lauren. "How Everyday Misogyny Feeds the Incel Movement." *The Walrus.* May 7, 2018. http://thewalrus.ca/how-everyday-misogyny-feeds-the-incel-movement/.

15. Solon, Olivia. "'Incel': Reddit bans misogynist men's group blaming women for their celibacy." *The Guardian.* November 8, 2017. https://www.theguardian.com/technology/2017/nov/08/reddit-incel-involuntary-celibate-men-ban.

16. Since the time the author originally reported on these comments, the domain incel.me has been shut down. The forum was later reopened under a new domain name, incels.co. For a general impression of the conversations that took place on this subreddit, you

can look at the quarantined Reddit page for "Braincels" at https://www.reddit.com/r/Braincels/?count=350&after=t3_8f31de.

17. Cain, Patrick. "What we learned from Alek Minassian's Incel-linked Facebook page—and what we'd like to know." *Global News.* April 24, 2018. https://globalnews.ca/news/4164340/alek-minassian-facebook-page/.

18. Rodger, Elliot. "My Twisted World: The Story of Elliot Rodger." https://www.documentcloud.org/documents/1173808-elliot-rodger-manifesto.html.

19. Again, see the quarantined Reddit page for "Braincels" at https://www.reddit.com/r/Braincels/?count=350&after=t3_8f31de.

20. We Hunted the Mammoth (blog)."Incels hail 'our savior St. Nikolas Cruz' for Valentine's Day school shooting."

21. Barrouquere, Brett. "Florida man who killed two women at yoga studio spoke of 'incel' hero Elliot Rodger in online video." *Southern Poverty Law Center.* November 3, 2018. https://www.splcenter.org/hatewatch/2018/11/03/florida-man-who-killed-two-women-yoga-studio-spoke-incel-hero-elliot-rodger-online-video; McDonnell-Parry, Amelia. "Florida Yoga Studio Shooter Is Latest in String of Violence By Incels." *Rolling Stone.* November 5, 2018. https://www.rollingstone.com/culture/culture-news/yoga-shooter-scott-paul-beierle-talahassee-751946/; Danner, Chas. "What to Know About the Tallahassee yoga Studio Attack." *New York Magazine.* November 4, 2018. http://nymag.com/intelligencer/2018/11/what-to-know-about-the-tallahassee-yoga-studio-attack.html.

22. Lach, Eric. "Trump's Mocking of Christine Blasey Ford and the Dark Laughter of His Audience." *New Yorker.* October 3, 2018. https://www.newyorker.com/news/current/trumps-mocking-of-christine-blasey-ford-and-the-dark-laughter-of-his-audience.

23. Stieb, Matt. "Why Is Jordan Peterson Selling Lobster Merch?" *New York Magazine.* March 18, 2019. http://nymag.com/intelligencer/2019/03/why-is-jordan-peterson-selling-lobster-merch.html; Peterson, Jordan B. "Goodbye to Patreon." YouTube video. January 1, 2019. https://www.youtube.com/watch?v=h8_OrrvaVVw.

24. Penguin Random House. *12 Rules for Life*, descriptive copy. https://www.penguinrandomhouse.com/books/258237/12-rules-for-life-by-jordan-b-peterson--foreword-by-norman-doige-md-illustrated-by-ethan-van-sciver/9780345816023/.

25. The Liberty Hound. "'Why Do Women Wear Makeup At Work?' Jordan Peterson STUMPS *Vice* Reporter." YouTube video. February 9, 2018. https://web.archive.org/web/20180209231924/https://www.youtube.com/watch?v=VSOwhAjhjdQ.

26. Peterson, Jordan. *12 Rules for Life: An Antidote to Chaos*. Toronto: Random House Canada, 2018, 298.

27. Peterson, Jordan. *12 Rules for Life: An Antidote to Chaos*, 303.

28. Teespring. Jordan B. Peterson Official Merchandise Store. https://teespring.com/stores/jordanbpeterson.

29. Marche, Stephen. "The 'debate of the century': what happened when Jordan Peterson debated Slavoj Žižek." *The Guardian*. April 20, 2019. https://www.theguardian.com/world/2019/apr/20/jordan-peterson-slavoj-zizek-happiness-capitalism-marxism.

30. Glick, Peter, and Susan T. Fiske. "An Ambivalent Alliance: Hostile and Benevolent Sexism As Complementary Justifications for Gender Inequality." *American Psychologist* 56, no. 2 (February 2001), 109–18.

31. Jacobsen, Margaret e. "Actually, Donald Trump, Motherhood Isn't The 'Most Important Job' I'll Ever Have." Romper. October 4, 2016. https://www.romper.com/p/actually-donald-trump-motherhood-isnt-the-most-important-job-ill-ever-have-19679; June, Laura. "Stop Telling Women Motherhood Is the Most Important Job." *New York Magazine*. October 4, 2016. https://www.thecut.com/2016/10/stop-telling-women-motherhood-is-the-most-important-job.html.

32. CNN Entertainment. "2005: Donald and Melania Trump as newlyweds." May 7, 2005. https://www.cnn.com/videos/entertainment/2016/05/06/donald-trump-melania-trump-2005-entire-larry-king-live-intv.cnn.

33. Jeltsen, Melissa. "Trump's Backwards Views On Parenting Could Have Disastrous Implications." *Huffington Post*. June 29, 2016. http://huffingtonpost.ca/entry/trumps-backwards-views-on-parenting-are-dangerous-as_n_57717819e4b379f6; Ioffe, Julia. "Melania Trump on Her Rise, Her Family Secrets, and Her True Political Views: 'Nobody Will Ever Know.'" *GQ* magazine. April 27, 2016. https://www.gq.com/story/melania-trump-gq-interview.

34. Bergeron, Manon. *L'Enquête Sexualité, Sécurité et Interactions en Milieu Universitaire*. http://essimu.quebec/wp/wp-content/uploads/2015/12/Rapport-ESSIMU-UQAM.pdf.

35. Bergeron, Manon. *L'Enquête Sexualité, Sécurité et Interactions en Milieu Universitaire*; Enos, Elysha. "Sexual violence widespread at Quebec universities, study finds." *CBC News*. January 16, 2017. https://www.cbc.ca/news/canada/montreal/sexual-assault-campus-quebec-victimization-1.3937527.

36. This refers to the Canadian Symposium on Sexual Violence in Post-Secondary Education Institutions held at McGill University, May 30 to May 31, 2018.

37. Radio-Canada. "Manon Bergeron, Scientifique de l'année 2018 de RADIO-CANADA." January 22, 2019. https://communiques.radio-canada.ca/radio/8590/MANON-BERGERON-Scientifique-De-Lannee-2018-De-RADIO-CANADA.

38. Boisvert, Yves. "Pauvre science." *La Presse*. January 24, 2019. https://www.lapresse.ca/debats/chroniques/yves-boisvert/201901/23/01-5212182-pauvre-science.php.

39. Radio-Canada. "La scientifique de l'année 2018." Facebook post, video. https://www.facebook.com/RadioCanada/videos/la-scientifique-de-lann%C3%A9e-2018/1965361626917364/.

40. Descarries, Francine, and Sandrine Ricci. "À la défense de savoirs scientifiques responsables et engages." *University Affairs/Affaires universitaires*. February 14, 2019. https://www.affairesuniversitaires.ca/opinion/a-mon-avis/a-la-defense-de-savoirs-scientifiques-responsables-et-engages/.

41. UNESCO. "Recommendation on Science and Scientific Researchers." November 2017. http://portal.unesco.org/en/ev.php-URL_ID=49455&URL_DO=DO_TOPIC&URL_SECTION=201.html.

42. Catalyst. *Quick Take: Women in Science and Medicine*. June 18, 2018. https://www.catalyst.org/research/women-in-science-and-medicine/.

43. Veldhuis, Caroline. "Women and work in the nonprofit sector." Charity Village. September 19, 2011. https://charityvillage.com/cms/content/topic/women_and_work_in_the_nonprofit_sector#.XKd1DetKjdQ.

44. Timmons, Vianne. "Closing the Gender Gap at Canadian Universities." *Policy Magazine*. September 2016. http://www.policymagazine.ca/pdf/21/PolicyMagazineSeptemberOctober-2016-Timmons.pdf; Wiart, Nikki. "Canadian colleges have more women at the helm than universities." *Maclean's*. November 28, 2016. https://www.macleans.ca/education/college/canadian-colleges-have-more-women-at-the-helm-than-universities/.

45. Ward, Susan. "Statistics on Canadian Women in Business: What women entrepreneurs in Canada are like." The Balance: Small Business. February 28, 2019. https://www.thebalancesmb.com/statistics-on-canadian-women-in-business-2948029.

46. Ratner, Rebecca K., and Dale T. Miller. "The Norm of Self-interest and Its Effects on Social Action." *Journal of Personality and Social Psychology* 81, no. 1 (2001), 5–16.

CHAPTER 4: THIS IS WHAT EQUALITY LOOKS LIKE

1. Forté Foundation. "Women's MBA Enrollment Rises to 38% in 2018—First U.S. Business School Reaches Gender Parity Milestone, Forté Foundation Finds." November 14, 2018. http://www.fortefoundation.org/site/DocServer/Forte_-_Women_MBA_Enrollment_Rises_to_38__in_2018.pdf?docID=25209.

2. Rosenzweig & Company. "14th Annual Rosenzweig Report: Women in Canada Continue to Face Incremental Growth in

Leadership Positions." Ciston PR Newswire. March 08, 2019. https://www.prnewswire.com/news-releases/14th-annual-rosenzweig-report-women-in-canada-continue-to-face-incremental-growth-in-leadership-positions-300809374.html; Rosenzweig & Company. *The 14th Annual Rosenzweig Report*. March 2019. https://www.rosenzweigco.com/media-1/the-14th-annual-rosenzweig-report-on-women-at-the-top-levels-of-corporate-canada.

3. Catalyst. *Quick Take: Women in Law*. October 2, 2018. https://www.catalyst.org/research/women-in-law/; Federation of Law Societies of Canada. "Statistical Report of the Federation of Law Societies of Canada: 2016 Membership." https://flsc.ca/wp-content/uploads/2018/04/Statistics-2016-FINAL.pdf.

4. Canadian Centre for Diversity and Inclusion. "Diversity by the Numbers: The legal profession." November 30, 2016. https://ccdi.ca/attachments/DBTN_TLP_2016.pdf.

5. Fine, Sean. "Ottawa appointing more female judges, but bench still short of gender parity." *Globe and Mail*. June 19, 2018. https://www.theglobeandmail.com/canada/article-ottawa-appointing-more-female-judges-but-bench-still-short-of-gender/; Office of the Commissioner for Federal Judicial Affairs Canada. "Number of Federally Appointed Judges as of September 3, 2019." September 2019. http://www.fja.gc.ca/appointments-nominations/judges-juges-eng.aspx.

6. Civitella, Anabel Cossette. "Women academics are still outnumbered at the higher ranks." *University Affairs*. June 13, 2018. https://www.universityaffairs.ca/news/news-article/women-academics-are-still-outnumbered-at-the-higher-ranks/.

7. Statistics Canada. "Number and salaries of full-time teaching staff at Canadian universities, 2016–2017." *The Daily*. November 28, 2017. https://www150.statcan.gc.ca/n1/daily-quotidien/171128/dq171128b-eng.htm.

8. Hannay, Chris, Mayaz Alam, and James Keller. "Politics Briefing: Across Canada, women are still underrepresented." *Globe and Mail*. March 8, 2018. https://www.theglobeandmail.com/news/politics/politics-briefing-across-canada-women-are-still-underrepresented/

article38247083/; OECD Data. "Women in politics." International Development Statistics: Gender, Institutions and Development. 2014. https://data.oecd.org/inequality/women-in-politics.htm; Orr, Erin. "Transforming Local Government: An update on women's status." *Public Sector Digest*. April 2018. https://publicsectordigest.com/article/transforming-local-government-update-women%E2%80%99s-status.

9. Bachman, Eric. "An Appreciation of Ann Hopkins, A Glass Ceiling Pioneer." *Forbes*. July 19, 2018. https://www.forbes.com/sites/ericbachman/2018/07/19/an-appreciation-of-ann-hopkins-a-glass-ceiling-pioneer/#5980e4525681.

10. Bachman, Eric. "An Appreciation of Ann Hopkins, A Glass Ceiling Pioneer."

11. Price Waterhouse v. Hopkins. U.S. Supreme Court. 490 U.S. 228. May 1, 1989. https://www.law.cornell.edu/supremecourt/text/490/228.

12. Barnes, Brooks. "Ann Hopkins, Who Struck an Early Blow to the Glass Ceiling, Dies at 74." *New York Times*. July 17, 2018. https://www.nytimes.com/2018/07/17/obituaries/ann-hopkins-winner-of-a-workplace-bias-fight-dies-at-74.html.

13. McGregor, Jena. "Yahoo CEO Carol Bartz gets fired by phone, gets real by email." *Washington Post*. September 7, 2011. https://www.washingtonpost.com/blogs/post-leadership/post/yahoo-ceo-carol-bartz-gets-fired-by-phone-gets-real-by-email/.

14. Shankland, Steven. "It's official: Bartz becomes Yahoo CEO." CNET. January 15, 2009. https://www.cnet.com/news/its-official-bartz-becomes-yahoo-ceo/.

15. Bartz, Carol. "Former Yahoo CEO Carol Bartz on the messed up excuses execs give for paying women less than men." Market Watch. March 7, 2018. https://www.marketwatch.com/story/former-yahoo-ceo-carol-bartz-on-the-messed-up-excuses-execs-give-for-paying-women-less-than-men-2018-03-07.

16. Sellers, Patricia. "Carol Bartz exclusive: "Yahoo 'f—ed me over.'" *Fortune*. September 8, 2011. http://fortune.com/2011/09/08/carol-bartz-exclusive-yahoo-f-ed-me-over/.

17. Covert, Bryce. "The first high-profile person blamed in the financial crisis is a woman." ThinkProgress. October 23, 2013. https://thinkprogress.org/the-first-high-profile-person-blamed-in-the-financial-crisis-is-a-woman-71e618827f61/.

18. Covert, Bryce. "How women may take the blame for a man's disastrous trade at JP Morgan." ThinkProgress. May 16, 2013. https://thinkprogress.org/how-women-may-take-the-blame-for-a-mans-disastrous-trade-at-jp-morgan-9391b9be77cc/.

19. Sherman, Erik. "If Elon Musk were a woman, he'd have been fired already." *Inc.* Dec 10, 2018. https://www.inc.com/erik-sherman/if-elon-musk-were-a-woman-hed-have-been-fired-already.html.

20. Viglucci, Andres, and Nicholas Nehamas. "FIU had grand plans for a 'signature' bridge. But the design had a key mistake, experts say." *Miami Herald*. June 14, 2018. https://www.miamiherald.com/news/local/community/miami-dade/article212571434.html.

21. Sherron, Alisha. "A female-led construction company built the Florida bridge that collapsed." Squawker. March 16, 2018; Evon, Dan. "Was an all-female construction company responsible for the FIU-Sweetwater bridge collapse?" Snopes. March 19, 2018. https://archive.is/CegL1, https://www.snopes.com/fact-check/was-all-female-responsible-bridge-collapse/.

22. Rhode, Deborah L. *Women and Leadership*. Oxford: Oxford Unversity Press, 2016.

23. Valian, Virginia. "The Cognitive Bases of Gender Bias." *Brooklyn Law Review* 65, no. 4 (1999).

24. Swim, Janet, and Lawrence J. Sanna. "He's Skilled, She's Lucky: A Meta-Analysis of Observers' Attributions for Women's and Men's Successes and Failures." *Personality and Social Psychology Bulletin* 22, no. 5. (May 1996).

25. Bertrand, Marianne, and Sendhil Mullainathan. "Are Emily and Greg More Employable than Lakisha and Jamal? A field experiment on labor market discrimination." *American Economic Review* 94, no. 4. (September 2004), 991–1013.

26. Stevenson, Jane Edison, and Evelyn Orr. "We Interviewed 57 Female CEOs to Find Out How More Women Can Get to the Top." *Harvard Business Review*. November 8, 2017. https://hbr.org/2017/11/we-interviewed-57-female-ceos-to-find-out-how-more-women-can-get-to-the-top.

27. Fitzsimons, Grainne, Aaron Kay, and Jae Yun Kim. "Lean In messages and the illusion of control." *Harvard Business Review*. July 30, 2018. https://hbr.org/2018/07/lean-in-messages-and-the-illusion-of-control.

28. Girlboss. "The Girlboss Rally." https://girlbossrally.com/.

29. Amoruso, Sophia. *#GirlBoss*. New York: Penguin Publishing Group, 2015, 6.

30. Nike. "Dream Crazier." YouTube video. February 24, 2019. https://www.youtube.com/watch?v=whpJi9RJ4JY.

31. Del Valle, Gaby. "Nike debuted a moving Serena Wiliams ad at the Oscars." Vox. February 24, 2019. https://www.vox.com/2019/2/24/18239151/serena-williams-nike-ad-dream-crazier-oscars.

32. Curcio, Jenna. "Serena Williams speaks out about female empowerment in Nike ad." *CR Fashion Book*. February 25, 2019. https://www.crfashionbook.com/culture/a26519254/nike-dream-crazier-serena-williams-campaign/.

33. Harvey, Olivia. "This Nike ad about women getting called 'crazy' and 'irrational' was secretly the best part of the 2019 Oscars." Hello Giggles. February 25, 2019. https://hellogiggles.com/news/nike-ad-about-women-getting-called-crazy-best-part-of-2019-oscars/.

34. Coffman, Julie, and Bill Neuenfeldt. "Everyday Moments of Truth: Frontline managers are key to women's career aspirations." Bain &

Company. June 17, 2014. https://www.bain.com/insights/everyday-moments-of-truth/.

35. Judge, Elizabeth. "Women on board: help or hindrance?" *The Times*. November 11, 2003. https://www.thetimes.co.uk/article/women-on-board-help-or-hindrance-2c6fnqf6fng.

36. Ryan, Michelle K., and S. Alexander Haslam. "The Glass Cliff: Exploring the Dynamics Surrounding the Appointment of Women to Precarious Leadership Positions." *The Academy of Management Review* 32, no. 2 (April 2007), 549–57.

37. Geir, Ben. "GM's Mary Barra: Crisis manager of the year." *Fortune*. December 28, 2014. http://fortune.com/2014/12/28/gms-barra-crisis-manager/; Bloomgarden, Kathy. "What Marissa Mayer can learn from Mary Barra about crisis management." *Fortune*. January 14, 2016. http://fortune.com/2016/01/14/marissa-mayer-mary-barra-crisis-management/.

38. Cook, Alison, and Christy Glass. "Research notes and commentaries above the glass ceiling: When are women and racial/ethnic minorities promoted to CEO?" *Strategic Management Journal* 35, no. 7 (June 2013).

39. Reingold, Jennifer. "Why top women are disappearing from corporate America." *Fortune*. September 9, 2016. http://fortune.com/women-corporate-america/.

40. Darouei, Maral, and Helen Pluut. "The paradox of being on the glass cliff: Why do women accept risky leadership positions?" *Career Development International*. September 2018.

41. Rockefeller Foundation. "Does the media influence how we perceive women in leadership?" October 28, 2016. https://assets.rockefellerfoundation.org/app/uploads/20161028122206/100x25_MediaLanguage_report1.pdf.

42. Gupta, Vishal K., Sandra C. Mortal, Sabatino Silveri, et al. "You're Fired! Gender Disparities in CEO Dismissal." *Journal of Management*. November 5, 2018.

43. Gupta, Vishal K., Seonghee Han, Sandra C. Mortal, et al. "Do Women CEOS Face Greater Threat of Shareholder Activism Compared to Male CEOS? A Role Congruity Perspective." *Journal of Applied Psychology* 103, no. 2 (October 2017).

44. Quadlin, Natasha. "The Mark of A Woman's Record: Gender and Academic Performance in Hiring." *American Sociological Review* 83, no. 2 (2018).

45. Macdonald, David. "The Double-Pane Glass Ceiling: The Gender Pay Gap at The Top Of Corporate Canada." Canadian Centre for Policy Alternatives. January 2019.

46. Maass, Anne, and Mara Cadinu. "Sexual Harassment Under Social Identity Threat: The Computer Harassment Paradigm." *Journal of Personality and Social Psychology* 85, no. 5 (December 2003), 853–70.

47. Sobczak, Anna. "The Queen Bee Syndrome: The paradox of women discrimination on the labour market." *Journal of Gender and Power* 9, no. 1 (2018).

48. Cooper, Marianne. "Why women (sometimes) don't help other women." *The Atlantic.* June 23, 2016. https://www.theatlantic.com/business/archive/2016/06/queen-bee/488144/; Khazan, Olga. "Why do women bully each other at work?" *The Atlantic.* September 2017. https://www.theatlantic.com/magazine/archive/2017/09/the-queen-bee-in-the-corner-office/534213/; Sandberg, Sheryl, and Adam Grant. "Sheryl Sandberg on the myth of the catty woman." *New York Times.* June 23, 2016. https://www.nytimes.com/2016/06/23/opinion/sunday/sheryl-sandberg-on-the-myth-of-the-catty-woman.html; Ludwig, Dr. Robi. "Bad female boss? She may have the Queen Bee Syndrome." *USA Today.* April 12, 2011. https://www.today.com/money/bad-female-boss-she-may-have-queen-bee-syndrome-2D80555922.

49. Derks, Belle, Naomi Ellemers, Colette van Laar, and Kim de Groot. "Do sexist organizational cultures create the Queen Bee?" *British Journal of Social Psychology* 50 (2011).

50. Sterk, Naomi, Loes Meeussen, and Colette Van Laar. "Perpetuating Inequality: Junior Women Do Not See Queen Bee

Behavior as Negative but Are Nonetheless Negatively Affected by It." *Frontiers in Psychology*. September 20, 2018.

CHAPTER 5: NO BOYS ALLOWED

1. Conger, Kate. "Exclusive: Here's the full 10-page anti-diversity screed circulating internally at Google." Gizmodo. August 8, 2017. https://gizmodo.com/exclusive-heres-the-full-10-page-anti-diversity-screed-1797564320.

2. Levin, Sam. "Women say they quit Google because of racial discrimination: 'I was invisible.'" *The Guardian*. August 18, 2017. https://www.theguardian.com/technology/2017/aug/18/women-google-memo-racism-sexism-discrimination-quit.

3. Smith College Libraries. Sorosis Records. Sophia Smith Collection of Women's History, SSC-MS-00356. https://asteria.fivecolleges.edu/findaids/sophiasmith/mnsss336.html.

4. General Federation of Women's Clubs. "History and Mission." https://www.gfwc.org/who-we-are/history-and-mission/.

5. General Federation of Women's Clubs. "History and Mission."

6. Croly, J. C. *The History of the Women's Club Movement in America*. New York: Allen, 1898. Quoted in Hobbs, Amy. "The Women Woke Up: Women's Clubs' Progressive Rhetoric in Gilman's Early Utopian Novels." CEA *Critic* 70, no. 2 (2008).

7. Blair, Karen K. "Limits of Sisterhood: The Women's Building in Seattle, 1908–1921." *Frontiers: A Journal of Women's Studies* 8, no. 1 (1984), 45–52.

8. Chase, Lucetta C. "The Work of Women's Organizations: The Social Program of the General Federation of Women's Clubs, One Index of Fifty Years of Progress." *Journal of Social Forces* 1, no. 4 (May 1923).

9. Cleveland, Grover. "Woman's mission and woman's clubs." *Ladies Home Journal*. May 22, 1905.

10. Ames, Alice. "Women's Clubs Today." *North American Review* 214, no. 792 (November 1921), 636–40.

11. Strong-Boag, Veronica. "Women's suffrage in Canada." *The Canadian Encyclopedia.* June 21, 2016. https://www.thecanadianencyclopedia.ca/en/article/suffrage.

12. Chase, Lucetta C. "The Work of Women's Organizations."

13. Anderson, Jackie. "Separatism, Feminism, and the Betrayal of Reform." *Signs* 19, no. 2 (1994), 437–48.

14. Joeres, Ruth-Ellen Boetcher, and Naomi Scheman. "Separatism Re-Viewed: Introduction." *Signs* 19, no. 2 (1994), 435–6.

15. Feminist Press. "History." https://www.feministpress.org/mission.

16. Thompson, Jane. *Words in Edgeways.* Leicester: National Institute of Adult Continuing Education, 1996. Quoted in Leathwood, Carole. "Doing difference in different times: Theory, politics, and women-only spaces in education." Women's Studies International Forum. November 2004.

17. McCarthy, Ellen. "Is 'The Wing' too hopelessly Manhattan for the working women of Washington?" *Washington Post.* April 10, 2018. https://www.washingtonpost.com/lifestyle/style/the-wing-is-opening-its-exclusive-doors-to-dcs-witches-but-will-they-accept-the-invitation/2018/04/09/c8950102-3aac-11e8-8fd2-49fe3c675a89_story.html?utm_term=.6f48dcd269f0.

18. Ferro, Shane. "The legality of a women-only club in the #MeToo era." Above The Law. August 15, 2018. https://abovethelaw.com/2018/08/the-legality-of-a-women-only-club-in-the-metoo-era/?rf=1

19. North, Anna, and Chavie Lieber. "The big, controversial business of The Wing, explained." Vox. February 7, 2019. https://www.vox.com/2019/2/7/18207116/the-wing-soho-dc-coworking-feminism-gelman.

20. New York State Department of Labor. "Minimum Wage." https://www.labor.ny.gov/workerprotection/laborstandards/workprot/minwage.shtm.

21. Retail Council of Canada. "Minimum Wage by Province: Minimum hourly wage rates as of June 1st, 2019." https://www.retailcouncil.org/resources/quick-facts/minimum-wage-by-province/.

22. Trotter, J. K. "The New York Human Rights Commission is investigating The Wing." Jezebel. March 12, 2018. https://jezebel.com/the-new-york-human-rights-commission-is-investigating-t-1823334726.

23. James E. Pietrangelo II v. Refresh Club Inc. and The Wing DC, LLC. Case 1:18-cv-01943-DLF. August 20, 2018. https://drive.google.com/file/d/180C_WPLgJ2CQ5n2dE3urdEfrVW98YSFC/view; Trotter, J. K. "Women's club The Wing quietly dropped its practice of banning men after a man filed a $12 million discrimination lawsuit." *Insider.* January 7, 2019. https://www.thisisinsider.com/the-wing-changed-membership-policy-to-allow-men-after-gender-discrimination-lawsuit-2019-1.

24. Holman, Jordyn. "Men cry discrimination in legal attack on women's organizations." *Bloomberg Businessweek.* May 11, 2018. https://www.bloomberg.com/news/articles/2018-05-11/men-cry-discrimination-in-legal-attack-on-women-s-organizations.

25. iFundWomen. "Ladies Get Paid." https://ifundwomen.com/projects/ladies-get-paid.

26. Ladies Get Paid. "Ladies Get Sued" (blog post). https://www.ladiesgetpaid.com/blog/ladies-get-sued.

27. Levintova, Hannah. "These men's rights activists are suing women's groups for meeting without men." *Mother Jones.* January 15, 2016. https://www.motherjones.com/politics/2016/01/men-rights-unruh-act-women-discrimination/.

28. Giordano, Chiara. "German man sues for discrimination over female-only parking space introduced after woman was raped."

The Independent. January 23, 2019. https://www.independent.co.uk/news/world/europe/women-only-parking-spaces-man-lawsuit-discrimination-german-eichstatt-a8742981.html.

29. The Wing. "Dear Wing family" (letter re membership). https://drive.google.com/file/d/1-h37Gq353_fDr6I2BDEI57-WhLVvUtvB/view.

30. James E. Pietrangelo II v. Refresh Club Inc. and The Wing DC, LLC. Case 1:18-cv-01943-DLF. "Exhibit 1." October 16, 2018. https://drive.google.com/file/d/1grfsfH31a8mosmTmAfWorcQ_koN3Bwo3/view.

31. Smith, Mary Jane. "The Fight to Protect Race and Regional Identity within the General Federation of Women's Clubs, 1895–1902." *The Georgia Historical Quarterly* 94, no. 4 (Winter 2010), 479–513.

32. Ruby, Jennie. "Women-Only And Feminist Spaces: Important Alternatives to Patriarchy." *Off Our Backs* 33, no. 5/6 (May–June 2003), 13–15.

33. Browne, Kath. "Womyn's Separatist Spaces: Rethinking Spaces of Difference and Exclusion." *Transactions of the Institute of British Geographers* 34, no. 4 (October 2009), 541–56.

34. Macdonald, Jocelyn. "Setting the record straight about MichFest." AfterEllen. October 24, 2018. https://www.afterellen.com/general-news/565301-setting-the-record-straight-about-michfest; Best, Jonathan. "The truth about Michigan Womyn's Music Festival and trans women—a correction." Medium. August 21, 2018. https://medium.com/@JonnnyBest/the-truth-about-michigan-womyns-festival-and-trans-women-a-correction-899d8e49f655.

35. Merlan, Anna. "Trans-excluding Michigan Womyn's Music Festival to end this year." Jezebel. April 22, 2015. https://jezebel.com/trans-excluding-michigan-womyns-music-festival-to-end-t-1699412910.

36. Borysiewicz, Kaitlyn. "Washington Post, we have a new title: Is 'The Wing' too white for Women of Colour?" The Melanin Collective (blog post). April 11, 2018. https://www.themelanincollective.org/

ideas/2018/4/11/washington-post-we-have-a-new-title-is-the-wing-too-white-for-women-of-color.

37. Rhana, Sahil. "Research: the gender gap in startup success disappears when women fund women." *Harvard Business Review.* July 19, 2016. https://hbr.org/2016/07/research-the-gender-gap-in-startup-success-disappears-when-women-fund-women.

38. Flabbi, Luca, Mario Macis, Andrea Moro, and Fabiano Schivardi. "Do Female Executives Make a Difference? The Impact of Female Leadership on Gender Gaps and Firm Performance." IZA Institute of Labor Economics: Discussion Papers. October 2014.

39. Hancock, Adrienne B. and Benjamin A. Rubin. "Influence of Communication Partner's Gender on Language." *Journal of Language and Social Psychology* 34, no. 1 (January 1, 2015), 46–64.

40. Karpowitz, Christopher F., Tali Mendelberg, and Lee Shaker. "Gender Inequality in Deliberative Participation." *American Political Science Review* (August 2012), 1–15.

41. Bever, Lindsey, Kayla Epstein, and Allyson Chiu. "Why NASA's historic all-female spacewalk isn't happening." *Washington Post.* March 26, 2019. https://www.washingtonpost.com/science/2019/03/26/nasas-first-all-female-spacewalk-isnt-happening-blame-wardrobe-malfunction/.

42. Frye Marilyn. "Some reflictions on separatism and power." Feminist Reprise (blog). Originally published in *The Politics of Reality: Essays in Feminist Theory.* New York: Crossing Press, 1983. https://feminist-reprise.org/library/resistance-strategy-and-struggle/some-reflections-on-separatism-and-power/.

43. Sisterhood and After research team. "The domestic division of labour." British Library: Sisterhood and After. March 8, 2013. https://www.bl.uk/sisterhood/articles/the-domestic-division-of-labour.

CHAPTER 6: MORE WOMEN, MORE MONEY

1. Gender Equity Advisory Council. "Advancing Gender Equality and Women's Empowerment." Government of Canada. 2018. publications.gc.ca//collections/collection_2018/amc-gac/FR5-144-2018-21-eng.pdf.

2. "Feminist Visions for the G7." Communique. April 26, 2018. http://w7canada.ca/wp-content/uploads/2018/05/W7-Communique_Apr-26-2018_Final2_w-recs_Final.pdf.

3. Justin Trudeau, Prime Minister of Canada. "Prime Minister concludes successful G7 Summit focused on creating economic growth that benefits everyone." June 10, 2018. https://pm.gc.ca/eng/news/2018/06/10/prime-minister-concludes-successful-g7-summit-focused-creating-economic-growth; Justin Trudeau, Prime Minister of Canada. "Canada concludes successful G7 Presidency." December 31, 2018. https://pm.gc.ca/eng/news/2018/12/31/canada-concludes-successful-g7-presidency.

4. Tolentino, Jia. "How empowerment became something for women to buy." *New York Times Magazine.* April 12, 2016. https://www.nytimes.com/2016/04/17/magazine/how-empowerment-became-something-for-women-to-buy.html.

5. Blume. "Know Your Flow: A guide to periods." https://cdn.shopify.com/s/files/1/0003/4580/0755/files/first-period-guide.pdf?12845690963815836305.

6. Lee, Matthew and Laura Huang. "Women entrepreneurs are more likely to get funding if they emphasize their social mission." *Harvard Business Review.* March 7, 2018. https://hbr.org/2018/03/women-entrepreneurs-are-more-likely-to-get-funding-if-they-emphasize-their-social-mission.

7. Hinchliffe, Emma. "Funding for female founders stalled at 2.2% of VC dollars in 2018." *Fortune.* January 28, 2019. http://fortune.com/2019/01/28/funding-female-founders-2018/.

8. Kanze, Dana, Laura Huang, and Mark A. Conley. "Male and female entrepreneurs get asked different questions by VCs—and it affects

how much funding they get." *Harvard Business Review.* June 27, 2017. https://hbr.org/2017/06/male-and-female-entrepreneurs-get-asked-different-questions-by-vcs-and-it-affects-how-much-funding-they-get.

9. Malmstrom, Malin, Jeaneth Johansson, and Joakim Wincent. "We recorded VCs' conversations and analyzed how differently they talk about female entrepreneurs." *Harvard Business Review.* May 17, 2017. https://hbr.org/2017/05/we-recorded-vcs-conversations-and-analyzed-how-differently-they-talk-about-female-entrepreneurs.

10. First Round. "The 10 Year Project." http://10years.firstround.com/.

11. Moore, McKenna. "Women entrepreneurs are optimistic about their businesses and the U.S. economy, study finds." *Fortune.* August 29, 2018. http://fortune.com/2018/08/29/women-entrepreneurs-business-economy/.

12. Lee, Matthew, and Laura Huang. "Women entrepreneurs are more likely to get funding if they emphasize their social mission."

13. Advisory Council on Economic Growth. "The path to prosperity—resetting Canada's growth trajectory: Executive summary." October 20, 2016. https://www.budget.gc.ca/aceg-ccce/pdf/summary-resume-eng.pdf.

14. Council on Foreign Relations. "Growing Economies Through Gender Parity." https://www.cfr.org/interactive/womens-participation-in-global-economy/.

15. Woetzel, Jonathan, Anu Madgavkar, Kweilin Ellingrud, et al. "How advancing women's equality can add $12 trillion to global growth." McKinsey Global Institute. September 2015. https://www.mckinsey.com/featured-insights/employment-and-growth/how-advancing-womens-equality-can-add-12-trillion-to-global-growth.

16. Kari, Shannon. "A woman's place." *Canadian Lawyer.* June 25, 2018. https://www.canadianlawyermag.com/author/shannon-kari/a-womans-place-15861/.

17. Needham, Breanna. "Law Society of Ontario (LSO) response: 'Change is coming!'" Petition at Change.org. February 20, 2019. https://www.change.org/p/treasurer-lso-ca-retire-the-lady-barrister-robing-room-at-osgoode-hall/u/24199177; Gallant, Jacques. "Lawyers will get gender-neutral room at Osgoode Hall following petition." *Toronto Star*. February 20, 2019. https://www.thestar.com/news/gta/2019/02/20/lawyers-will-get-gender-neutral-robing-room-at-osgoode-hall-following-petition.html.

18. Gallant, Jacques. "Lawyers will get gender-neutral room at Osgoode Hall following petition."

19. McLaughlin, Heather, Christopher Uggen, and Amy Blackstone. "The economic and career effects of sexual harassment on working women." *Gender & Society* 30, no. 3 (June 2017), 333–58.

20. Thomson, Stéphanie. "#MeToo is having unexpected consequences for women at work." World Economic Forum. March 7, 2018. https://www.weforum.org/agenda/2018/03/metoo-campaign-women-isolated-at-work/.

21. Lean In. "Working relationships in the #MeToo era: Key Findings." 2019. https://leanin.org/sexual-harassment-backlash-survey-results.

22. Government of Canada, Department of Justice. *An estimation of the economic impact of violent victimization in Canada, 2009.* https://www.justice.gc.ca/eng/rp-pr/cj-jp/victim/rr14_01/p10.html.

23. 30% Club. "FAQs: Why 30%?" https://30percentclub.org/resources/faqs.

24. Carlile, Luismaria Ruiz, Lori Choi, Patricia Farrar-Rivas, and Alison Pyott. "Women, Wealth & Impact: Investing with a Gender Lens 2.0." Veris Wealth Partners. March 2015. https://www.veriswp.com/wp-content/uploads/2018/02/CA_Women-Wealth-and-Impact-2.0_2015-03-05.pdf.

25. Flabbi, Luca, Mario Macis, Andrea Moro, and Fabiano Schivardi. "Do Female Executives Make a Difference? The Impact of Female

Leadership on Gender Gaps and Firm Performance." IZA Institute of Labor Economics: Discussion Papers. October 2014.

26. Bezanson, Kate. "Why the gender budget is important to Canada—and what it got wrong." *Globe and Mail*. March 14, 2018. https://www.theglobeandmail.com/opinion/article-why-the-gender-budget-is-important-to-canada-and-what-it-got-wrong/.

27. Government of Canada, Department of Finance. "Backgrounder: Gender Equality and a Strong Middle Class." March 3, 2018. https://www.fin.gc.ca/n18/data/18-008_1-eng.asp.

28. Government of Canada, Employment and Social Development Canada. "Backgrounder: Proactive Pay Equity." December 14, 2018. https://www.canada.ca/en/employment-social-development/news/2018/10/backgrounder-pay-equity.html.

29. Canadian Centre for Policy Alternatives. "No Time to Lose: Alternative Federal Budget 2019." https://www.policyalternatives.ca/afb2019.

30. Bezanson, Kate. "Why the gender budget is important to Canada—and what it got wrong."

31. Boesveld, Sarah. "A Boost for Parental Leave and More Key Takeaways from Trudeau's 'Gender Equality' budget." *Chatelaine*. February 27, 2018. https://www.chatelaine.com/living/politics/federal-budget-2018/.

32. Women Deliver. "The investment case for girls and women." May 7, 2016. https://womendeliver.org/2016/the-investment-case-for-girls-and-women/.

33. Cannivet, Michael. "Why women are better at investing." *Forbes*. December 29, 2018. https://www.forbes.com/sites/michaelcannivet/2018/12/29/why-women-are-better-at-investing/#39306cf16f37; Wilson, Pip. "Women invest differently than men and get better results." *Entrepreneur*. June 7, 2018. https://www.entrepreneur.com/article/313972.

34. Hicks, Coryanne. "Ellevest co-founder Sallie Krawcheck helps women invest." *U.S. News*. January 7, 2019. https://money.usnews. com/investing/investing-101/articles/ellevest-co-founder-helps-women-invest.

CHAPTER 7: I SEE YOU NOW

1. Geena Davis Institute on Gender in Media. "The Scully Effect: I Want to Believe…in STEM." 2018. https://seejane.org/research-informs-empowers/the-scully-effect-i-want-to-believe-in-stem/.

2. Geena Davis Institute on Gender in Media. "Female characters in film and TV motivate women to be more ambitious, more successful, and have even given them the courage to break out of abusive relationships." February 25, 2016. https://seejane.org/gender-in-media-news-release/female-characters-film-tv-motivate-women-ambitious-successful-even-given-courage-break-abusive-relationships-release/.

3. Women's Media Center and BBC America. "Superpowering Girls, Female Representation in the Sci-Fi/Superhero Genre." October 2018. http://www.womensmediacenter.com/reports/bbca-wmc-superpowering-girls-infographic.

4. Smith, Stacy L., Marc Choueiti, Ashley Prescott, and Katherine Pieper. "Gender Roles & Occupations: A Look at Character Attributes and Job-Related Aspirations in Film and Television: Executive Report." Geena Davis Institute on Gender in Media and Annenberg School for Communication & Journalism. 2012. https://annenberg.usc.edu/sites/default/files/MDSCI_Gender_Roles_%26_Occupations_in_Film_and_Television.pdf.

5. Smith, Stacy L., Marc Choueiti, and Katherine Pieper. "Inclusion or Invisibility? Comprehensive Annenberg Report on Diversity in Entertainment." Institute for Diversity and Empowerment at Annenberg (IDEA). February 22, 2016. https://annenberg.usc.edu/sites/default/files/2017/04/07/MDSCI_CARD_Report_FINAL_Exec_Summary.pdf.

6. Annenberg Inclusion Initiative. "Inequality across 1,200 popular films: Examining gender and race/ethnicity or leads/co leads from 2007 to 2018." Research brief. February 12, 2019. http://assets.uscannenberg.org/docs/inequality-in-1200-films-research-brief_2019-02-12.pdf.

7. Smith, Stacy L., Marc Choueiti, Angel Choi, and Katherine Pieper. "Inclusion in the Director's Chair: Gender, Race, & Age of Directors Across 1,200 Top Films from 2007 to 2018." Annenberg Inclusion Initiative. January 2019. http://assets.uscannenberg.org/docs/inclusion-in-the-directors-chair-2019.pdf.

8. Smith, Stacy L., Marc Choueiti, Katherine Pieper, et al. "Inclusion in the recording studio? Gender and Race/Ethnicity of Artists, songwriters & producers across 700 popular songs from 2012–2018." Annenberg Inclusion Initiative. February 2019. http://assets.uscannenberg.org/docs/inclusion-in-the-recording-studio.pdf.

9. King, Michelle. "Three advantages to investing in women of colour." *Forbes*. September 26, 2018. https://www.forbes.com/sites/michelleking/2018/09/26/three-advantages-to-investing-in-women-of-color/#6a6112852f9a.

10. Center for American Women and Politics. "Women of Color in Elective Office 2018: Congress, Statewide, State Legislature, Mayors." Rutgers Eagleton Institute of Politics. 2018. https://cawp.rutgers.edu/women-color-elective-office-2018.

11. Choueiti, Marc, Stacy L. Smith, and Katherine Pieper. "Critic's Choice 2: Gender and Race/Ethnicity of Film Reviewers Across 300 Top Films from 2015–2017." Annenberg Inclusive Initiative in partnership with Time's Up Entertainment. September 2018. http://assets.uscannenberg.org/docs/critics-choice-2.pdf.

12. The Record.com. "Solange Knowles blasts Grammy Awards on Twitter." February 14, 2017. https://www.therecord.com/whatson-story/7139078-solange-knowles-blasts-grammy-awards-on-twitter/.

13. Kaufman, Gil. "Solange suggests 'build your own institutions' after Beyonce's 'Lemonade' Album of The Year Grammy snub." *Billboard*. February 14, 2017. https://www.billboard.com/articles/

news/grammys/7693175/solange-beyonce-grammys-snub-reaction-twitter.

14. Sundance Institute. "2018 Sundance film festival awards announced." January 27, 2018. https://www.sundance.org/blogs/news/2018-film-festival-awards.

15. Dhillon, Sunny. "Journalism while brown and when to walk away." Medium. October 29, 2018. https://medium.com/s/story/journalism-while-brown-and-when-to-walk-away-9333ef61de9a.

16. Yasmin, Seema. "A survival kit for journalists of color." Poynter. June 12, 2018. https://www.poynter.org/newsletters/2018/a-survival-kit-for-journalists-of-color/.

17. Zoledzlowski, Anya. "Working as the newsroom's 'diversity hire.'" *The Tyee*. March 12, 2019. https://thetyee.ca/Culture/2019/03/12/Women-Colour-Newsroom-Diversity/.

18. Women's Media Center. "The Status of Women in the U.S. Media 2019." February 2019. http://www.womensmediacenter.com/reports/the-status-of-women-in-u-s-media-2019.

19. Women's Media Center. "The Status of Women of Color in the U.S. News Media 2018." March 2018. https://www.womensmediacenter.com/reports/the-status-of-women-of-color-in-the-u-s-media-2018-full-report.

20. Worth, Nancy, Akim Karaagac, Shari Graydon, and Samantha Luchuk. "Counting Ourselves In: Understanding Why Women Decide to Engage with the Media." Informed Opinions. October 2018. https://informedopinions.org/wp-content/uploads/2018/10/Counting-Ourselves-In-Final-Report-Oct-2018.pdf.

21. Informed Opinions. "First of its kind Gender Gap Tracker measures data in real time to motivate news outlets to more equitably reflect women's voices." News release. February 3, 2019. https://informedopinions.org/first-of-its-kind-gender-gap-tracker-measures-data-in-real-time-to-motivate-news-outlets-to-more-equitably-reflect-womens-voices/; Informed Opinions. "Gender Gap Tracker." https://gendergaptracker.informedopinions.org/.

22. Leibbrandt, Andreas, and John A. List. "Do Equal Employment Opportunity Statements Backfire? Evidence From a Natural Field Experiment on Job-Entry Decisions." Cato Institute: Research Brief in Economic Policy no. 152. February 27, 2019. https://www.cato.org/publications/research-briefs-economic-policy/do-equal-employment-opportunity-statements-backfire.

23. Sodexo, Rohini Anand, and Mary-Frances Winters. "A Retrospective View of Corporate Diversity Training From 1964 to the Present." *Academy of Management Learning & Education* 7, no. 3 (2008), 356–72.

24. Dobbin, Frank, and Alexandra Kalev. "Why diversity programs fail." *Harvard Business Review* (July–August 2016). https://hbr.org/2016/07/why-diversity-programs-fail.

25. Oluo, Ijeoma. "Confronting racism is not about the needs and feelings of white people." *The Guardian.* March 28, 2019. https://www.theguardian.com/commentisfree/2019/mar/28/confronting-racism-is-not-about-the-needs-and-feelings-of-white-people.

26. DiAngelo, Robin. "How white people handle diversity training in the workplace." Medium. June 27, 2018. https://medium.com/s/story/how-white-people-handle-diversity-training-in-the-workplace-e8408d2519f.

27. Rivera, Lauren A. "Hiring as Cultural Matching: The Case of Elite Professional Service Firms." *American Sociological Review* 77, no. 6 (November 2012). https://journals.sagepub.com/doi/10.1177/0003122412463213.

28. Dobbin, Frank, and Alexandra Kalev. "Why diversity programs fail." *Harvard Business Review.* July–August 2016. https://hbr.org/2016/07/why-diversity-programs-fail.

29. Dastin, Jeffrey. "Amazon scraps secret AI recruiting tool that showed bias against women." Reuters. October 9, 2018. https://www.reuters.com/article/us-amazon-com-jobs-automation-insight/amazon-scraps-secret-ai-recruiting-tool-that-showed-bias-against-women-idUSKCN1MK08G.

30. Mason, Paul. "The racist hijacking of Microsoft's chatbot shows how the internet teems with hate." *The Guardian*. March 29, 2016. https://www.theguardian.com/world/2016/mar/29/microsoft-tay-tweets-antisemitic-racism.

31. *The Economist*. "Facebook's ad system seems to discriminate by race and gender." April 4, 2019. https://www.economist.com/business/2019/04/04/facebooks-ad-system-seems-to-discriminate-by-race-and-gender; Biddle, Sam. "Facebook's ad algorithm is a race and gender stereotyping machine, new study suggests." The Intercept. April 3, 2019. https://theintercept.com/2019/04/03/facebook-ad-algorithm-race-gender/.

CHAPTER 8: SLAY ALL THE TROLLS

1. Ciston, Sarah. "ladymouth: Anti-Social-Media Art as Research." *Ada: A Journal of Gender, New Media, and Technology*, no. 15 (2019).

2. "Updated Glossary of Terms and Acronyms." Reddit post (r/TheRedPill). 2015. https://www.reddit.com/r/TheRedPill/comments/2zckqu/updated_glossary_of_terms_and_acronyms/.

3. "Updated Glossary of Terms and Acronyms." Reddit post (r/TheRedPill).

4. Brown, Danielle. "Google diversity annual report 2018." https://static.googleusercontent.com/media/diversity.google/en//static/pdf/Google_Diversity_annual_report_2018.pdf.

5. Apple: Inclusion and Diversity. "Different together." December 2018. https://www.apple.com/diversity/.

6. Facebook: Diversity. "2019 Diversity Report." December 2018. https://www.facebook.com/careers/diversity-report.

7. Packer, George. "Change the World." *New Yorker*. May 27, 2013. https://www.newyorker.com/magazine/2013/05/27/change-the-world.

8. Uber Technologies. "Uber Diversity and Inclusion Report 2019." Link to download at https://www.uber.com/en-CA/about/diversity/ under "Diversity and Inclusion."

9. Fowler, Susan J. "Reflecting on one very, very strange year at Uber" (blog post). February 19, 2017. https://www.susanjfowler.com/ blog/2017/2/19/reflecting-on-one-very-strange-year-at-uber.

10. West, Tony. "Turning the lights on." Uber Newsroom. May 15, 2018. https://www.uber.com/en-CA/newsroom/turning-the-lights-on/.

11. Kunkle, Fredrick. "Uber changes policy on sexual-misconduct claims, allowing victims to pursue charges." *Washington Post*. May 15, 2018. https://www.washingtonpost.com/news/tripping/ wp/2018/05/15/uber-changes-policy-on-sexual-misconduct-claims-allowing-victims-more-leeway/.

12. Bloomberg. "Uber HR head quits after accusations she ignored allegations of racial discrimination." *Fortune*. July 11, 2018. http:// fortune.com/2018/07/11/uber-liane-hornsey-whistle-blower-racial-discriminiation/; Recode Staff. "Recode Daily: Uber's newest HR problem is its HR boss." Vox. July 12, 2018. https://www. recode.net/2018/7/12/17563060/uber-liane-hornsey-resign-racial-discrimination-comcast-sky-fox-twitter-followers-magic-leap-esports.

13. Jean-Baptiste, Keesha. "To further embrace diversity, agencies need to focus on equity." *Adweek*. July 10, 2018. https://www.adweek. com/agencies/to-further-embrace-diversity-agencies-need-to-focus-on-equity/.

14. Davies, Hannah J. "Does Tinder's Menprovement initiative do enough to protect women?" *The Guardian*. October 9, 2017. https://www.theguardian.com/lifeandstyle/2017/oct/09/tinder-menprovement-protect-women-dating.

15. Davidblacksheep. "Tinder's #menprovement campaign is looking like some cheap misandric bullshit." Eyes of a Black Sheep (blog post). October 11, 2017. https://eyesofablacksheep.com/2017/10/11/ tinders-menprovement-campaign-is-looking-like-some-cheap-

misandric-bullshit/; "Tinder's Menprovement Initiative." Reddit posts. 2018. https://www.reddit.com/r/MGTOW/comments/76r3sj/tinders_menprovement_initiative/.

16. Lautenback, Kyle. "Cancelled Lego MMO's biggest problem was a penis filter." IGN Africa. June 1, 2015. https://za.ign.com/lego-universe/91181/news/cancelled-lego-mmos-biggest-problem-was-a-penis-filter.

17. Satell, Greg. "Think technology moves faster today? Think again." *Inc.* March 3, 2018. https://www.inc.com/greg-satell/think-technology-moves-faster-today-think-again.html.

18. Rotman, David. "Tech slowdown threatens the American dream." MIT *Technology Review.* April 6, 2016. https://www.technologyreview.com/s/601199/tech-slowdown-threatens-the-american-dream/.

19. Ehrenfreund, Max. "We were promised jetpacks and flying cars, and all we got was this lousy chart." *Washington Post.* March 8, 2016. https://www.washingtonpost.com/news/wonk/wp/2016/03/08/we-were-promised-jetpacks-and-flying-cars-and-all-we-got-was-this-lousy-chart/.

20. Maney, Kevin. "Silicon Valley Needs Moms!" *Newsweek.* November 8, 2015. https://www.newsweek.com/2015/11/20/silicon-valley-working-replace-mothers-391794.html.

21. Nitrozac and Snaggy. *The Joy of Tech.* (Webcomic). https://pbs.twimg.com/media/CFWnoVIVIAACzqV.jpg.

22. Sharma, Sarah. "Going to work in mommy's basement." *Boston Review.* July 19, 2018. http://bostonreview.net/gender-sexuality/sarah-sharma-going-work-mommys-basement.

23. Kaufman, Sarah M., Christopher F. Polack, and Gloria A. Campbell. "The Pink Tax on Transportation: Women's Challenges in Mobility." NYU Rudin Centre for Transportation. November 2018. https://wagner.nyu.edu/files/faculty/publications/Pink%20Tax%20Report%2011_13_18.pdf; Kaufman, Sarah. "The Pink Tax on Transportation: The Challenges Women Face in Mobility." Newcities: Women in Cities 2019. March 8, 2019. https://newcities.

org/the-big-picture-the-pink-tax-on-transportation-womens-challenges-in-mobility/.

24. Goldsmith, Belinda. "Exclusive: Safety and time are women's biggest concerns about transport—global poll." Reuters. November 14, 2018. https://www.reuters.com/article/us-transport-women-poll/exclusive-safety-and-time-are-womens-biggest-concerns-about-transport-global-poll-idUSKCN1NK04K.

25. Kooti, Farshad, Mihajlo Grbovic, Luca Maria Aiello, et al. "Analyzing Uber's Ride-sharing Economy." Paper presented at the 26th Annual International World Wide Web Conference, April 3–7, Perth, Australia. http://papers.www2017.com.au.s3-website-ap-southeast-2.amazonaws.com/companion/p574.pdf.

26. UN Women. "Creating safe public spaces." http://www.unwomen.org/en/what-we-do/ending-violence-against-women/creating-safe-public-spaces.

27. Smith, DeAnne. "Montreal ladies love Meow Mix." *Xtra*. December 3, 2008. https://www.dailyxtra.com/montreal-ladies-love-meow-mix-37371.

28. Mukurtu. "About." http://mukurtu.org/about/.

CHAPTER 9: UNCONVENTIONAL WOMEN

1. Koon, Rebecca. "The politics of framing Hillary Clinton as 'The best mother in the world." *Bitch*. July 29, 2016. https://www.bitchmedia.org/article/politics-framing-hillary-clinton-best-mother-world-dnc-motherhood-feminism-speeches.

2. Martin, Patrick. "Don't have kids? Neither do some of the world's most powerful leaders." *Washington Post*. May 25, 2017. https://www.washingtonpost.com/news/worldviews/wp/2017/05/25/dont-have-kids-neither-do-some-of-the-worlds-most-powerful-leaders/.

3. Interview with Nagwan Al-Guneid, March 8, 2019.

4. Keith, Tamara. "Best way to get women to run for office? Ask repeatedly." NPR "She Votes." May 5, 2014. https://www.npr.org/2014/05/05/309832898/best-way-to-get-women-to-run-for-office-ask-repeatedly; Snell, Kelsey. "Wanted: Female candidates for federal office." *Washington Post*. September 13, 2016. https://www.washingtonpost.com/news/powerpost/wp/2016/09/13/wanted-female-candidates-for-federal-office/?utm_term=.69f4176c8952; Miller, Clair Cain. "The problem for women is not winning. It's deciding to run." *New York Times*. October 25, 2016. https://www.nytimes.com/2016/10/25/upshot/the-problem-for-women-is-not-winning-its-deciding-to-run.html.

5. Lawless, Jennifer L., and Richard L. Fox. "Girls Just Wanna Not Run: The Gender Gap in Young Americans' Political Ambition." Women and Politics Institute (American University, School of Public Affairs). March 26, 2013. https://www.american.edu/spa/wpi/upload/girls-just-wanna-not-run_policy-report.pdf.

6. Mendelberg, Tali, and Christopher F. Karpowitz. "Power, Gender and Group Discussion." *Advances in Political Psychology* 37 (January 22, 2016).

7. Lawless, Jennifer L. "Female Candidates and Legislators." *Annual Review of Political Science* 18 (May 2015).

8. Roper Center for Public Opinion Research. "Madame President: Changing attitudes about a woman president" (blog post). March 17, 2016. https://ropercenter.cornell.edu/blog/madame-president-changing-attitudes-about-woman-president-blog.

9. Lawless, Jennifer L. "Female Candidates and Legislators."

10. Anastasopoulos, Lefteris. "Estimating the gender penalty in House of Representative elections using a regression discontinuity design." *Electoral Studies* 43 (September 2016), 150–7.

11. Begley, Sarah. "Hillary Clinton leads by 2.8 million in final popular vote count." *Time*. December 20, 2016. http://time.com/4608555/hillary-clinton-popular-vote-final/.

12. Fox, Richard L., and Jennifer L. Lawless. "Gendered Perceptions and Political Candidacies: A Central Barrier to Women's Equality in Electoral Politics." *American Journal of Political Science* 5, no. 1 (January 2011), 59–73.

13. Lawless, Jennifer L., and Richard L. Fox. "A Trump Effect? Women and the 2018 Midterm Elections." *The Forum: A Journal of Applied Research in Contemporary Politics* 16, no. 4 (February 22, 2019), 665–86.

14. Okimoto, Tyler G., and Victoria L. Brescoll. "The Price of Power: Power seeking and backlash against female politicians." *Personality and Social Psychology Bulletin* 36, no. 7 (2010).

15. Mendelberg, Tali, and Christopher F. Karpowitz. "Power, Gender and Group Discussion."

16. Lawless, Jennifer L. "Female Candidates and Legislators."

17. Lawless, Jennifer L., and Richard L. Fox. "A Trump Effect? Women and the 2018 Midterm Elections."

18. Okimoto, Tyler G., and Victoria L. Brescoll. "The Price of Power: Power seeking and backlash against female politicians."

19. Lawless, Jennifer L., and Sean M. Theriault. "Will She Stay or Will She Go? Career Ceilings and Women's Retirement from the U.S. Congress." *Legislative Studies Quarterly* 30, no. 4 (November 2005), 581–96.

20. Okimoto, Tyler G., and Victoria L. Brescoll. "The Price of Power: Power seeking and backlash against female politicians."

21. Brescoll, Victoria L. "Who Takes the Floor and Why: Gender, Power, and Volubility in Organizations." *Administrative Science Quarterly* 56, no. 4 (2011), 622–41.

22. Lawless, Jennifer L. and Sean M. Theriault. "Will She Stay or Will She Go? Career Ceilings and Women's Retirement from the U.S. Congress."

23. Correll, Shelley, Stephan Benard, and In Paik. "Getting a job: Is there a motherhood penalty?" *American Journal of Sociology* 112, no. 5 (2007), 1297–339.

24. Fox, Michelle. "The 'motherhood penalty' is real and it costs women $16,000 a year." CNBC Make It. March 25, 2019. https://www.cnbc.com/2019/03/25/the-motherhood-penalty-costs-women-16000-a-year-in-lost-wages.html.

25. Ali, Safia Samee. "'Motherhood penalty' can affect women who never even have a child." NBC News. April 11, 2016. https://www.nbcnews.com/better/careers/motherhood-penalty-can-affect-women-who-never-even-have-child-n548511.

26. Killewald, Alexandra. "A Reconsideration of the Fatherhood Premium: Marriage, Coresidence, Biology, and Fathers' Wages." *American Sociological Review* 78, no. 1 (December 20, 2012), 96–116.

27. Zalis, Shelley. "The Motherhood Penalty: Why we're losing our best talent to caregiving." *Forbes.* February 22, 2019. https://www.forbes.com/sites/shelleyzalis/2019/02/22/the-motherhood-penalty-why-were-losing-our-best-talent-to-caregiving/#5ec271ae46e5.

28. Antecol, Heather, Kelly Bedard, and Jenna Stearns. "Equal but Inequitable: Who Benefits from Gender-Neutral Tenure Clock Stopping Policies?" IZA Institute of Labor Economics: Discussion Papers. April 2016.

29. McKeon, Lauren. "How to Build a Life Without Kids." *The Walrus.* May 2, 2018. https://thewalrus.ca/is-motherhood-good-for-women/.

30. Rosa, Christopher. "Beyoncé's pregnancy announcement is the most-liked Instagram photo of 2017." *Glamour.* November 29, 2017. https://www.glamour.com/story/beyonce-pregnancy-announcement-most-liked-instagram-photo-of-2017.

31. Lang, Cady. "Here's the Instagram post that just dethroned Queen Beyoncé from the top spot." *Time.* February 7, 2018. http://time.com/5138005/most-instagram-likes/.

32. Carroll, Laura. *The Baby Matrix: Why freeing our minds from outmoded thinking about parenthood and reproduction will create a better world*. LiveTrue Books, 2012.

33. Peck, Ellen. *The Baby Trap*. New York City: Pinnacle Books, 1971.

34. Andersen, Christopher P. "Non-mother Ellen Peck advises couples who don't want children: Stop feeling guilty." *People*. February 9, 1976. http://people.com/archive/non-mother-ellen-peck-advises-couples-who-dont-want-children-stop-feeling-guilty-vol-5-no-5/.

35. Carroll, Laura. *The Baby Matrix*.

36. Pharr, Mary F., and Leisa A. Clark, eds. *Of Bread, Blood and The Hunger Games: Critical Essays on the Suzanne Collins Trilogy*. Critical Explorations in Science Fiction and Fantasy. Jefferson: McFarland and Company, 2012.

37. Aggeler, Madeleine. "Even female robots can't avoid the 'Do you want kids?' question." *The Cut*. November 29, 2017. https://www.thecut.com/2017/11/sophia-the-saudi-arabian-robot-wants-to-have-kids.html.

38. Norwood, Candice. "A classic prep for parenthood, but is the egg all it's cracked up to be?" NPR Ed. April 9, 2015. https://www.npr.org/sections/ed/2015/04/09/398074310/the-egg-baby-project-a-lesson-in-sex-education and http://www.educationworld.com/a_curr/curr128.shtml.

39. Grand View Research. "Baby Products Market Size worth $16.78 billion by 2025." Press release, January 2019. https://www.grandviewresearch.com/press-release/global-baby-products-market.

40. Vicks. "Moms Don't Take Sick Days." iSpot.tv (video). https://www.ispot.tv/ad/wRg4/vicks-nyquil-severe-moms-dont-take-sick-days.

41. Donath, Orna. *Regretting Motherhood: A Study*. Berkeley: North Atlantic Books, 2017.

42. McKeon, Lauren. "How to Build a Life Without Kids." *The Walrus*. May 2, 2018. https://thewalrus.ca/is-motherhood-good-for-women/.

43. O'Connor, Joe. "Trend of couples not having children just plain selfish." *National Post*. September 19, 2012. http://nationalpost.com/opinion/joe-oconnor-selfishness-behind-growing-trend-for-couples-to-not-have-children.

44. Siegal, Harry. "Why the choice to be childless is bad for America." *Newsweek*. February 19, 2013. http://www.newsweek.com/why-choice-be-childless-bad-america-63335.

45. Sandler, Lauren. "Having it all without having children." *Time*. August 12, 2013. http://content.time.com/time/subscriber/article/0,33009,2148636,00.html.

46. Fox News Insider. "Time Magazine's 'Childfree Life' controversy: What message does it send?" August 3, 2013. http://insider.foxnews.com/2013/08/03/time-magazines-childfree-life-controversy-what-message-does-it-send.

47. Bodenner, Chris. "Women choosing to go childless: your thoughts." *The Atlantic*. April 28, 2015. https://www.theatlantic.com/sexes/archive/2015/04/your-thoughts-on-women-choosing-to-go-childless/391712/.

48. Kirchgaessner, Stephanie. "Pope Francis: not having children is selfish." *The Guardian*. February 11, 2015. https://www.theguardian.com/world/2015/feb/11/pope-francis-the-choice-to-not-have-children-is-selfish.

CHAPTER 10: REBEL GIRL

1. Hamkins, SuEllen, and Renée Schultz. *The Mother-Daughter Project: How Mothers and Daughters Can Band Together, Beat the Odds, and Thrive Through Adolescence*. New York: Plume, 2008; The Mother-Daughter Project. "The Story of the Mother-Daughter Project." https://themother-daughterproject.com/ourstory.htm.

2. Girl Guides of Canada. "Sexism, Feminism & Equality: What Teens in Canada Really Think." October 2018. https://www.girlguides.ca/WEB/Documents/GGC/media/thought-leadership/201SexismFeminismEquality-WhatTeensinCanadaReallyThink.pdf.

3. Shipman, Claire, and Katty Kay. "The Confidence Code for Girls: The Confidence Collapse and Why it Matters for The Next Gen." YPulse poll. 2018. https://static1.squarespace.com/static/588b93f6bf629a6bec7a3bd2/t/5ac39193562fa73cd8a07a89/1522766258986/The+Confidence+Code+for+Girls+x+Ypulse.pdf.

4. Simmons, Rachel. *The Curse of the Good Girl*. New York: Penguin Publishing Group, 2009, 2.

5. Association for Psychological Science. "Teenage girls are exposed to more stressors that increase depression risk." News release, October 8, 2014. https://www.psychologicalscience.org/news/releases/teenage-girls-are-exposed-to-more-stressors-that-increase-depression-risk.html.

6. Fisher, Maryanne, L., ed. *The Oxford Handbook of Women and Competition*. Oxford: Oxford Library of Psychology, 2017.

7. Burton, Laura J., and Sarah Leberman. *Women in Sport Leadership: Research and Practice for Change*. Abingdon: Routledge, 2017.

8. Johnson, Holly. "A look at the link between playing sports and success in business." CEO *Magazine*. May 7, 2018. https://www.theceomagazine.com/business/management-leadership/look-link-playing-sports-success-business/.

9. Zarya, Valentina. "What do 65% of the most powerful women have in common? Sports." *Fortune*. September 22, 2017. http://fortune.com/2017/09/22/powerful-women-business-sports/.

10. EY. "Research: Does it pay to let girls play?" https://web.archive.org/web/20180122024151/http://www.ey.com/br/pt/about-us/our-sponsorships-and-programs/women-athletes-global-leadership-network---research-does-it-pay-to-let-girls-play.

11. Hensely, Laura. "Catsuits ruled OK for the tennis courts thanks to Serena Williams." *Global News*. December 18, 2018. https://globalnews.ca/news/4773018/catsuits-tennis-court/; Nittle, Nadra. "The Serena Williams catsuit ban shows that tennis can't get past its elitist roots." Vox. August 28, 2018. https://www.vox.com/2018/8/

28/17791518/serena-williams-catsuit-ban-french-open-tennis-racist-sexist-country-club-sport.

12. Fisher, Maryanne L., ed. *The Oxford Handbook of Women and Competition*.

13. OBOS Abortion Contributors. "Aspiration Abortion." *Our Bodies Our Selves* (blog post). April 2, 2014. https://www.ourbodiesourselves.org/book-excerpts/health-article/vacuum-aspiration-abortion/.

14. Weber, Jasmine. "Judy Chicago responds to criticisms about the 'Dinner Party." Hyperallergic. August 13, 2018. https://hyperallergic.com/455572/judy-chicago-responds-to-criticisms-about-the-dinner-party/.

15. Chicago, Judy. "A place at the table: an exchange." *New York Review of Books*. July 2018. https://www.nybooks.com/daily/2018/07/11/a-place-at-the-table-an-exchange/.

CHAPTER II: BECAUSE IT'S 2020

1. Justin Trudeau, Prime Minister of Canada. "Government of Canada makes historic investment to promote the health and rights of women and girls around the world." News release, June 4, 2019. https://pm.gc.ca/eng/news/2019/06/04/government-canada-makes-historic-investment-promote-health-and-rights-women-and.

2. Garber, Megan. "The Real Meaning of Trump's 'She's not my type' defense." *The Atlantic*. June 25, 2019. https://www.theatlantic.com/entertainment/archive/2019/06/trump-e-jean-carroll-rape-allegation-not-my-type-defense/592555/; D'Antonio, Michael. "'She's not my type' tells us all we need to know about Trump." CNN Opinion. June 27, 2019. https://www.cnn.com/2019/06/27/opinions/carroll-rape-allegation-trump-dantonio/index.html.

3. North, Anna. "Why the president is feuding with Megan Rapinoe, star of the U.S. women's soccer team." Vox. July 3, 2019. https://www.vox.com/identities/2019/7/3/20680073/megan-rapinoe-trump-world-cup-soccer; Helmore, Edward. "Trump congratulates USA on World Cup despite confrontation with Rapinoe." *The Guardian*.

July 7, 2019. https://www.theguardian.com/football/2019/jul/07/trump-usa-world-cup-win-megan-rapinoe.

4. NDP. "NDP: Liberals must match feminist rhetoric with actions for women's equality." News release, September 25, 2018. https://www.ndp.ca/news/ndp-liberals-must-match-feminist-rhetoric-action-womens-equality.

5. Boesveld, Sarah. "A Beer with Andrew Scheer: Conservative leader, popcorn addict...Feminist?" *Chatelaine*. August 2, 2017. https://www.chatelaine.com/living/politics/andrew-scheer-interview/.

6. MacDonald, Fiona, and Jeanette Ashe. "MacDonald and Ashe: Wilson-Raybould and Philpott are showing us what feminist governance looks like." *Ottawa Citizen*. March 5, 2019. https://ottawacitizen.com/opinion/columnists/macdonald-and-ashe-wilson-raybould-and-philpott-are-showing-us-what-feminist-governance-looks-like.

7. Walsh, Marieke, Michelle Zilio and Kristy Kirkup. "Trudeau apologizes again for wearing blackface, cannot say how many times he wore racist makeup." *Globe and Mail*. September 19, 2019. https://www.theglobeandmail.com/politics/article-new-blackface-video-surfaces-a-day-after-trudeau-apologizes-for-two/.

8. Max Bell School of Public Policy. Digital Democracy Project Research Memo #5: Fact-Checking, Blackface and the Media. October 2019. https://ppforum.ca/articles/ddp-research-memo-5/.

9. "Read the full text of Justin Trudeau's victory speech: Liberal leader says he's on Alberta and Saskatchewan's side." *National Post*. October 22, 2019. https://nationalpost.com/news/politics/election-2019/canada-full-text-justin-trudeau-victory-speech-liberals.

10. Smart, Amy. "Former Liberal Jody Wilson-Raybould wins her Vancouver seat as Independent." *BNN Bloomberg*. October 22, 2019. https://www.bnnbloomberg.ca/former-liberal-jody-wilson-raybould-wins-her-vancouver-seat-as-independent-1.1335146.

Acknowledgements

Thank you firstly to my editor, Michelle MacAleese. You are brilliant. Your endless support and keen insight made me better; I appreciate each gentle "haircut" and every tough question. (Also, I would be remiss not to thank you for your dedication to ensuring all meetings have gluten-free cookies.)

A huge thank you as well to the rest of the team at House of Anansi Press for your belief in this book and your care and enthusiasm at every step. To Shelley Ambrose and Sarah MacLachlan: thank you both for dreaming up The Walrus Books; I am honoured to be part of it.

A particular thank you to Maria Golikova for your grace, humour, and patience throughout the production process; to Catherine Marjoribanks for a sharp, incredibly thoughtful, and bang-on copyedit; to Gemma Wain for your fine-tooth comb; to Siusan Moffat for a delightful and comprehensive index; to Laura Brady for speedy and attentive typesetting; to Alysia Shewchuk for a beautiful, perfect cover; and to Curtis Samuel, for his work in shining a spotlight on my work.

And to the entire team at The Walrus: you are amazing; you create wonderful, compelling, important things every day in that basement. Thank you especially to Carmine Starnino for your guidance on and astute editing of all *The Walrus* pieces that sparked the ideas in this book, and to Jessica Johnson for being supportive during a very hectic year. And, of course, to the Coven: you are magic, always. Thank you, digital witches.

I also couldn't have done this book without the support of the Chawkers Foundation. The foundation invests in journalism that propels the Canadian conversation, and it supports projects writers may not otherwise have the opportunity to make. It's vital work, and I'm grateful for it.

Thank you also to my agent, Hilary McMahon, for always going to bat for me. And to my closest, oldest friends: you know who you are. Thank you for being your awesome selves, for putting up with my ridiculous schedule and general delinquency as I worked on this book, and also for ensuring I took much-needed breaks. I am so lucky to have you all. To my family: you are all powerful, incredible, dynamic, generous women. Thank you for teaching me, thank you for being there, thank you for everything.

Kylan, you make everything brighter. Thank you for bringing me plants during tough times (even when they continue to have a 50 percent survival rate). Thank you for listening, for going on your own journey into feminism, and for joining me on every adventure.

A final thank you to everyone I interviewed and who shared their visions for a more equitable, kinder, interesting world. Your time and insights were appreciated. You are all inspiring. You are all fierce. Your work is so worthy. I cannot wait to see what you create. Let's tear up the rule book and start building.

Index

LAUREN MCKEON's critically acclaimed first book, *F-Bomb: Dispatches from the War on Feminism*, was a finalist for the Kobo Emerging Writer Prize. She is the winner of several National Magazine Awards, and her writing has appeared in *Hazlitt, Flare, Reader's Digest*, and *Best Canadian Essays 2017*, on TVO.org, and in the book *Whatever Gets You Through: Twelve Survivors on Life After Sexual Assault*. McKeon has taught long-form writing at Humber College and holds an M.F.A. in Creative Nonfiction from the University of King's College. She was the editor of *This Magazine* from 2011 to 2016 and is currently a contributing editor at *Toronto Life* and the digital editor at The Walrus.